The Best Year of Their Lives

The Best Year of Their Lives

KENNEDY,
JOHNSON,
AND NIXON
IN 1948

Learning the
Secrets of Power

LANCE MORROW

BASIC
BOOKS

A Member of the Perseus Books Group

New York

Copyright © 2005 by Lance Morrow

Published by Basic Books,
A Member of the Perseus Books Group

Books published by Basic are available at special discounts for bulk purchases in the United
States by corporations, institutions, and other organizations. For more information, please
contact the Special Markets Department at the Perseus Books Group, 11 Cambridge Center,
Cambridge, MA 02142, or call (617) 252-5298, (800) 255-1514, or e-mail special.
markets@perseusbooks.com.

Design by Jane Raese
Text set in Garamond 3

A CIP catalog record for this book is available from the Library of Congress.
ISBN 0-465-04723-8

05 06 07 08 / 10 9 8 7 6 5 4 3 2 1

FOR HENRY GRUNWALD

CONTENTS

INTRODUCTION

THREE CRISES

On the cool, cloudy morning of August 3, 1948, Richard Nixon met Whittaker Chambers.

Chambers was a senior editor for *Time* magazine. He appeared at 9:30 that morning to testify before the House Un-American Activities Committee in a hearing room in the House Office Building in Washington, D.C. Chambers, a short, dumpy man, wore a wrinkled suit and a haunted expression that, in the weeks ahead, would become a front-page fixture peering from smudgy black-and-white newspaper photographs: porcine, woebegone, an enigmatic Humpty-Dumpty. There would be sworn testimony about his bad teeth—not that Chambers was given to smiling. Someone would joke that Chambers, a man in whom dark clouds and doom coagulated, was the only American character in Dostoevski.

Nixon, an over-earnest, near-handsome freshman congressman from Whittier, California, appraised Chambers with a lawyerly eye connected to a rapidly evolving political brain. That first day, Nixon listened mostly in silence. He was the most intelligent and professionally polished member of the House Un-American Activities Committee. Nixon, a reserved and self-possessed young man, knew how to activate an instinct for the theatrical when he judged the time was right.

Chambers was a man much given to meditation; Nixon was much given to premeditation.

Almost inaudibly (the microphones weren't working), Chambers began to tell the committee about his activities in the 1930s as a Communist undercover agent collecting U.S. government secrets and reporting them to the Soviet military's Fourth Branch (Intelligence). He mentioned a man named Alger Hiss.

That morning launched Richard Nixon's career.

With the August 3 committee meeting, the Hiss case started—a gaudy, sensational two-year-long pageant of congressional hearings and court trials that would bring the Cold War home, divide Americans, and introduce Nixon as a national figure, the intense young star of the Republican Party.

The Hiss case also began an ideological and cultural civil war. Americans lined up on either side of the question of whether it was true, as Whittaker Chambers told the committee, or not true, as Alger Hiss indignantly responded, that Hiss—a man as elegant as Fred Astaire, an impressive member of the New Deal liberal establishment, a former clerk to Justice Oliver Wendell Holmes, a highly placed State Department official, a veteran of the Yalta conference, and now head of the Carnegie Endowment—had conducted a second, covert life as a Communist agent. The case touched the rawest postwar American anxiety—Communist infiltration of American life.

Nixon became the Javert and impresario of the Hiss case. It made him suddenly famous. Speaking invitations poured in from around the country. Nixon leveraged his fame to run for the U.S. Senate in 1950 against Helen Gahagan Douglas. He won, and in 1952 became the thirty-nine-year-old vice presidential candidate on the Republican ticket with Dwight Eisenhower. After eight years as vice president, he was the Republicans' inevitable presidential nominee in 1960.

None of this would have happened without the Hiss-Chambers drama that Nixon presided over in 1948.

AT THE SAME MOMENT in the summer of that year, Lyndon Johnson was locked in a fight for his political life in Texas—a run for the U.S. Senate against the popular conservative former governor, Coke Stevenson.

John Connally, who managed the campaign, told the biographer Robert Caro forty years later that Johnson's 1948 race against Stevenson "was the beginning of modern politics . . . the dawn of a whole new era." Stevenson, a slow-moving, slow-talking Texas archetype—laconic, judicious, the embodiment, as some thought, of an Old West ideal, was happiest when working his goat ranch down on the Llano River. He campaigned by riding around the state in an old Plymouth driven by his nephew, turning up virtually unannounced to shake hands around the courthouse square and then say a few words to the local civic group. He relied on the unstated antique Texas premise, a sort of mystic masculinity that was the equivalent of the judgment used by the British ruling class when deciding whether a man was "sound"—a shared mystique of right and wrong, honor and duty: the old virtues compounded by old faults, such as racial bigotry. Into that static politics Johnson injected fiercely manipulative new instruments—huge sums of money raised from corporate donors who would be rewarded later, cash that bought big media and mass mailings and almost daily tracking polls, along with an expensive novelty: the Johnson campaign helicopter. "Johnson's 1948 Senate race was the first modern mass media campaign in Texas," according to one biographer. The level of corruption had an aspect of modernity as well—a foretaste of the era when money and media would come to dominate and all but overwhelm the political process.

The campaign was also an astonishing display of Johnson's political ingenuity, energy and will, and of his capacity to endure intense physical suffering. Early in the race, in May 1948, Johnson developed a kidney stone that, as the days of campaigning went on, inflicted "unbearable pain," high fevers (his temperature climbing above 104 degrees) and sudden chills that forced him to change shirts eight or nine times a day.

At one point in May 1948—in Dallas, fifteen years before John Kennedy was assassinated in that city and LBJ took the oath of office as president—a moment occurred that raised interesting counterfactual possibilities. Johnson gave in to the pain. He dictated a statement withdrawing from the Senate race. He told his aide, Woody Woodward, to telephone the Dallas newspapers and read it to them. "Do it right now," he ordered. "I'm out of this." Woodward stalled until Lady Bird Johnson flew to Dallas and talked her husband out of withdrawing.

If Johnson had withdrawn, or if he had lost the election to Stevenson, his political career (after eleven years in the House, where he was bored and stale and still relatively obscure) would have come to an end. In the years that followed, he would have settled into middle age as a prospering Texas rancher, a radio station owner, or perhaps a corporate lobbyist in Washington. He would have been out of elected office, out of government—and out of history. "This is the crisis," Johnson wrote to the old New Dealer Tommy Corcoran in June 1948. "I am either in the Senate or I'm out completely."

Johnson won the Senate race, or rather, he "won." He beat Stevenson by the famous eighty-seven votes from Box 13 in Boss George Parr's Duval County. Johnson's victory, challenged all the way to the U.S. Supreme Court and ratified only through a brilliant manipulation of technicalities (Justice Hugo Black ruled that the federal government did not have jurisdiction to interfere in the counting of ballots in a state primary election) made him "Landslide Lyndon," a title that, for a time, he boasted of, in a raffish, winking way.

The meaning of 1948 for Richard Nixon and Lyndon Johnson was decisively public. The meaning of the year for John Kennedy was decisively private.

Kennedy's crisis had begun a year earlier, in the late summer of 1947, just after he visited his sister Kathleen at Lismore Castle in Ireland; Kathleen was the widow of Billy Hartington, killed in France in 1944. Lismore was one of the castles that belonged to Billy's father, the Duke of Devonshire. Just after the holiday with his sister, Kennedy went to London, and there he suffered his first onset of Addison's disease, a potentially fatal insufficiency of the adrenal glands. A London doctor who examined Kennedy told Pamela Churchill (later Pamela Harriman): "That American friend of yours hasn't got more than a year to live."

Kennedy, attended by a nurse, returned to the United States on the *Queen Mary;* at the dock in New York, a priest gave him the last rites (the first of four times he would receive the Sacrament of Extreme Unction, the last time being on the afternoon of November 22, 1963, in Dallas). After weeks of treatment in Boston, Kennedy's health improved, and for the rest of his life (that is, for the next sixteen years) he managed to get along by injecting himself with cortisone—which was just coming into use as a treatment for Addison's—and other drugs that arrested or suppressed the symptoms of Addison's but caused further medical problems, including a deterioration of the spine, complications that would in themselves become life threatening.

From the time of the first attack in 1947, Kennedy and his family concealed the truth of his Addison's disease; if voters had known that the ostensibly vigorous young Kennedy suffered from a dangerous and debilitating illness, his subsequent political career, and his election as president, would have been impossible. Kennedy and his father knew that. For the rest of his life, Kennedy lied about this health. As he told an interviewer in 1959: "From 1946 through 1949, I underwent treatment . . . for malaria—the fevers ceased—there was complete rehabilitation." At the 1960 Democratic convention in Los Angeles, supporters of Lyndon Johnson (who still hoped he would be drafted for the presidential nomination) tried to head Kennedy off by spreading the word that the vigorous young senator from Massachusetts suffered from Addison's. It did not work; the Kennedy camp's denials (deflecting attention from Addison's to malaria) were sufficient to kill it as an issue. Kennedy offered Johnson the second spot on the ticket, which Johnson unexpectedly accepted. After the 1960 election, Kennedy declared flatly: "I have never had Addison's disease."

Addison's was a physical ordeal that had, or should have had, moral dimensions for Kennedy: Is it a political sin for a politician to lie about having a potentially fatal disease? And at what stage of his career does the public interest supersede medical privacy and make the continuing lie immoral? When he is a congressman? A senator? A presidential candidate? A president?

Then in May 1948, Kennedy's sister Kathleen died, along with her married lover, Peter Fitzwilliam, in a plane crash in the Rhone Valley of France. Kick was the sibling to whom Jack Kennedy was closest. In their grief, the Kennedys lied about the circumstances of her death—at least, about her scandalous relationship with Fitzwilliam—as they lied about Jack's illnesses. Kathleen hoped to marry Fitzwilliam, a war hero and something of a rake, after he had divorced his wife. Joseph Kennedy put the word out that Fitzwilliam, with whom Kick was traveling for a weekend on the Riviera, was merely a casual acquaintance with whom she had hitched a ride on the chartered plane.

Her death plunged John Kennedy into a period of distraction and morbidity that became a turning point in his life.

THE YEAR 1948 is a tangle of counterfactual possibilities:

If Johnson had not become senator, and thence, vice president, and thence, via Dallas, president, would there have been a Vietnam War? Would there have been a Voting Rights Act of 1965?

If there had been no Vietnam War, would there have been a Watergate? After all, most of the Watergate scandal arose from the illegal activities of Nixon's men to investigate and discredit antiwar dissenters.

If there had been no Hiss case, might there have been no President Nixon, and therefore no opening to China?

And what if Kennedy's Addison's disease had been frankly acknowledged, and the truth of his medical fragility had combined with his depression after Kathleen's death to drive him out of politics? Would Camelot have remained only an Arthurian myth—or a Broadway musical?

Nineteen forty-eight was a year when three future American presidents, whose careers were densely interbraided during the sixties, passed through formative ordeals and emerged, in one sense or another, reborn—launched toward their destinies, all three of which were either literally or politically fatal. Nineteen forty-eight was, for all three, a rite of passage and the moment of their political maturing.

Secrets were the drama and the key to the three ordeals. Nixon delved into the hidden Communist lives of Alger Hiss and Whittaker Chambers. John Kennedy locked the truth of his medical condition in a secret compartment, where it remained for years. "Landslide Lyndon" went to desperate legal lengths to keep Box 13 in Duval County sealed, its ballots hidden.

Those secrets converged with a year, with an era, of secrets—political, personal, atomic. The nascent Cold War took form upon a battleground of deadly concealed knowledge, of espionage and counterespionage the great, terrible prize of which was nothing less than the secret of the power to destroy the world. The United States possessed the power, and had twice demonstrated it upon inhabited cities, Hiroshima and Nagasaki. With the power came the fear—that the Soviet Union, yesterday's wartime ally, might steal the secret tomorrow, and might do to America what America had done to Japan.

The three future presidents, so different from one another in almost all ways (physically, intellectually, culturally, socially—in their geographical origins, in their accents), shared a tendency toward elaborately deliberated amorality; all three behaved as if rules were for others, not for them. All chose a course of advancement that demanded, among other things, forms of deceit. It was in 1948 that the three committed themselves to a mature and focused political ruthlessness.

They had in common a fierce ambition. Up to 1948, the driving force in Kennedy's political career was more his father's tribal ambition than his own desire. But after 1948, John Kennedy's political ambition—and his life—began to become his own.

The three men represented, on the dark side of their maneuvers, a convergence of personal ambition with secrecy, amorality, and a ruthless manipulation of the truth. These energies and techniques were all brought to bear at a critical moment: at the dawn of the atomic age, the start of the television age, and the onset of the real "American century," which eventually globalized American consumer democracy and popular culture.

If Franklin Roosevelt founded the modern presidency, Kennedy, Johnson, and Nixon, for better and for worse, were the founders of the postmodern presidency. Roosevelt accumulated enormous new power in the White House and, after more than three terms in residence there, achieved apotheosis—became, in vast stretches of America, a household god, a benevolent omnipotence. Kennedy's assassination in 1963 began not only his own apotheosis but also a radical new sense of presidential vulnerability: to an assassin's bullets and, with Johnson and Nixon, to an eventual demystification of the office. Dallas showed America that a president, even a young one, might suddenly die. Johnson and Nixon—through their entanglements in Vietnam and Watergate—showed Americans that presidents could, and did, lie. On Marx's dictum that history enacts itself first as tragedy and then as farce, it might be said that the presidential tragedies of Johnson and Nixon yielded a generation later to the farce of Bill Clinton and Monica Lewinsky. In any event, a process of diminution, the end of an inherent American reverence, or at least respect for the office of the presidency, began with Kennedy, Johnson, and Nixon in the sixties.

What's striking in the three beginnings in 1948 is the way in which they predict the ends, years later. The three tales have a symmetry—a Newtonian reciprocity, or a Shakespearean dynamic of comeuppance. A cold poetic justice manifests itself in each denouement.

Nixon's prosecution of Alger Hiss's secrets in 1948 predicts the prosecution of his own secrets, his undoing in Watergate. He would be hounded as relentlessly and fatally as he had hounded Hiss. (One of the hounds of Watergate would be Carl Bernstein, a young *Washington Post* reporter whose own father, a labor organizer in Washington and a member of the Communist Party, had sometimes been hounded into hiding by subpoenas from Nixon's House Un-American Activities Committee.)

Lyndon Johnson's theft of the Senate seat from Coke Stevenson in 1948 foreshadowed his own downfall, twenty years later, when the techniques of deceit that defeated Stevenson ultimately failed. In 1948, LBJ destroyed Stevenson, in part, by means of lies (claiming, for example, with outrageous aplomb, that the conservative Stevenson was a virtual socialist, in bed with Big Labor) and by having a friendly south Texas satrap diddle the returns. In 1968, Johnson ensnared and immobilized himself in webs of his own cunning and lies, especially about Vietnam. His fierce, elemental personal will, so powerful in 1948 against Coke Stevenson, became, in 1968, the energy of his own destruction.

As for Kennedy, his formal mythmaking began in 1948; he ended by vanishing after his death in a cloud of myth that apparently no revisionism can completely dispel. He became the myth, and the man all but disappeared into the elaborately spun confection. His beginning and end reverberated with the family theme of death. Kennedy's private grief for his sister Kathleen in

1948 foreshadowed the public grief over his own death in 1963. The last rites he received in 1947 took effect in 1963.

Among the Kennedys, there came to be much foreshadowing of this kind—a heartbreaking and almost hackneyed motif of doom, a trail of early death (by airplane or by assassination) from Joe Kennedy Jr. (blown to bits when his plane exploded over the English Channel in 1944) to Kathleen to Jack to Bobby to John Kennedy Jr., the pattern that has been melodramatized in folklore as The Kennedy Curse.

KENNEDY, JOHNSON, AND NIXON have become archetypes—media-generated archetypes, the memory's collages of tabloids and high history and television clips, embedded in the subsoil of the American mind.

Symbols and motifs recur—the interwoven, or interacting, imageries of American memories of the men, and of their shared era.

One might bracket Nixon's "Checkers" presentation in 1952 at one end and his strange, sad White House farewell ("My mother was a saint!") in 1974 at the other. Kennedy's snowy "Ask Not What America Can Do for You . . ." inaugural in 1961 can be paired with Dallas in 1963, and the riderless horse at the funeral and John Jr. saluting the casket, beside his mother in a black veil, and the eternal flame. Johnson's "We *shall* overcome" speech to Congress in 1965, a moment of historical grace and redemption when a Southern president invoked the anthem of the Black civil rights movement, is annulled by his heavy, drawling, hound-dog excruciations on the nation's television screen for the years and years of Vietnam.

At his political beginning and his end, Johnson conjured, strangely enough, a bracketing theme of helicopters. In his 1948 race for the Senate, Johnson became the first politician to use a helicopter while campaigning, an inspired novelty that became known as the "Johnson City Windmill," that dropped the candidate out of the hot blue sky (Lyndon *ex machina*) onto small towns and West Texas ranches. Nearly twenty years later at the vast American base at Danang, Vietnam, on a tarmac crowded with a thousand battle-ready choppers, a young officer would tell him, "Mr. President, your helicopter is waiting," and LBJ would reply, "Son, they are all my helicopters." Johnson took Texas by helicopter; in Vietnam, helicopters became the vehicles and symbols of the immense American military power that his grandiosity commanded; but the helicopters, descending upon a peasant nation, ultimately failed and gave Johnson the fate of George Armstrong Custer, but without the glory. In April 1975, when North Vietnamese Communist armies rolled into Saigon to put a belated end to the war that had ruined Johnson, the world watched the last overloaded American helicopters lifting off the embassy roof, people clinging to the skids; the helicopters would set down on aircraft carriers in the South China Sea and, to make room on the flight deck for more incoming choppers, the sailors simply pushed the helicopters, each worth millions of dollars, off the carrier deck into the sea. All of Lyndon Johnson's helicopters sank to the bottom.

AS PRESIDENT in the White House, a man becomes himself, squared—his hyperself, flaws and virtues enlarged by world attention and brought to fulfillment by the nature of the work and the power, and by the inescapability of the buck that stops on the desk in the Oval Office.

The coming of the nuclear age raised the moral stakes in presidential elections (from 1948 on, voters would know they were making a decision about the steadiness of the finger on the world-destroying red button) and therefore introduced considerations of the presidential stability and character from a new angle.

The character and mental stability of Richard Nixon, Lyndon Johnson, and John Kennedy would be examined in the new light of nuclear possibility; but perhaps they were not examined in that light nearly enough. All three suffered from what can only be called personality disorders. Nixon and Johnson would be accused of clinical paranoia, or, at least, of displaying, from time to time, unbalanced minds; Kennedy's personal recklessness raised an imponderable question about his common sense and, as it were, his moral sanity.

Further, the addition of nuclear weapons to the forces available to the commander-in-chief—the apocalypse that might conceivably be set loose at his discretion—changed the power and the nature of the American presidency. The obliteration of two cities—Hiroshima and Nagasaki—that ended a world war, ushered in a new metaphysics of the planet; and yet the decision to do all that had been made, in the end, by a man who was not even elected president (surely few voters in 1944 considered Harry Truman when they cast their ballots for Roosevelt), who made the decision in near-absolute secrecy to exercise, in the name of the world's greatest democracy, an annihilating power that had been unavailable to any previous ruler or autocrat in history. During the New Deal and World War II, Franklin Roosevelt had concentrated immense new power in the executive branch. Now the atomic bomb had given the president the power to destroy the world.

In the years to come, nuclear weapons—forbidden, potentially apocalyptic, hidden in silos under farmers' fields—would become so familiar as to be almost domesticated in a political sense, and half-forgotten, a kind of low-level background anxiety except in moments of crisis. But at such moments, they would present Kennedy, Johnson, and Nixon with dramatic dilemmas—in the Cuban missile crisis of 1962, in the conduct of the Vietnam War, and in Nixon's work to demilitarize the Cold War with the Soviet Union and China—and in doing so, they altered the yardsticks by which presidencies are judged.

THE ANXIETY OF THE OVERDOG

THE MOVIE WAS CALLED *The Best Years of Our Lives,* and it won the Oscar for Best Picture of 1946.

In the final scene of the movie, Dana Andrews (who played an ex-air force captain, Fred Derry) took Teresa Wright (in the role of Peggy Stephenson) in his arms, kissed her with a taut, mail-slot mouth, and then delivered a surprisingly grim proposal of marriage.

Fred warned Peggy:

"You know what it will be like? We'll have no money . . . no decent place to live. . . . We'll have to work. . . . We'll get kicked around!"

The proposal was a caveat emptor. It savored of anger, of self-pity. It sounded, weirdly, like Richard Nixon—a premonition of Nixon's famous "last press conference" in 1962, when he told reporters bitterly that they "won't have Nixon to kick around anymore."

And that was the end of the movie in 1946.

That was the future that Fred offered Peggy in postwar America.

Fred's speech sets off odd if remote bells when you listen to it a couple of times. Fred's least festive of marriage proposals might remind you of the future that John Milton set forth for Adam and Eve after they had sinned and God threw them out of Paradise: The shamed and disobedient pair would earn their living by the sweat of their brows, God warned, homeless and taking their chances in a fallen, bitter world; they would be . . . kicked around.

The movie told us that, for some reason difficult to understand at the moment of American victory, the American Adam and

Eve, Fred and Peggy, would go forth into a postlapsarian nation, as if they had just committed original sin—an interestingly un-triumphant thought for Hollywood to offer the country at the end of a world war that America had so unconditionally won. It was as if the scriptwriter, Robert Sherwood, had felt the undercurrent American sense of transgression. America had bitten a very dangerous apple. The great victory was also, in some sense, a Fall.

During the war, the poet Archibald MacLeish was enlisted to preside over the making of a series of propaganda films called *America at War.* A sample of dialogue from one of the movies: "We Americans are affable enough. We've never made killing a career, although we happen to be pretty good with a gun . . . a sentimental people, a sympathetic people."

But that American self-image, essential to Americans' sense of their own virtue, had by 1948 been compromised. During the Great Depression, the nation's popular culture had evolved an elaborately moving self-mythology of the American Underdog. Frank Capra, the Sicilian-born movie director whose movie *It's a Wonderful Life,* was the runner-up for the Best Picture Oscar in 1946, losing to *The Best Years of Our Lives,* had contributed memorable American fables to the underdog mythology—*It Happened One Night, Mr. Deeds Goes to Town, Mr. Smith Goes to Washington, Meet John Doe.*

Capra's vision of America worked when he portrayed endearing, vulnerable, ordinary people struggling against cynical wealth and power. In 1948, Capra came out with a different kind of movie, *State of the Union,* whose hero is a tycoon running for president and trying to restore decency to a corrupted political system. In April 1948, Truman attended the premiere of the movie at a Washington theater and loved it; later an article in *Variety* claimed that as a result of that movie Truman vowed to run in 1948, despite the odds against him, doing what the Spencer Tracy character did in the movie, taking his case directly to the people. Plenty of reviewers liked *State of the Union.* A critic for the *Scotsman,* seeing America from a distance, described the Spencer Tracy hero as "the idealist seeking a working basis for a capitalist democracy." Exactly: Frank Capra, and America itself, might be seen as an idealist seeking a working basis for a capitalist democracy.

But *State of the Union* is not as good as Capra's earlier work; it fails because in some crucial way America itself had lost the vulnerability that was its pathos and self-justification. America had morally as well as politically and economically changed by war's end. Hiroshima and Nagasaki, among other things, had changed it. America by 1948 had just begun to become enmeshed in the moral dilemmas of the Overdog. How can the overdog—especially an overdog armed with a bomb that can blow up the world—be virtuous?

THE MIND HAS BILLIONS of unfiltered sources, and a reading of any period profits from the perception of Herodotus, at the dawn of the writing of history, that although it is important to record what actually happened, it may be equally important to consider what people think happened. You need to see the connections people make, the myths they accept: How could anyone study the presidency of Ronald Reagan, for example, without grasping the importance of the American imagery he evoked—a version of the nation that was in some measure derived from 1930s movies—and the power of that imagery in the American imagination of the 1980s?

The Dana Andrews character in *The Best Years of Our Lives*—which was filmed just about the time Lieutenant Commander Richard Nixon mustered out of the navy and began his first run for Congress—superimposes himself upon the historical Nixon, in something of the same sleight-of-hand that was involved when the actor George C. Scott impersonated General George S. Patton in making the movie *Patton,* which, as things turned out, became President Richard Nixon's favorite—a film that he screened repeatedly in the White House during the days of the Cambodian invasion and that he used as a sort of moral text and spine-stiffener.

The playwright Arthur Miller once remarked that "Richard Nixon's character is our history." This might be said of all three men. They were the vivid, oversized protagonists who dominated the formative years of the baby boom generation, for example, in the dramas of Dallas and Vietnam and Watergate, of civil rights and all the rest of the historic cultural earthquake in the midst of which America substantially reinvented itself. Kennedy and Johnson and Nixon had been formed by World War II, by the precedent of Munich (never appease aggressors) and by the later logic of Munich's child, the Domino Theory (if Vietnam falls to communism, then other dominoes such as Laos and Cambodia and Thailand and—who knows?—India, will fall as well). At length, Kennedy, Johnson, and Nixon themselves became dominoes, toppling, one after another, losing their power to an assassin's bullets, to a long, misbegotten war, and to a scandal of misused power: the burst appendix of Watergate.

Historical images materialize slowly, like a Polaroid picture developing. Perceptions evolve into opinions, which mature into beliefs, which in time achieve the apotheosis of myth—actualities-once-or-twice-or-several-times-removed. Before you know it, they have become tabloid fairy tales. If one were fashioning fairy tales of Kennedy, Johnson, and Nixon out of spare parts from Jung and Joseph Campbell, from iconic news footage, from political celebrity journalism and docudrama, from clichés of characterization so highly polished that they have ascended into a sort of vivid media heaven, they might unfold like this:

Once upon a time, there lived a Light Prince and a Dark Prince.

Now, the Dark Prince sweated on his upper lip, and he walked on the beach in business shoes. He had black wavy hair, Bryll-cremed straight back, a five-o'clock shadow and a Bob Hope nose. His piano-key smile (false teeth) did not synch with his darting eyes. In public, he talked like a lawyer. In private, he talked like a foulmouthed thug. He played dirty tricks on people (including himself, whom he tape-recorded), and finally he was driven away from his castle, disgraced, and he went to live in a lonely house on the other side of the country, beside the Pacific Ocean.

But the Light Prince was a dreamboat. He was rich and handsome, with a tussock of brown-reddish hair that he pushed back in a charming, boyish way. When he rode through the streets in an open car, girls jumped up and down. He went to Harvard and he said "Cuber" instead of "Cuba." He died in Dallas, shot dead in his prime while riding in an open car, and later, in memory, he would become the American sungod.

John Kennedy would be Apollo.

Richard Nixon would be Vulcan, god of the American under-earth.

And between Kennedy's Camelot and Nixon's Shadowland, there would fall the interval of the False Claimant.

Lyndon Johnson was a shapeshifter; if you knew him of old, you knew his cruel genius for mimicry, for slipping into men's skins like a burglar to rummage through their secrets. In November 1963, Johnson came to the throne as a benign Uncle-Guardian ("We are not going to send American boys to do a job that Asian boys should be doing . . ."), but that was, it seems, a lie of political convenience (in the narrative of 1964, Barry Goldwater was the warmonger, the nuclear nut, and Johnson the nation's wise grief counselor and steward). LBJ revealed himself (too late) to be a devouring Cyclops: a warmaker, a child-killer, a Macbeth.

In later versions of the myth, Johnson the false claimant is half reprieved, granted a gentler reading as a tragic Monster-Idealist, himself a victim, and a sad case altogether—King Lear on the heath of the mad 1960s. After he abdicated, he went back to the ranch in the Hill Country of Texas and drank whisky and started smoking cigarettes again and let his hair grow long (like the young Furies who had driven him out of Washington) . . . and waited to die.

Fragments of myth commingle with one another. A woman who knew John Kennedy in the late forties said that he reminded her of Edwin Arlington Robinson's poem "Richard Cory." The poet presented "Richard Cory" as "a gentleman from sole to crown, / clean favored, and imperially slim." Like Kennedy, Richard Cory "fluttered pulses." Like Kennedy, he "glittered when he walked."

The woman who knew Kennedy did not pursue the comparison to the end of the poem, for, of course, it ended: "And Richard Cory, one calm summer night, / Went home and put a bullet through his head."

What does "Richard Cory" mean? It is a haunted little parable that on the surface warns against the envy of the rich and beautiful and seemingly all-favored for—who knows?—at the secret core of Richard Cory and perhaps of American success may be rot and a will to self-destruction.

But the myth of the poem, especially if set beside the myth of John Kennedy, is haunted by blurred traces of earlier god-stories. There is also the motif of ritual sacrifice—as if, for example, John Kennedy were Democracy's Osiris. The Egyptian god was slain, and resurrected, in a dramatization of the Earth's continuing fertility: The young and beautiful are sacrificed to appease the gods.

If—to pursue the conceit—Kennedy was a ritual sacrifice to appease some god or other, fancy would have to conclude that the gesture did not work. The gods were not appeased by Kennedy's death, but inflamed. Osiris was killed by his brother Seth, who is chaos. What followed Kennedy's death was the chaos of the sixties—a journey through the underworld.

All three presidents, Kennedy, Johnson, and Nixon, journeyed through the realm of Seth, and all of them were, in varying degrees, destroyed by it. All three presidents ended their careers in dramas that might be construed as American sacrifices. But if so, it is not clear to what they were sacrificed, by whom, and for what. Were they the older, World War II generation—with an exhausted ethos and worldview—sacrificed so that the baby boom generation and its new energies might supplant them? Were the sixties merely the forest fire clearing off old growth and nourishing the soil for the coming of new life?

Kennedy was young and beautiful, so that his sacrifice might be pleasing to the gods. Johnson and Nixon were not young and beautiful. They were not so much ritually sacrificed as ignominiously shouldered aside by destructive energies that originated, to a Shakespearean degree, within themselves.

When Nixon was a student at Whittier College, he and some classmates founded a club called the Orthogonians—the squares, the poorer boys and scholarship students. The established club on campus, called the Franklins, comprised the more privileged, sleeker students, who sponsored black-tie dinners and dances for themselves and rejoiced in a social ease that, throughout his life, eluded Richard Nixon. The Orthogonians in defiance gave hot dog and baked bean dinners to which they wore open-collar shirts.

All his life Richard Nixon harbored an Orthogonian's resentment of the Franklins of the world.

John Kennedy was a quintessential privileged Franklin; so, indeed, was Richard Cory.

Lyndon Johnson, too—a child of hard times in the Texas Hill Country, where his father was a failure and his mother felt she had married beneath herself—resented and envied Kennedy's beauty and privilege and money and Harvard education. When he became vice president under Kennedy, "the Harvards," as he called them, treated him like an uncouth has-been, like the hired help.

But in America, of course, the difference between a Franklin and an Orthogonian (or someone far poorer than an Orthogonian) may be just a matter of time. Joe Kennedy, as a young Boston Irishman, harbored a deep Orthogonian outsider's hatred of the ruling Boston Brahmin class that had so long kept the Irish down and, even at Harvard, had kept him out of the good clubs. The same fuel of resentment that propelled Joe Kennedy to make millions and build a sort of Prospero's island of money and privilege and immunity around his tribe also drove Richard Nixon's efficient engine.

And Lyndon Johnson's, as well. In 1948, Johnson began to tell friends that he had become a millionaire. A million dollars is not an unusual personal fortune now, but in the America of 1948, it was still an almost mythic amount that, above all, signaled invulnerability, a kind of untouchability in a world that remembered—keenly, with a dark chill that touched the bones—what it meant to be poor in the Great Depression. Johnson had started out his political career as a selfless and generous school teacher and New Dealer. Now, in the late 1940s, he had rich and powerful friends in Texas, and Franklin Roosevelt and the New Deal were gone.

ANNUS MIRABILIS

IT WAS A COLD WINTER—a little postwar Ice Age, a literal-minded siege of weather to mark the start of the Cold War. Twenty-five inches of snow fell on New York just after Christmas 1947. Over the Midwest, the temperature sank to fifty-four below. Ice enameled the Deep South. In Washington, people could skate across the Potomac to Virginia. Oil tankers on the Atlantic were held up in winter storms for days; when they made it to America they might find themselves locked in rivers by the ice.

America burned more oil that year than it ever had, and the cold stirred a longer-range anxiety. Oil reserves were low: In 1947, U.S. demand was 300,000 barrels more per day than the voracious wartime demand of 1944. When spring finally arrived in 1948, Secretary of State George C. Marshall would tell Harry Truman that he opposed American recognition of Israel; the new Jewish state, Marshall thought, would enrage the Arabs and jeopardize the nation's oil supplies.

Palestine would plunge into full open war in May.

World War II had settled so much (the Japanese Empire, anyway, and the Third Reich), but it had also set loose terrible new energies that followed, almost without pause, on the old destruction.

America froze. France and Italy and Greece contemplated Communism. What Winston Churchill had called an Iron Curtain hardened from the Baltic to the Adriatic.

In newly independent India, the seventy-nine-year-old Mahatma Gandhi fasted—moral blackmail to persuade Muslims and Hindus to stop killing one another. Kashmir would go up in flames. There were massacres in the Punjab. Sikh and Hindu refugees demanded revenge against Pakistan. Prime Minister

Liaquat Ali Khan of Pakistan caught the spirit of things: "Every Pakistani is an atom bomb in himself." Gandhi sipped hot water while his liver deteriorated.

Then a wave of nonsectarian remorse swept across India and, as *Life* reported, "Delhi's frayed citizens began to organize meetings and processions around the single motto, 'Save Gandhi's life.'" Post office employees stamped every letter mailed in New Delhi with the message, "Keep communal peace and save Mahatma Gandhi." Gandhi agreed to break his fast. A Muslim politician handed Gandhi a glass of orange juice mixed with dextrasol. He drank it.

But then, on the same day that Orville Wright died in America, in New Delhi a young man named Nathu Ram Vinayak Godse knelt at Gandhi's feet as the Mahatma walked toward his prayers.

The young man said, "You are late today for the prayer."

Gandhi replied, "Yes, I am."

The young man fired a Beretta automatic pistol three times into Gandhi's chest and stomach. Gandhi fell backward. He muttered, "Ai Ram, ai ram (O Rama, O Rama)."

The assassin was a member of a militant Hindu organization called Mahasabha (The Great Society).

As Gandhi lay dying, his grandniece Ava chanted his favorite verse from the Bhagavad-Gita: "Arjuna asked: 'My lord, how can we recognize the saint who has attained pure intellect, who has reached this state of bliss, and whose mind is steady? How does he talk, how does he live, and how does he act? . . . The sage whose mind is unruffled in suffering, whose desire is not to rouse by enjoyment, who is without attachment to anger or fear—take him to be one who stands at that lofty level."

It was said that the night before he died, Gandhi recited a Gujarati couplet known in Porbandar, where he was born: "This is a strange world. How long have I to play this game?"

That note of metaphysical disorientation reverberated in 1948. So much of the world had been torn loose from its moorings—by world war, of course, but also by science. Orville Wright died only a couple of months after a test pilot named Chuck Yeager, flying a projectile called the X-I in the skies over Muroc Field in California, burning a cocktail of alcohol and liquid oxygen, became the first man to punch through the sound barrier, a mystical and supposedly fatal wall, beyond which, many thought, lay death, or some other dimension.

Yeager had said that was nonsense, and he was right. Gandhi had said, "I heartily detest this mad desire to destroy distance and time." The world was poised on an ambivalence, as it were, between Chuck Yeager and Mahatma Gandhi.

J. Robert Oppenheimer, the director of the atomic project at Los Alamos, found himself deeply reproved by his own mystical conscience. On the day in May 1945, when he had set off the first atomic bomb, in the American desert, he, too, quoted the Bhagavad-Gita: "I am become death, the destroyer of worlds."

Now, in early 1948, Oppenheimer was the director of the Institute for Advanced Study at Princeton (home, as well, to Albert Einstein, another genius in whose mind science and mysticism circled round to meet one another in an unexpected, apocalyptic rendezvous). In *Technology Review,* Oppenheimer published an article reflecting his bad conscience. He wrote:

> The experience of the war . . . has left us with a legacy of concern. . . . Nowhere is this troubled sense of responsibility more acute . . . than among those who participated in the development of atomic energy for military purposes. . . . The atomic bomb came straight out of our laboratories and our journals. . . . In some sort of crude sense which no vulgarity, no humor, no overstatement can quite extinguish, the physicists have known sin. And this is a knowledge which they cannot lose.

On the day of his death, Gandhi talked to the photographer Margaret Bourke-White. She mentioned to him that he had told her once that he hoped he would live to be 125 years old. Now he said, "I have lost that hope. . . . I do not want to live in darkness and in madness. I cannot continue."

Bourke-White said that Americans, too, were filled with foreboding, especially about the atomic bomb.

"How would you use nonviolence against the atomic bomb?" she asked.

"Ah, ah," he said. "How should I answer that?" He worked his spinning wheel for a moment.

Then he said, "By prayerful action."

Bourke-White replied, "You would pray while the planes are overhead?"

Gandhi shook his head. "I said prayerful *action*. I would come out in the open and let the pilot see I had not the face of evil against him."

Gandhi paused.

The pilot would not see my face from such a height. . . . But that longing in our hearts that he won't come to harm would reach up to him and his eyes would be opened. Those who were done to death in Hiroshima by the bomb, if they had died with that prayerful action, died openly with prayer in their hearts, without uttering a groan, the war would not have ended as disgracefully as it has. It is a question now whether the victors are really the victors or the victims. The world is not at peace. It is still more dreadful.

That was the terrible disquiet—the sense now crystallizing in 1948 that so much death and sacrifice had merely opened the door upon still more death and sacrifice, that the war had among other things served mostly to perfect the instruments of destruction and to introduce the human conscience to forms of killing that, so to speak, lay beyond the moral sound barrier, in dimensions previously unthinkable or in any event impossible.

Mankind seemed to have picked the lock to the last room in Bluebeard's castle. And so what Oppenheimer and his physicists saw within that room threw them back, atavistically, into something as primitive as the sense of sin.

Just at the time of Gandhi's death, in January 1948, *Life* magazine, Henry Luce's catalog of postwar American prosperity and possibility, published a strange parable about Satan on New Year's Eve. The subheading of the article said: "When the Age of Reason began, he went underground. . . . His strategy is to make men think he doesn't even exist. . . . And although theologians are now discovering him anew, he never had it so good."

The story was written by a then-obscure editor of Luce's *Time* named Whittaker Chambers. In Chambers's tale, the devil, "a massive and immaculate stranger with a rich Miami tan," suddenly materializes toward midnight in "a New York nightclub" much like the Rainbow Room, sixty-five stories above Rockefeller Center.

Chambers, who wrestled with devils all his life, casts himself in the role of a character he calls "the Pessimist." The devil asks the Pessimist, "Do you still doubt my existence? Then I will give you evidence that even you cannot refute. *Si monumentum requiris, circumspice.* If you are seeking my monument, look around you." The devil draws the Pessimist to a window overlooking the city and the harbor and says, "Behold the world! Behold my handiwork!"

The article continues: "In the room behind them the band had struck up 'Bongo, Bongo, Bongo, I Don't Want to Leave the Congo'. . . Below them the sheer walls of Rockefeller Center, abstractly glittering with their geometry of electrically lighted windows, plunged gray and chasmic to the city at their base.

"'A proud architecture,' said the devil. 'We have a view in hell rather like that. And certain it is that in all human history man has never before closed such a haughty edifice above his head to fend off the wind and rain.'"

The devil tells the Pessimist: "I have brought man to the point of intellectual pride where self-extermination lies within his power. There is not only the bomb, of which I frankly am a little tired of hearing, there are the much less discussed delights of bacteriological annihilation. And it is only a question of time until whole populations can be driven ultrasonically insane in time of war by sound which their ears cannot hear but their nerves cannot bear." Death by ultrasound!

The devil finishes his sermon to the Pessimist: "It still lies with man to make the choice (after all, the filthy beetles have free will): a skeleton beside a broken wall on a dead planet purged of all suffering because purged of all life; or Him, with all that that entails. Personally, as I glance around this room, I have never felt my chances to be so good."

IT WAS A SIGN of Henry Luce's indulgence that *Life* published the devil parable, which appealed (as Chambers himself did) to the melodramatic, theological side of Luce's nature.

In 1948, Luce's magazines (articulating a kingdom of God on Earth by way of American ingenuity and American virtue in close alliance, profit and prophet hand in glove, materialism under divine sponsorship), worked intensely at the theme of the repentant sinner. In another issue that January, *Life* published "The Failure of Marxism," by the former Marxist believer, the author John Dos Passos. He, too, had been to the devil's camp and brought back hard-won experience from hell: "Revolutions have happened and regimes and empires have crashed in the mud, but the old problem of how to control man's domination of man remains unsolved." Both Dos Passos and Chambers (though Chambers's Communist past was, for the moment, concealed from the general public) would appear before the mass audience of the

Luce press in the manner of sinners coming to the front of the church and witnessing to the congregation their former lives of sin.

With the end of World War II, America's manifest destiny had been validated on a global scale . . . and yet history quickly devolved, by 1948, to a theologically classic struggle between good and evil: Between the Soviet Union's godless barbarism and America's prospering freedom. America's wartime ally against Hitler "now rules," wrote Dos Passos, "a depraved and exhausted people by brute force. . . . The Russian socialized state has been allowed to develop into a military force for pillage and conquest."

Dos Passos told the American congregation: "The dilemma of our time, under the cover of the dazzle of socialist illusions, and just at the moment when our technology is opening up the certainty of really widespread well being in material things, the masses of mankind are being plunged back into a regime of misery and servitude such as has not existed in the west since the days of serfdom."

Early 1948 was exactly the moment the chill set in. The Communists took over Czechoslovakia. The Truman Doctrine went to the aid of Greece and Turkey. The Marshall Plan was in motion. Before long, the Berlin airlift would save the city where, fourteen years later, Kennedy would appeal to the myth of 1948 by proclaiming, *"Ich bin ein Berliner."*

In 1948, the emergent Cold War was Manichaean and invited vocabularies of the absolute. The world was now given to speaking of irreconcilable categories (good and evil, God and devil, freedom and communism) because it had recently seen such vivid enactments of the absolute at such places as Auschwitz and Hiroshima—had seen war advance, or degenerate, into new dimensions of annihilation. Civilizations had vanished. Empires had fallen. Much of Europe had been reduced to rubble. Six million Jews had been destroyed.

Miracles (even of the blackest kind) and revolutions had become commonplace. And above all, the terrible secrets of atomic energy—that form of negative transubstantiation whereby the rearrangement of an atom might blow up the planet—gave to the bipolarization of the world an apocalyptic urgency.

In his magazines, Henry Luce, tycoon and moralist, worked an uneasy borderline between God and Mammon. Luce liked Whittaker Chambers because Chambers could (amid the ads for liquor and cigarettes and new cars) sound the note of the Prophet Amos: "Woe to them that are at ease in Zion."

Chambers's heavy, mordant prose in the devil parable ("How well I know the rationalist and liberal mind," says the devil, "the modern mind that still does not understand the nature of a commonplace like electricity but does not hesitate to question the existence of heaven and hell; the mind that cannot grasp the mystery of the universe in which it has lived 600,000 years, let alone those greater universes beyond the myopia of man's greatest telescopes, but does not hesitate to doubt that its creator and the creation are divine . . .") is sandwiched, after all, in a super-sized glossy picture magazine that was, for its millions of readers across America, a much-awaited weekly event and a sort of metaphysical bridge—a mass medium indeed—that interpreted postwar America to itself in all its political, economic, social, artistic, and moral dimensions. In *Life,* the very advertising came to speak in curiously religious and world-historical terms.

Not far from Whittaker Chambers's parable, the reader found an advertisement for Dr. West's "Miracle Tuft Brush" and Dr. West's "Miracle Tooth Paste." Madison Avenue naturally tended toward the absolute, the supernatural. Jesus' miracles cured lepers. Dr. West's miracles cure stained teeth.

America set its course for material paradise. It was the beginning of the great historical pivot from depression and world war to what became America's vast peacetime imperial consumerism—the automobile-and-suburb culture, the blossoming triumph of the middle class in the avid reciprocity of demanding and supplying, an Aladdin's cave of good things long denied, and even undreamed of.

Accordingly, the word "revolution" came off the barricades and into the shops. Gillette introduced the "revolutionary new Gillette Blue Blade dispenser: blade changing a cinch and shaving faster and more convenient than ever before." Not far from the Chambers piece on the devil, *Life* published an article on the dress designer Christian Dior: "Like all great revolutionists, Christian Dior is a creature of destiny." *Life* was referring to Dior's decision on what to do with hemlines.

The baby boom was in utero, or in diapers. George W. Bush and Bill Clinton were approaching their terrible twos.

In *Life,* an ad for Mutual Life Insurance showed a drawing of a young man just about Richard Nixon's age (thirty-five)—hair slicked back like Nixon's—bending over a child, about two years old, sleeping in a crib with a teddy bear.

The father says, "Goodnight, Mr. President . . . and big dreams."

CHAPTER ONE

THREE YOUNG MEN

JACK'S FAVORITE MOVIE

IN 1948, John Kennedy was a gauntly boyish freshman congressman from the Eleventh District of Massachusetts. He lived in Georgetown in a row house, along with his sister Eunice and his aide, Billy Sutton, and a cook and a butler sent down by his father to keep the place in some kind of order. Kennedy never had a strong sense of home—growing up, he and his brothers and sisters would return from boarding school or college and, instead of having rooms of their own at Hyannisport or Palm Beach, they would simply take whatever bedrooms were unoccupied. So the Georgetown house had that bivouac frat house air. Kennedy attended to his always fragile health, and to a variety of attractive women. He went to New York as often as he could to see the Broadway shows. The day-to-day business of his congressional office was tedious; he left it to his staff.

Sargent Shriver, a young Yale graduate, ran the Merchandise Mart in Chicago for Joe Kennedy. Shriver moved into a house nearby, on N Street. He told the Kennedy biographers Joan and Blair Clark: "[Eunice and Jack] had a lot of dinner parties. That's where I first met Richard Nixon and Joe McCarthy . . . both young veterans. Nixon was a freshman congressman, like Jack, and I saw him there several times. Joe McCarthy was a freshman senator from Wisconsin, a colorful, dynamic outspoken, frank, Irish-type fellow. It was natural for them—Jack and Mc-Carthy—to be friendly. . . . It was an intelligent group. Young. Optimistic."

Other freshmen congressmen, among them Henry M. ("Scoop") Jackson of Washington and George Smathers of Florida, came to dinner.

Joe McCarthy dated Eunice for a while, with Joe Kennedy's approval. (Joseph P. Kennedy took careful note of everything his children did, including whom they dated). Joe Kennedy liked McCarthy. So did Jack Kennedy. McCarthy played shortstop on the Kennedys' "Barefoot Boys" softball team at Hyannis, but was taken out of the game after he made four errors.

A few years later, after McCarthy had become notorious, a speaker at the one-hundredth anniversary of the Spee Club at Harvard remarked that he was glad the Spee had not produced a Joe McCarthy or an Alger Hiss. Kennedy was there that night and he demanded, with uncharacteristic anger, "How dare you couple the name of a great American patriot with that of a traitor?" Kennedy stalked out of the room. In 1952, when Kennedy was running for the Senate against Henry Cabot Lodge, McCarthy, then hunting Communists and at the height of his garish fame, campaigned for Republican candidates all over the country, but stayed out of Massachusetts partly because Joe Kennedy (who had contributed money to McCarthy's war chest) asked him to stay away, and partly because McCarthy had picked up rumors that Lodge and other moderate Republicans were plotting against him. When it came time for the Senate to vote on the censure of McCarthy in 1954, Kennedy (recovering from a back operation) stayed away and did not vote.

In those early days, before drink and his own recklessness ruined him, McCarthy set himself up as a sort of blue-collar Kennedy. He had a boorish charm. Like Jack, McCarthy dated many women. A bachelor living in an aide's spare bedroom in the Anacostia section of the city—where the postwar housing shortage remained acute—McCarthy, the former chicken farmer from Appleton, Wisconsin, had a remarkable appetite for Washington social life. When he arrived in the Senate in 1947, having defeated Robert LaFollette, he set out to accept every invitation he received. As one Wisconsin journalist wrote, "He is handsome in a dark, square-jawed way that has kept the Washington society columnists chirping excitedly ever since he alighted on the capital roost. . . . The scratching for the decorative McCarthy's presence at dinners and cocktail parties is particularly furious."

Jack Kennedy and Joe McCarthy shared a kind of juvenile indifference to their own appearance. McCarthy wore inexpensive dark blue, double-breasted suits, which he bought four at a time and wore until they were frayed and shiny. McCarthy's biographer, Thomas C. Reeves, reported: "Joe was extremely careless about clothing. Stockings and underwear were frequently scattered all over his room; he left a trail of hats wherever he went. When packing a suitcase, he would grab whatever was in sight. He borrowed spare clothes when necessary. His shirts were often rumpled and dirty. . . . His often garish ties were frequently askew and soiled."

Congressman Kennedy's secretary, Mary Davis, reported: "He . . . left clothes all over the place. He was constantly replacing or trying to retrieve his coats."

Kennedy's favorite movie in 1948 was *Red River.* He went to see it several times with Billy Sutton. Howard Hawkes's epic Oedipal Western reflected, in a way almost too pat, John Kennedy's struggle that year to break away from his father's autocratic control and to assert an identity of his own.

In the movie, Matt (Montgomery Clift) even resembled Kennedy—at least, he was Kennedy's physical type: gaunt, youthfully handsome. Clift held himself in a wary, crouched posture, shoulders hunched, a tautness of abdominal muscles. The overall effect, in profile, made him look like a tense parenthesis. Kennedy held himself in the same gingerly posture because of his back trouble.

Both Matt and young John Kennedy had intelligent eyes that searched the father's face for instructions; but as the story proceeded, Matt's eyes reflected the young man's transition to a will of his own.

The part of Joe Kennedy in the movie was taken by John Wayne, who played the primal prairie tyrant, Tom Dunson, a self-made cattleman and archetype of ruthless American imperial energy—a law unto himself. All his business life, Joe Kennedy had operated roughly along the lines of Tom Dunson, making his own rules, creating, out of nothing, his own empire. John Kennedy, always acutely and lovingly and uncomfortably aware of his powerful and sometimes embarrassing father, responded to the movie.

In 1948, Franklin Roosevelt, the great god, was gone. Winston Churchill was out of office. The evil gods Hitler and Mussolini were dead and buried in their ignominy. Stalin had vanished behind his Iron Curtain. The race of giant-fathers was much diminished. The postwar years marked the beginning of the transition of power to a new generation—to men such as Richard Nixon, Lyndon Johnson, and Jack Kennedy. *Red River* was an exact parable of the process: the story of a young man earning the right to take over the outfit, to inherit the cattle ranch, to supersede his foster father. To be The Man himself.

Joe Kennedy was by no means a broken man, but he had decided that his dreams would now be enacted and fulfilled not by him, but by his surviving children—starting with Jack. Joe Kennedy had botched his own chance at history, as he hard-headedly admitted; his mythmaking gifts could work magic for his family, but not for himself. Balzac said that every great fortune begins with a great crime; Kennedy's great fortune—some $400 million (about $3 billion in contemporary dollars)—had at the least been acquired by sharp dealing, by stock churning and bootlegging, and other maneuvers that were not always in line with Marquis of Queensberry's rules.

After his disastrous tenure as the U.S. ambassador in London at the start of the war, after saying things that had hurt him publicly (he was enraged at Harry Truman for accepting the nomination for vice president in 1944 and asked him angrily: "Harry, how can you go on a ticket with that crippled son of a bitch that killed my son?"), Joe Kennedy's reputation was irretrievable. He emerged from the war as a disgraced appeaser, a defeatist, and probably an anti-Semite. Anti-Semitism before the war had been a commonplace informal inclination of America's Christian ruling classes—a sort of snobbery, a reflex of class. After Auschwitz, anti-Semitism became sinister in a previously unthinkable way; the meaning of anti-Semitism passed from the realm of the comparative/social to the absolute/moral. To be an anti-Semite was, by inference, to be an accomplice of Hitler, of evil itself. Public figures in America so tainted would be, for official purposes at least, beyond the pale. Joe Kennedy had become El Sordo in the cave—Hemingway's corrupted clan leader: shrewd, repudiated, past his prime.

So he receded. He sold his liquor interests to clear the stage morally for Jack's career; it was a way of laundering the Kennedy fortune. The old man would remain out of sight backstage for the duration, except for the memorable snowy day in January 1961 when he would sit in the viewing stand in front of the White House to watch Jack ride by as the new president—the son rising in his open car and tipping his silk top hat to his father in eloquent acknowledgement of all that had come before: acknowledgement that the cattle drive was over, and that it had been great success, and that, as the son had just announced at the Capitol, "the torch [had] passed to a new generaton." Inauguration day of 1961 completed the transfer of power from Joe to Jack that had begun in 1948.

WHEN JACK FIRST CAME to Washington as a congressman in January 1947, he seemed lackadaisical. He took little interest in his congressional work; it was as if something lingered from adolescence and made him dig in his heels and resist performing the duties that his father had imposed upon him. His Washington secretary, Mary Davis, who had extensive experience on Capitol Hill, reported later that Jack "did not know the first thing about what he was doing." Davis worked for him for six years and would never see much improvement in that regard: "He never did involve himself in the workings of the office. He wasn't a methodical person. Everything that came into the office was handed to me." Kennedy was accustomed to having servants pick up after him.

Joe Kennedy exerted an astonishing degree of detailed personal control over all his children. He had agents who spied on them. He had his man Frank Morrissey take charge of Jack's Boston office. The office secretary kept a log of every visitor to the office and gave it to the father as a matter of course. In *A Question of Character,* Thomas C. Reeves reported that "Timothy ('Ted') Reardon, Joe Junior's ever-loyal Harvard roommate, was put in charge of the Washington office, and the ambassador offered him money to report on Jack's activities. There was even a maid in Jack's Georgetown home who reported to the ambassador."

Jack never carried money. Almost everyone who knew him (friends, members of his staff, dates) told stories about having to pick up the check in restaurants, or about his putting the touch on them for small loans, which were rarely repaid. Joe Kennedy covered most of Jack's expenses, whether for the office or for personal items. As a congressman, Jack earned $12,000 a year, but he had a rich child's innocence about money. The ambassador had succeeded almost too well in his desire to accumulate so much money that he could liberate his children from financial concerns and free them for pursuits of public service.

Jack seemed resigned to his father's overbearing control. He joked about it: "I guess Dad has decided that he's going to be the ventriloquist," he told his friend Lem Billings, "so I guess that leaves me the role of dummy."

Joe Kennedy's grip upon his tribe was something close to totalitarian. The sheltered, isolated dynamics of John Kennedy's upbringing produced an unusual young man who in certain ways remained dangerously innocent of elementary facts of American life—the everyday realities of money, for example, and how people acquire and spend it; or the realities of race. He could approach an issue such as the advisability of the Taft-Hartley Act—proposing to outlaw the closed union shop, a hot issue in 1948—with modulated good sense (he joined most Democrats in opposing the act but saw some useful provisions in it), but his views on such matters were almost totally divorced from anything in his personal experience.

In later years, almost all portraits of John Kennedy would speak of a coolness or a detachment in his character. The famous detachment, beloved of Kennedy's iconographers, originated, it may be, not in some Olympian dispassion of Kennedy's brain but rather in the fanatical exclusivity of the Kennedy tribe ("Take it from me," said Patsy Mulkern, one of the family retainers, "there's nobody close to them") and the consequent detachment from many of the dimensions of American life. Kennedy possessed a gift of friendship, a sharp and wry sense of humor, and a fund of human kindness that was unusual. His friend George Smathers remarked, "He loved people, not in the intimate sense, perhaps, but he loved their humanness. He loved conversation. The more personal and gossipy the more he loved it. Whenever you had inside, salacious stuff, he wanted to hear it." And yet Kennedy did not possess a second-nature instinct about people's lives that comes from having existed on quite the same plane on which others normally struggle.

Still, his numerous chronic physical frailties had given him an education in what it means to suffer. The pain of his ailments—and of his brother Joe's death and his sister Kathleen's death and his sister Rosemary's mental retardation and lobotomy—taught him, on the good side, something about grace and good humor;

and on the reckless side, a Byronic comprehension of the evanescence of life and the advisability of taking sexual pleasures as you can and when you can and as often as possible. The admirably stoic detachment of his suffering, cheerfully borne, was balanced by the paradoxical detachment of debaucheries, recklessly and even cruelly pursued.

The debaucheries were cruel when he persisted in them after he was married; even before that, Jack displayed something of the ambassador's goatish narcissism.

The ambassador flirted with and pursued his son's girlfriends. Jack may have recognized the moment in *Red River* when John Wayne calls upon Matt's girlfriend (Joanne Dru). In an ugly scene, the old man looks her over as if she were breeding stock, offers to marry her, and give her a cut of his kingdom if she will bear his children. *Droit du seigneur* as incest. In something of the same spirit, Joe Kennedy apparently attempted to bed Inga Arvad, Jack's beautiful Danish girlfriend, with whom Jack had been, it seems, in love, even as the old man broke the couple up, forbidding Jack to see her again. Arvad's son said years later: "The Kennedy family was weird. The family was just an extension of the old man's schizophrenic condition. . . . She thought old Joe was awfully hard—a really mean man. He could be very charming when she and Jack were with him, but if she left the room, he'd come down on Jack about her, and if Jack left the room, he'd try and hop in the sack with her. . . . She thought it was a totally amoral situation, that there was something incestuous about the whole family."

Cis McLaughlin, another friend of Jack's, was a married woman when the ex-ambassador invited her out in New York and suggested that she come to his private apartment in Miami and have sex with him. "'You are a good-looking girl and what are you wasting your time for?' he said. 'I pay my butler more than your husband will ever make for a living, you know you can do better.'"

There would be hundreds of Joe Kennedy dirty-old-man stories—ranging in tone from the hilarious to the repellent. One
story managed to be both. Jack told friends about the time one
of his sister's friends woke up in the middle of the night when
she was visiting the Kennedys at Hyannis Port. The ambassador
was standing beside the bed, removing his robe. He whispered to
her: "This is something you'll always remember."

That much was surely true.

At Hyannis, Jack would sometimes warn female guests as they
were about to go to bed: "Be sure to lock the bedroom door. The
Ambassador has a tendency to prowl late at night." The ambassador appeared at a young woman's room at the Cape—one of his
sister Eunice's friends—told her he wanted to say goodnight, and
then kissed her full on the mouth. When this happened, the door
to Eunice's room was open. The friend recalled: "I remember
thinking, 'How embarrassing for Eunice.'"

Two seemingly contradictory sides of John Kennedy's nature—his cool intellectual detachment on the one hand, and his
reckless sexual hedonism on the other—were both the responses
of his nature to the peculiar, powerfully distorting presence of his
father.

The cool detachment represented, to some degree, Jack's un-
trained temperament. He had grown up on what amounted to a
different planet, the planet Kennedy. He came to American politics as an immigrant from that other world and therefore—although he savored the "Sweet Adeline" blarney of the Honey
Fitz world (the lore of shrewd Boston Irish localism) and grasped
political issues and strategy intellectually—he did not have a
visceral feel for the lives of his constituents. It eventually came to
be fashionable in the media to refer to the Kennedys as "America's Royal Family," and although it was a mawkish line, it carried some truth—not least in its implication that the Kennedys,
like the royals of England, lived lives radically apart from those
of commoners.

Kennedy's reckless hedonism belonged as well to the idea of royal males on another planet not quite fully wired up to the value systems of the bourgeois planet Earth. One seeks in vain for evidence that either Joe Kennedy or Jack Kennedy suffered spasms of remorse, for example, when they betrayed their wives. "Betrayed their wives," in fact, is not a phrase that would have occurred to either of them. Jack was on a yacht in the Mediterranean, with Senator George Smathers, enjoying a procession of beautiful young women, when Jackie Kennedy's first child was stillborn. Jack, even when he heard the news, seemed reluctant to return home from the frolic.

One of the reasons for the Kennedy charisma was precisely its freedom from guilt. Aristocratic insouciance in matters of sex was scandalously appealing. Kennedy admired it in the Whig aristocracy. He caught the spirit that Plutarch was thinking of when he wrote of Marc Antony: "He did not fear the audit of his copulations, but obeyed the urgings of nature, and in doing so, left behind him the foundations of many a noble Roman house."

Jack Kennedy was certainly imitating his father's competitive tomcat amorality. More deeply than that, he seems to have felt untrammeled in his sexual life because, like his father, he was unrestrained either by the teachings of his Church or by the inhibitions of a conventional conscience.

He very likely would have pursued the same energetic extracurricular sexual life even if he had not been oppressed by the *memento mori* of his Addison's and other ailments, or by the tragic warnings of his brother's, and then his sister's, death. His energetic sexual behavior was also a symptom of a primitive moral detachment that he inherited from his father—it signaled, not a passionate involvement with others, but, instead, a paradoxical kind of isolation, even a poignant cluelessness.

THE TRANSFORMATION OF
A QUAKER BOY

THE NIXON LIBRARY in Yorba Linda has in its files a flier from May 1947 announcing a breakfast meeting of the Los Angeles Sales Executives Club to discuss the theme of "Communism V. American Business."

One speaker at the breakfast would be Art Linkletter, of the *People Are Funny* show.

The other speaker would be freshman United States Congressman Richard Nixon. The headline of the flier proclaims: "He's Dynamic—He's Honest—He's American—He Pulls No Punches."

That is the young Richard Nixon of historic memory—or at least, that is Nixon as he wished to present himself: an earnest veteran, back from the war, and, as his sponsors saw him, a political comer, a future leader of the Republican Party. The political editor of the *Los Angeles Times,* Kyle Palmer, wrote that Nixon represented a "brand of Americanism in our national political affairs which is unmixed by any other ideology, which sees clearly, thinks straight and deals squarely."

But the black-and-white close-up photo portrait that accompanies the words in the brochure is obscurely disturbing—unexpected, even mysterious. Surely the man in the photograph cannot be the man described in the headline.

In the photograph the young Nixon wears an enigmatic half-smile, lips closed but wet, his black eyes sanpaku and strangely sleepy, almost as if (by a shocking improbability) there were seductive thoughts occurring behind them. But what, exactly, was the object of his desire? The answer is a secret. The man is a sphinx.

The face, as in later life, is a slightly odd, distinctive off-handsome, a face broad and bottom-heavy (the famous jowls, rounded like an eggplant), bisected, upper from lower, by the line of the ears and eyes, as if the head comprised two hemispheres that do not quite go together: that clash. One senses an architecture of discrepancy and contradiction. The mystery seems to deepen the more you contemplate his face.

The dark, watchful-but-dreamy eyes are baldachinned by shading eyebrows. A capacious brow above counterbalances jowl-and-jaw below. On top, tense, Brillantined black hair ripples straight back from the forehead, like rapids.

Nixon's nose descends straightforwardly between caterpillar eyebrows, but two-thirds of the trip down, it turns Cyrano, acquiring a gravid fleshy mass that belongs to the rounded heaviness of the lower hemisphere.

The disconcerting impression of the photograph is, at first, one of prissy smugness; and then, after a moment, of what (in a parallel universe) would look—can it be?—like a weirdly opiated come-hither in the eyes; and farther on, behind those, the promise of menace. The closed, half-smiling mouth intimates anger, determination, secret thoughts.

The face broadcasts a dozen signals, one after another—mixed, difficult to read. Who could decipher this cuneiform?

Nixon's chronic discomfort arose from something unsynched, unintegrated—struggling—in the components of his personality. That agitation has always made it difficult to see him clearly—partly because he did not wish to be seen clearly, one suspects, and partly because he never quite saw himself clearly.

Odd, in any case, to behold such an . . . unwholesome face looking out from a hearty, can-do postwar American businessmen's club brochure, which praises Nixon as a patriot who "pulls no punches." Patriotic Americans do not send mixed signals; if all were as it should be, a young Quaker congressman, as anti-Communist and all-American as the Chamber of Commerce, would not present himself as an ambiguously sinister Italian renaissance courtier whose Mona Lisa smile suggests daggers hidden in his sleeves and a nuanced knowledge of poisons.

But that was just one take, one instant in a photographer's studio. People looked at Nixon and saw different things—a variety of characters.

House Speaker Sam Rayburn called him "that ugly man with the chinkapin eyes" who had "the cruelest face of any man I ever met," referring to the lustrous little brown nuts produced by chinkapin trees in the South.

The secret of the historic hatred of Richard Nixon was to a certain extent aesthetic. Kennedy's appearance and story were aesthetically appealing. Nixon's appearance and story (the sweating upper lip, the out-of-synch smile, the five o'clock shadow) were aesthetically unappealing. It may be that the ultimate popular judgment of the man has been made in the part of the American brain that renders judgments on movies and television shows. The American people's pupils dilated when they beheld Jack Kennedy. They contracted to pinpoints when they beheld Dick Nixon.

But there were contrary impressions.

The men serving under Nixon in the Pacific saw him as a good guy and benefactor, as "Mr. Roberts"—the loveable Henry Fonda character in the Josh Logan–John Ford hit about a naval officer in the Pacific. A smiling photograph of Nixon taken in 1944 in the South Pacific shows a beaming, happy, humorous young man with an air of self-confident competence and pleasant mischief.

One of the happiest periods of his life was his time in the U.S. Navy, a time when, even under military discipline, in wartime, he discovered, along with many men at war, that he enjoyed an immense release of freedom—from the constraints of civilian life and family life, from Quaker Whittier, the Wingert & Bewley law firm, and the obligations of his past and future, and finally, a no doubt welcome freedom from himself.

Nixon had joined the navy after serving some months with the OPA (Office of Price Administration) in Washington. After officer candidate school in Rhode Island, he was ordered, deflatingly enough, to Ottumwa, Iowa, in October 1942, to work as an administrative aide at the Naval Air Station. But by the summer of 1943, he was on his way at last to the war. The navy ordered him to Espiritu Santo in the New Hebrides, where he supervised the movement of military passengers to and from the battle zones. MacArthur's American forces were island-hopping through the Treasury and Solomon archipelago following the Japanese retreat from Guadalcanal. As one writer described it: "It was a strange, half-lit theater of the war, the military actions now bloody frontal assaults and flashing sea battles, now feints and phantom landings and fitful, sporadic forays. The fighting took place against a setting at once ominous and majestic. Jungles of emerald lushness rose suddenly off the beaches toward wild, sweeping mountain peaks and smoking volcanoes."

The object of the American drive was the Japanese Gibraltar, the fortress at Rabaul to the north, the key to Tokyo's hold on this part of the Pacific. In the autumn of 1943, the great struggle would be for Bougainville. The way there involved bloody, memorable actions—Rendova, Munda, Kula Gulf, the Tokyo Express, the Slot. One dark night in August, not far up the archipelago from where Nixon was stationed, Lieutenant (jg) John F. Kennedy waited aboard *PT-109,* engines idling in the eerily phosphorescent water, for the high-speed Japanese supply convoy to make its nightly run through the Blackett Strait. While Nixon slept or played poker or wrote a daily ardent letter to his bride, Pat, a Japanese destroyer steamed out of nowhere and ran over Kennedy's boat.

The war made Nixon mostly a rear-echelon drudge, though he did become a sort of unexpected hero to his men. On Bougainville, and on Green Island, Nixon (nicknamed "Nick" Nixon by the men) inventively scrounged provisions and set up

"Nick's Hamburger Stand" to serve hard-to-get hamburgers and Australian beer to exhausted fighter and bomber crews passing through. "Some of the stuff was, shall we say, 'liberated,'" said one of his men, Edward McCaffrey, "but Nick could swap anything. Just a small trade would set in motion a series of bigger trades that not only had his men well-housed but kept the hamburger stand operating. If you ever saw Henry Fonda in *Mr. Roberts,* you have a pretty good idea of what Nick was like."

The war also brought out a shrewdly calculating and notably successful poker player in Nixon. He came back from the Pacific with a grubstake of poker winnings. He played cautious, observant poker, on the whole, but like any good poker player, varied that game with the occasional daring bluff. One fellow officer, James Udall, watched Nixon as he bluffed a lieutenant commander out of a $1,500 pot with only a pair of deuces. Nixon was particularly proud of his best hand in the Pacific: He drew a royal flush in diamonds, with an ace in the hole.

When Nixon moved to Bougainville, there were Japanese snipers near his airstrip. (He wrote to his parents that "the only things that really bothered me were lack of sleep and the centipedes.") Just before Christmas, the base came under heavy Japanese attack. "When it was over," he wrote later, "we counted thirty-five shell holes within a hundred feet of the air raid bunker six of us shared. Our tent had been completely destroyed."

He moved on to Green Island in March 1944, in the wake of the American offensive. There were bombing raids now and then, but Nixon's most indelible memory was of the moment when a crippled army air force B-29 from a raid over Rabaul came in for a crash landing. All the men cheered as the bomber slid down on its belly, apparently safe and intact; then the men "watched in horror," Nixon related, as the plane skidded into a bulldozer near the runway and burst into a ball of flames against the dusk. "The carnage was terrible," Nixon said later. He helped clear the bodies. "I can still see the wedding ring on the charred hand of one of the crewmen when I carried his body from the twisted wreckage."

Nixon proved to be an outstanding officer—efficient, effective, unpretentious, a hands-on leader. When emergency supply missions came in, planes teeming on the runways at Green Island or Bougainville with arms and supplies for the front to be unloaded and reloaded, Nixon, the officer in command of the work crews, "peeled off his shirt and sweated through the hard physical labor right along with the rest of the men," according to Edward McCaffrey.

Now Nixon, in the familiar social cross-fertilization of war, met Americans from every class and every part of the country—a "classic, almost Hollywood-cast cross section of the navy, young men from New York slums and the Midwest, one from a wealthy family in the South, a Mexican, an Indian, an Italian, and the inevitable Texas, J. 'Tex' Massingill." He wrote home about the men; his relatives thought they saw a change in him—a broadening, a wider understanding of people. His cousin Lucille Parsons observed: "He learned how to get along with people . . . boys from all over the country to work with. He said he never knew what it was like to be associated with people brought up in all these different ways. . . . When he came back from that he was really much more humble; I mean he saw how the other half lived."

He also learned to curse in the navy way. For the rest of his life, Nixon continued to voice, from time to time, a pietistic abhorrence of profanity (he once issued a particularly prissy statement about Harry Truman's use of "hell" and "damn")—but Green Island and Bougainville undoubtedly marked the start of Nixon's private habit of growling profanity in the company of men, punctuating his sentences with "expletives deleted": words such as "fuckers" and "shits" and "cocksuckers." John Kennedy and Lyndon Johnson used much the same vocabulary. Perhaps it was Nixon's hypocrisy on the subject that allowed his critics to make an issue of Nixon's own foul mouth in the Oval Office.

When Nixon's Pacific tour of duty was over, his men threw a party for him. A friend recalled: "They borrowed all the liquid they could find. . . . All of them were strong for him, and hated to see him go."

He left the Pacific with two battle stars and a commendation for his "meritorious and efficient performance as officer-in-charge" of the SCAT units on Bougainville and Green Island. The citation said that Nixon "displayed sound judgment and initiative" and praised his "able leadership, tireless efforts, and devotion to duty." His Marine commander rated him "outstanding."

A classmate at Duke Law School noted: "[Nixon] was popular in our class . . . but I would describe it as a sort of lonesome kind of popularity." That phrase—a lonesome kind of popularity—condenses the paradox of the entire political career of a man who was elected twice to the American presidency (the second time, in 1972, by a landslide), but was uncomfortable around people and rarely seemed to connect with them in a personal way.

Those who saw Nixon when he was alone and unaware of being watched reported that his default manner was a slumping, hunch-shouldered depressive posture, eyes down, the face rather bleak, as if, in his most private thoughts, the landscape that he beheld was desolation. The New York Times's Tom Wicker saw Nixon walking alone in a corridor of the U.S. Capitol one night: "I realized that I was seeing a man bound up in his inner being, unaware that he was meeting another person, unaware of the impression he was making, unaware even that he was making an impression, too absorbed in himself to present the façade with which . . . most of us guard the truth of that inner self, that secret life, we rarely share with anyone." Wicker thought that at that moment he had had a glimpse of the "real Nixon." But it is also possible that Nixon was simply tired after a long day.

Some insisted that the "real Nixon" was a warm-hearted, generous, humorous man. Or that the real Nixon was a solitary intellectual, happiest when alone, working out ideas on yellow legal pads. He said that if he could have been something else, he would like to have been a sports writer—an interesting choice, a fantasy of so much of what Nixon never permitted himself in his actual life: the careless masculine bonhomie of games and postgame locker room interviews, the debate over beers about nothing more consequential than baseball and batting averages and a rookie's curve ball.

But politics was his choice: In 1946, in his first campaign for the House, one of his backers worried that Nixon was working too hard, and persuaded the candidate to take an afternoon off to watch a baseball game. Nixon bought newspapers on the way to the stadium and sat in the stands underlining political stories.

The young Nixon was shy, especially with women, and he tended to avert his gaze when talking to them. A campaign adviser in 1946 warned him: "You have to look these people in the face or they won't think you are telling them the truth."

The shyness could be endearing, or quaint. When Nixon started working for the Whittier law firm of Wingert & Bewley just before the war, he was given a few divorce cases. He hated them. "I remember when I had just started law practice," he recalled, "I had a divorce case to handle, and this good looking woman, beautiful really, began talking to me about her problem of sexual incompatibility with her husband. . . . I turned fifteen colors of the rainbow. I suppose I came from a family too unmodern, really. Any kind of personal confession is embarrassing to me personally . . . any letting down of my hair, I find that embarrassing."

About sex, he was a prude. His distaste for confessions resonates ironically with Nixon's ultimate personal embarrassment thirty-five years later, when he was forced to resign as president.

If Nixon had decided on a confession (at least a partial one) instead of a stonewall, he might have saved his presidency.

Shyness is a boyish quality, an innocent trait—and there are moments when it is charming to glimpse the boy in Nixon: a sweetness, a vulnerability. But Nixon had in him, from boyhood on, a countertrait of somewhat disagreeable maturity: He was an earnest little man, and as the years went by, an increasingly calculating, devious one. Variations on the theme followed Nixon for all his political career: Tricky Dick. Herblock drew him as devious, or worse, as a busy politician/devil slopping muck from buckets, or scheming in his workshop complete with chronic beard-shadow, ski-jump nose, straight-back hair, dark burning eyes, sinister intensity. Enemies always cited his shifty eyes: "Would you buy a used car from this man?"

For such a calculating man, Nixon seems to have been intensely emotional. He was given sometimes to sudden collapse into despair—from which, in the typical course of one of his crises, he would rouse himself for action. Melodramatic, narcissistic emotionalism alternated with ruthless calculation. In Nixon an Emersonian sense of the universal individual, the self as a sort of metaphysical cynosure, became corrupted by self-pity, by his inflamed grievances about the injuries that the world had done him. The self-pity hardened, in the workshop of the Nixonian psyche, into aggressive political action made razor-sharp by the melodrama of Dick Nixon's feeling sorry for himself. The poignancy of his self-pity excused whatever amoral political course he might pursue.

It was a Balkan logic brought to American politics—deep historic consciousness of grievance and victimhood. Richard Nixon conceived of himself as a victim. It was a central truth of his character. His administration and his political career ultimately broke apart in the Watergate scandal, it may be, because the president of the United States, the most powerful man in the world, ultimately could not sustain the emotional conceit of his victimhood; without the energy of inveterate grievance that had energized him through so many crises, he no longer had moral ground to stand on, and when that happened, the fierce internalized judgment of his saintly mother fell upon him and cast him out of the White House and dismantled everything he had achieved. He might have saved himself. He could easily have destroyed the incriminating tapes that became the evidence against him. He might have taken charge of the scandal. But he could not. When a perennial victim, long accustomed to all the moral exemptions and perquisites of victimhood—which allow one, in effect, to display a "Handicapped" sign and park anywhere— loses the victim's privileges, and, worse, becomes, at last, exposed (to others, perhaps even to himself) as a notorious abuser of the weak and blameless and defenseless, then a crisis of identity occurs. The grievances for all of those years were his defenses and his rationale. Now he stands exposed to himself. And some part of his hypertrophied conscience, so long accustomed to accusing others, turns inwards and indicts himself, and participates in the drama of his own condemnation and punishment. All that is what Richard Nixon ultimately did to himself. John Kennedy, though physically afflicted and suffering pain for most of his life, seems never to have construed himself as a victim. Franklin Roosevelt, stricken by polio in the summer of 1921 and confined to a wheelchair for the remaining twenty-four years of his life, did not think of himself as a man unjustly treated by fate.

Now and then one senses in Nixon's story a heartbreaking American something. In *Walden,* Thoreau wrote this enigmatic line: "I long ago lost a hound, a bay horse, and a turtle dove, and I am still on their trail." Orson Welles was getting at the elusive something when he invented the rosebud on the little boy's sled. It is some sense of primal dislocation that is at the heart of the poignancy—a sense of loneliness and disconnection, it may be: the American version of the biblical Fall. If America from the start had been set up as Eden, the new beginning, under divine sponsorship, where Europeans, new Adams and Eves, would regain the grace that the corrupt Old World had forfeited, the reality did not match the theology. The vast American space conspired with the urgent American mobility to swallow up and banish the securities of Eden, and to condemn Americans to labor, like Adam and Eve, by the sweat of their brows, in barren, unsheltered places such as, for example, Yorba Linda or Whittier, California, at the western edge of a very hard trek and a somewhat disillusioning dream. Thoreau's wistful line about the hound, bay horse, and turtle dove has in it the vibration of threnody. So, somehow, deep down, does Nixon's story—beneath the drama of the struggle for power and the hurt and viciousness and ambition and manipulation of ideals . . . a thin strain of lamentation, barely audible, like a memory of bleached bones beside the trail.

In Nixon there was a multilayered unease, psychological, social, that arose—in part, at least, and far back in time—from the Nixons' lack of secure social position in the tight community of Whittier.

Three decades later, Judith Wingert, the wife of Nixon's partner in the law firm, described the Nixons as "lower middle class in Whittier," and said their grocery was a place where "you stopped on your way back from the golf course." Even after he became a partner in the firm, Nixon was not invited to have dinner at his partners' homes. His father, Frank Nixon, had been a brash, crude trolley car conductor when Hannah Milhous married him; it was deemed that she married beneath herself, beneath her genteel upbringing, and neither the Milhous family nor the fancier neighborhoods of Whittier ever accepted Frank Nixon's household on an equal footing.

When humiliation turns to anger, it becomes dangerous. A lonely, sensitive, intelligent child may be devastated by a sense of shame. In Richard Nixon, an early energy of shame seems to have turned first to resentment and then proceeded to the next step, aggression. In the process, shame may well have driven out, or overridden, the ethical sense.

There was in Nixon a touch of the odious Edmund, the bastard son of Gloucester, in *King Lear.* Edmund's illegitimacy made him an angry Orthogonian. He was born outside the ranks and rights of legitimate privilege, and therefore would seize it by illegitimate means.

Edmund is a malignant character, in the style of Iago, and Nixon borrowed traits of character from Edmund. The most important was the energy of exclusion and resentment, the dynamic by which resentment (his perception of the unfairness of life that favored the legitimate brother, the Kennedy, the Franklin) came in his own mind to excuse unethical behavior. He would act in devious ways to make up the privilege and power of which he had been deprived, and the gods would stand up for bastards.

Something in Nixon's straitened family background and emotional poverty—and something in the detachment of his ruthlessness—bears a sort of subterranean resemblance to that of another Californian and public figure of his generation—the actress Lana Turner.

Lana Turner was born in Idaho, eight years after Nixon, and moved to Southern California, where she became a famous movie actress and was married seven times. Her book, *The Lady, the Legend, the Truth: Lana,* strangely suggests that she and Nixon shared, deep down somewhere, a psychic common ground. You pick it up, oddly enough, in the emotional blanks, in a certain cluelessness and emotional bleakness, a periodic sense of hopelessness and abandonment that emerged, on the far side, in a kind of emotionless amorality.

It is, on the face of it, a preposterous and frivolous comparison, and it requires patience. But one cannot understand Richard Nixon without help from unusual quarters. Turner and Nixon were in something of the same line of work—one a professional movie actress, the other a career politician. A sex symbol is supposed to be sexy, but Lana Turner was, deep down, rather the reverse. A politician might be expected to be gregarious, or at least, to like people, and wish to be with them. But Nixon did not. Both Turner and Nixon were isolated, manipulative, calculating, detached.

Sex was her act. Politics was his. "I was the sexual promise, the object of desire," Lana wrote. Both the Turner and the Nixon acts were successful, and yet the lives of both were hollow, a vivid outer shell hiding a dark inner self, and a tendency to implosion.

During the war, sailors on an American battleship voted Lana Turner the most desirable companion on a desert island. Turner commented: "All those years that my image on the screen was 'sex goddess'—well, that makes me laugh. Sex was never important to me." Nixon seemed to dislike people as much as Turner disliked sex. He was, like Turner, watchful, calculating, self-absorbed.

Nor, for that matter, has much evidence turned up that Nixon liked sex, either. Most of the time, Nixon's sexuality—like Lana Turner's—seems to have been as neurotically suppressed as John Kennedy's was neurotically liberated. Nixon's idea of a relaxing good time was a long silent afternoon with Bebe Rebozo. Lana Turner wrote, "I might as well confess that I was not a great companion in bed." Repugnance for Nixon among the true Nixon-haters over the years focused sometimes—though not in print, not publicly, exactly—upon what was taken to be his almost sinister asexuality. Both Richard Nixon and Lana Turner were cross-grained by loneliness, unhappiness. In both one glimpsed a desolate inner landscape. Both of them projected resentment—resentment distilled, energized, turned into ruthlessness and danger. They were at home in the atmosphere of film noir. The character that Lana Turner played in the 1946 movie *The Postman Always Rings Twice*—Cora, a beautiful young blonde wife plotting the murder of her much older husband, the Greek-born owner of a diner on a desolate stretch of California coast—

was of course fictional, written by James M. Cain. But the ruthlessness and sexlessness, and the enigmatic capacity for betrayal (adultery with a young lover, followed by murder, represents, shall we say, an unambiguous violation of marriage vows)—these cold maneuvers were performed down in the same moral temperature range in which Lana Turner herself seemed to operate: a battered and fortified narcissism. One detects the same chill—an affectless and amoral ambition—in Richard Nixon. It is a geographical curiosity that *The Postman Always Rings Twice* was filmed on the stretch of California coast at San Clemente, which is where Pat Nixon accepted Dick's proposal of marriage, and where the Nixons retreated, wounded and disgraced, after his resignation in 1974.

Nixon ran against Jerry Voorhis in 1946, the same year that *The Postman Always Rings Twice* was released. In Cora, as in Dick Nixon, one is almost always aware of Nixon's line when he was asked about the amorality of his campaign against Voorhis: "You don't understand. We *had* to win." The same logic that murdered Cora's husband Nick also defeated Voorhis.

Both Turner and Nixon were impressive survivors—tough, complicated, Depression-bred survivors who left behind them a trail of collateral damage. Nixon lost two brothers to disease when he was young, as Lana had lost her father, who was murdered. Their own subsequent ruthlessness had about it a Darwinian urgency. Hard-bitten Frank Nixon told his young sons back in the East Whittier grocery: "Root hog, or die." Lana Turner reported: "Times were hard, and there were days when the money ran out. Once we lived on crackers and milk for half a week." Her parents had split up. "My mother found an apartment to share with two young women. There wasn't much space. When their men friends came to visit, the women would bed me down on the floor of a large closet, to get me out of the way."

Both Turner and Nixon detested the press and damned it as an oppressor. Lana wrote: "Despite the reams of copy that have been written about me, even the supposedly private Lana, the press never had any sense of who I am; they've even missed my humor, my love of gaiety and color." She ended the paragraph with a Nixonian retreat, the *noli me tangere* of a tough veteran abused, long ago, as a child: "My inner self—my mind and heart, my thoughts, opinions, and beliefs—I have kept for myself alone." Both Nixon and Turner thought that the intrusions of the press were, in an almost sexual sense, a violation, an outrage. And, of course, they had a point.

Lana Turner was "discovered" when she was a "fifteen-going-on-sixteen" student at Hollywood High School. She cut a class and walked across Highland Avenue to have a Coke at the Top Hat Café (not Schwab's, as movie magazine legend had it in the fifties). A man named W. R. Wilkinson, publisher of the *Holly-wood Reporter,* spotted her, kept staring at her, eventually had the soda jerk carry over his card and ask whether he might talk to her. He sent her to Zeppo Marx, the Marx Brother who had quit the act and become an agent. So she was "discovered," to use the miracle word with which Americans describe what happened in 1492. The producer Mervyn Leroy abolished her old name (Judy Turner) in favor of Lana (which she herself thought up on the spur of the moment), put her in a Deep South melodrama called *They Won't Forget,* in which she played a schoolgirl with a sexy walk who is presently excused from the rest of the story by being raped and murdered.

Nixon was himself "discovered"—first by the Republican businessmen who recruited him in 1946 for the Voorhis race (his Top Hat Café experience), and then, on the national scene, by the Hiss case, which was his version of the indelible Walk that Lana Turner had made in *They Won't Forget.*

Nixon, too, experienced a shock of discovery when, in the midst of the Hiss case, he heard from the American audience the political equivalent of the growls and wolf whistles that surprised and disconcerted Lana Turner when she first came onscreen as an adolescent girl. Those, too, were an expression of approbation and of a kind of lust. Nixon, like Lana Turner, had, almost by accident, hit on something primitive and powerful and, as they both found, malleable.

Nixon's face was often his enemy. It was not entirely under his control: a mask or a mirror of his thoughts, opacity, and transparency alternating, concealing or revealing, depending upon the shifting angles of his mind and mood, and the changing angles of his purposes. Perhaps—under the pressure of so much urgent business—there was nothing he could do about it.

In characteristic meet-the-public performance mode, Nixon set his face in an expression of manly earnestness and sincerity: The politician's preliminary ingratiating flash of smile would be followed by an efficient lawyerly gravity and focus on the business at hand.

His voice, distinctively basso-mellow, a mellifluous growl but not unpleasant, had the light rise and fall of dark water moving over smooth rocks—an amiable instrument until it turned to accusation. Then it would begin to quiver, in a black vibrato of indignation and paranoia . . . that would, nonetheless, be presently restored to the world of sane and decent people by a rising note, a disclaimer sung in a minor key, in a tenor voice, stating now that men of good will might disagree and that he (Nixon) did not wish to impugn motives, or to suggest that his opponent did not have the perfect right to his opinion in the matter, *but* (the voice descending again to basso profundo and the music to something like political Beethoven) . . . and now the original accusation would be driven home in the finale of earnest intimation. It was the distinctive Nixon music.

Dark hair, dark eyes, dark voice, dark shadow. Nixon emitted little light. Politics normally attracts extroverts: It is difficult to imagine why a person would wish to go into politics who did not much like people or enjoy their company. That, too, was part of the mystery of Nixon: He appeared so ill at ease and so neurotically unspontaneous in his dealings with them, almost incapable of small talk or of those unbidden and mostly unconscious sincerities that are the small change and lubrication of daily life. It sometimes seemed that Nixon regarded the most ordinary transactions with a wistful wonder. He wanted so much to be one of the guys. He prized the idea of manly camaraderie, and made stabs at it from time to time. One of the funniest Nixon stories goes like this: One Monday morning when he returned from a weekend break to resume taping his series of television interviews with David Frost, he and Frost were riding in the elevator up to the studio where they were filming. Nixon stared at the floor, and searched his mind for the appropriate thing for one man to say to another in the circumstances.

Nixon spoke at last. He said: "So, David. Did you do any fornicating over the weekend?"

In an acute essay written in the 1950s on Marx and Disraeli, Isaiah Berlin observed "a tendency to idealization . . . most frequently found among those who belong to minorities which are to some degree excluded from participation in the central life of their community. They are liable to develop either exaggerated resentment of, or contempt for, the dominant majority, or else over-intense admiration or indeed worship for it, or, at times, a combination of the two, which leads both to unusual insights and—born of overwrought sensibilities—a neurotic distortion of the facts."

Berlin makes the brilliant case that Disraeli idealized the British aristocracy and Marx idealized an abstract proletariat as a result of the dilemma both men experienced as outsiders cut off, during their fathers' generations, from the roots of their Jewish ancestry. Each man came from a long line of rabbis. Benjamin Disraeli was baptized in 1817, the same year that Heschel Marx, Karl's father, was received into the Lutheran Church and baptized Heinrich. Karl was baptized with his brothers and sisters in 1824. But both Marx and Disraeli remained outsiders, not quite Jewish any longer, not quite Christian—"the blank pages between the Old Testament and the New," as Donna Louisa says in Sheridan's *The Duenna.* Marx became a notorious anti-Semite. Disraeli in his novels elaborated for himself an exotic Hebraic pedigree with ancient roots—a pedigree that made him more than the equal of the British aristocracy that he aspired to lead against the vulgarization of the rising middle class. The dynamic that Berlin describes—outsiders driven by idealization or resentment, or both—is central in the American experience, in a nation settled by outsiders thrown upon their resources, a nation that enacted itself as a fairy tale among nations, a pageant of transformations, rags to riches, in which anything can happen.

Did Richard Nixon fit the pattern of Berlin's resentful/idealizing outsiders? He surely possessed an "overwrought sensibility." He was surely resentful—especially of the Franklins of the world, of the more privileged, who did not have to get up at four in the morning to fetch vegetables for the family store, who condescended to the Nixons (especially to his coarse father) and rejected Richard for the opulent big-city law firms and condemned him to a small-potatoes practice in Whittier. That he considered himself an outsider was clear for his entire career. Even as Nixon later advanced along an insider's track (financed and cheered on by corporate interests, businessmen, Rotarians), and as he commanded respect and wielded high-level power inside the party and inside government for thirty years, something in him remained obdurately and even neurotically outside of everything. His obscurely self-willed, self-propelled expulsion from the White House in the climax of Watergate merely ratified and formalized the psychology that had, it seemed, driven him for years. It might be said that he was happiest as an outsider—even happiest when quite simply alone.

THERE IS A STORY LINE that by some negative alchemy, the 1946 campaign against the incumbent Congressman Jerry Voorhis transformed Nixon from a basically good Quaker boy into a gutter fighter and political smear artist—the first of the long procession of "New Nixons." Earl Mazo's 1959 biography stated that "while some Whittier residents were never particularly friendly to Nixon, he had no enemies in his home town before he got into politics. . . . A close friend of his in high school and college said, 'There was never anything ruthless about Dick when we were growing up. If it was a fair fight, anything went . . . but not anything dirty. That's why I could never understand the positions he took in campaigns.'"

The Voorhis campaign merely sharpened aggressive tendencies in Nixon that some may not have noticed before, but that were surely there. His Whittier debating coach, Mrs. Clifford Vincent, would say, years later, "There was something mean in him, mean in the way he put his questions, argued his points." Another who knew him then remembered that "he offended some of his Quaker teachers by his willingness to justify bad means by the end. They said he cared too much about winning school contests. His schoolmates were proud of his winnings but admired rather than liked him." Still another from those days recalled, even then, a mechanical quality, something artificial: Nixon could easily be prompted to start talking and arguing on almost any subject—this was perhaps an inheritance from his blustering, opinionated father, the autocrat of the grocery store—but "it wouldn't be intriguing or creative. Well, it would be a dogmatic, pedagogical kind of argument that would be no fun at all." Nixon was, in short, developing certain sharp but humorless and Jesuitical gifts as debater and incipient lawyer, skilled at representing different sides of almost any question, and alert to the weaknesses of the opposition.

Some of the critical memories of Nixon from people who knew him before he went into politics were doubtless colored by their feelings about what he became in later years.

It would be true of all three men—Kennedy, Johnson, and Nixon—that peoples' memories would be edited by their knowledge of the fuller, later story as the three passed into history, and that interpretations of the early behavior would often depend on their feelings about the man whom their boyhood friend ultimately became. Richard Nixon probably suffered more than the two others from this censorious retrospection.

Nixon was just mustering out of the navy when a group of California Republican businessmen approached him about running against Jerry Voorhis for the seat from the state's Twelfth Congressional District. The prospect was not promising. Though a Democrat in a basically Republican district, Voorhis, a diligent, popular congressman, had carried it in five elections. For the GOP, the 1946 campaign would have to be "a sort of giant-killer operation," thought Kyle Palmer, the partisan Republican and political editor. "The man [Nixon] proposed to unseat was a very popular and well entrenched Democrat. The Republicans—including myself—generally felt it was a forlorn effort."

Nixon came in as the unknown and the underdog. He might well have lost (in which case he would not have been in Washington to reacquaint Alger Hiss with Whittaker Chambers) and according to one line of conventional political logic, he probably should have lost.

On the other hand, the argument has been made persuasively that Richard Nixon would have beaten Jerry Voorhis in 1946 regardless of whether or not Nixon had introduced the issue of Communist influence in the labor movement and Voorhis's relations with national and state labor political action committees.

Voorhis had problems. He was curiously inattentive to affairs in his district, and was late in recognizing the danger that his opponent presented. Nixon began campaigning early in 1946, as soon as he had left the navy and moved back to Whittier. Voorhis, accustomed to winning against inferior opponents without much serious campaigning, stayed in Washington for months, through a June primary (which he won handily, however), returning to the district only in August, late in the game.

Voorhis had first been elected in 1936, a Depression year, when his liberal social conscience and background as a onetime registered Socialist had a congenial resonance. Voorhis was resolutely anti-Communist; he had even served for a time as a member of the House Un-American Activities Committee. Most Americans rarely made the distinction between a Socialist and a Communist, however, so Voorhis, whatever his own careful principles, was vulnerable on the left.

By 1946, serving his fifth term in the House, Voorhis had to some extent lost touch with the voters back home, and his politics was more aligned to the Depression years. He had fallen out of synch with the mood of postwar America, with its newly released energies of enterprise driven by technological progress. Voorhis had not kept track of the changes in the district. In the wave of postwar immigration to California, there were twice as many Republicans as Democrats among new voters in a district that was already fundamentally Republican.

Over the years, Voorhis, an idealist with principled independence of mind and a habit of voting his convictions, had made influential enemies—among the bankers, the oil companies and other corporations, among farmers. In 1943, he had made a speech denouncing a government contract, secretly concluded, that would have allowed Standard Oil to exploit for private profit the vast U.S. Navy petroleum reserve at Elk Hills in central California. The contract gave Standard Oil five years of exclusive free drilling, with $20 million in immediate profit and the potential for billions more. After Voorhis's speech, the deal was cancelled.

The elections of 1946 occurred in an atmosphere of postwar turmoil and uncertainty. Labor unrest was everywhere. A wave of strikes shook the economy. At one point, nearly 2 million workers were on strike. Harry Truman, a Democrat who was supposed to be a friend of labor, had "proposed, with widespread public approval, to break the crippling railroad strike by drafting the strikers into the armed forces. The proposal was outrageous," Tom Wicker wrote, "but Truman had reason to be exasperated."

Truman had spent much of his sudden, unexpected presidency trying to moderate the wild energies of postwar American labor. He had seized the coal mines twice, had taken control of 134 meat-packing plants, the facilities of twenty-six oil-producing and refining companies. He had agreed to relax wartime wage controls, but the country nonetheless was torn apart by strikes against General Motors, United States Steel, and dozens of other industries.

And so Nixon in his maiden political campaign seized, in a canny debate-team way, upon an issue that in 1946 just began to be promising for Republicans. He worked at encouraging voters to accept the idea—unfair but with just enough elements of truth to work—that there existed a continuum (conscious or unconscious) from expansionist international Communism to American Big Labor (where some Communist influence undoubtedly was at work) to big labor's political friends, the Democrats.

The Roosevelt administration had indeed welcomed many officials (among them Alger Hiss) whose backgrounds included membership in what their apologists would consider a more innocent and idealistic Communist Party that should not be made to share the blame for Stalin's crimes. Whittaker Chambers had first reported the Alger Hiss Communist cell to a high State Department official, Adolph Berle, in September 1939; Berle apparently reported the cell to the White House. Roosevelt, with a world war on his hands (Hitler had just invaded Poland) was not interested.

In the minds of liberals, there was good communism and bad communism. Good communism was the early version that sprang from what seemed a justified despair of the capitalist system after the crash of 1929, and from a utopian idealism not yet disabused by knowledge of Stalin's crimes or of the inherent brutalities, corruptions, imbecilities, and injustices of Communist governance.

Good communism had its respectable flowering among Western intellectuals all through the thirties—an irony of timing, because that was the period when Stalin committed his greatest crimes—the Ukrainian genocide, the Great Terror, the Gulag, the slaughter of millions. Few respectable figures in the arts, few moviemakers, writers, and artists during the thirties deviated from at least a sentimental allegiance to the spirit of good communism.

Reports at last came in, postwar, that good communism was entirely an illusion. What had seemed an idealism on the side of the angels came to be seen as satanic. The transformation of communism from respectable humanitarian creed (a kind of Godless Quakerism, as it were) to a program of totalitarian enslavement was a matter of enormous political convenience for American conservatives. They could run against a man who had once, when younger perhaps, been a good Communist (if only a sentimental one) as if the fact of his communism back then made him, today, in 1946, an agent of bad communism. Good communism turned to bad communism, and therefore, by an opportunistic political logic, a good Communist then was a bad Communist now. This was deemed to be true even when, as happened in legions, the former good Communists recoiled from the crimes of Stalin and repudiated the faith of their naïve youth.

The postwar atmosphere in which the 1946 congressional races were fought was heavy with a sense of great stakes, vital issues, of life or death for the American future. By the following year, when the victors of those races had taken office, Harry Truman promulgated the Truman Doctrine, telling a joint session of Congress: "The time has come when nearly every nation must choose between alternative forms of life"—meaning must choose between totalitarian communism and the freedom of the West.

In the audience for the presidential address that night were Congressmen John Kennedy, Richard Nixon, and Lyndon Johnson.

Nixon said of his Voorhis race: "You don't understand, I had to win." To critics of his decision to drop nuclear bombs on Japan, Harry Truman responded, in effect: "You don't understand; we had to win." A corollary logic would even assert: It would have been amoral—if one possessed such weapons, such means of ending the war quickly and saving so many lives—*not* to drop the bombs. Similarly, a categorical mindset brought back from the war and applied to postwar politics would have instructed a man like Nixon, with his combative opportunist's mind, that it would have been immoral *not* to have seized all available means to win the congressional seat.

American politics had never been a pristine, chivalric arena. But the brutal education of two world wars coarsened the psychology and morals of American politics in a new way. The nation's perhaps dangerously inflated sense of its own inherent virtue after its triumphs in those world wars carried with it an implicit sanction of the techniques of ruthlessness. The moral unimpeachability—the righteousness, the invincibility—of the Allied cause gave moral cover to whatever wrongs the Allies may have committed in accomplishing the victory. But when that principle migrates into domestic politics, it becomes problematic: If you think you are right—if you know you are right— then you do what is necessary to win. It becomes easy enough to shave the first half off that sentence and proceed with the morally naked other half: You do what is necessary to win. That became Richard Nixon's unapologetic agenda.

The war sharpened another principle that made its way into the politics of Nixon, Kennedy, and Johnson: You must do it to them before they do it to you. It is the logic of preemptive savagery: If no rules restrain the other side (no chivalric old code) then one must as quickly as possible anticipate the worst—and then do the worst, first, yourself!

The logic of the preemptive (even if illegal or unethical) strike was seductive to Richard Nixon's instincts. He had a deep sense of the unfairness of his life, a sense of deprivation. Why not strike back?

In the drama of postwar supercession—veterans back from the war, validated by combat, and pushing their way into politics to displace the older generation—an attitude of amoral gamesmanship seemed appropriate enough. Politics was a game of calculation and chance. Poker gave Nixon a casual preliminary education in the dynamic art of secrets. In poker, Nixon learned to bluff. Poker is a game of chance in which the usual rules of ethics—the rules about lying, for example—are irrelevant. The whole point is precisely the secrets you possess in your hole cards, and the way you play those secrets to achieve your goal. Nixon learned to play in a rhythm of authentically strong hands and the occasional bluff in which he held worthless cards but, in his betting, lied about it. That was a pattern of artfully intermingled truth and lies that might be said to have carried over into his political career for the next thirty years.

There was no moral onus involved in bluffing. Anyone can bluff. Only a sucker goes into a game as a literal-minded moralist. Especially in the Depression-bred generation of Johnson and Nixon, there was for a man a high value placed upon being tough, and wise to the world, wise to the con. Movie heroes like Humphrey Bogart enforced the idea of manly savvy: "Wise up!" It was smart to play some angles. Only a sap would not. And only a sap, like Jerry Voorhis, would let Nixon get away with the dirty tricks and rhetorical rabbit punches that Nixon used in 1946.

There is a difference between a victim and a chump. Nixon always took the view that Voorhis was a chump for not playing his hand better in 1946—for letting his young challenger get away with a high school debater's tactics and with the slippery ellision of the somewhat left-tainted national CIO-PAC (not supporting Voorhis) with the less-tainted California PAC (that did support

Voorhis). Just below the surface of Nixon's defense of his campaign against Voorhis runs the assumption that he, Nixon, simply played a better hand of poker than Voorhis. A man who loses a hand of poker is not a victim. He is a loser.

The GOP had been through a long drought. Republicans had lived since 1933 under the immense shadow of Franklin Roosevelt and the triumphant, overriding ideas of the New Deal—leadership that had taken the country through the Great Depression and world war.

But the giant's successor, Harry Truman, seemed small, mediocre, incapable of governing. Senator Robert Taft's wife quipped, "To err is Truman." By the spring of 1946, the Gallup poll found the new president's popularity had fallen from 87 percent to 32 percent. There were meat and housing shortages. The Republican slogan that year was, "Had enough?"

The wartime alliance-of-convenience with Stalin's Soviet Union (a necessary, valuable, expensive arrangement that had been sentimentalized, but never sanitized, with nonsense about "Uncle Joe") was turning, by 1946, into a threatening antagonism. The Pentagon drafted secret plans for atomic war, code-named Broiler and Sizzle.

The great divide of American opinion over the Hiss case, McCarthy, and the "red scare" was often discussed in later years in rigid, immobile terms that did not take into account the changing nature of the American understanding of communism and the Soviet Union, from the somewhat starry-eyed, idealistic earlier 1930s through the shock of the Hitler-Stalin pact in 1939, through the wartime alliance with the USSR, and then into the postwar, post-Hiroshima era of incipient superpowers, of expansionist ideological colonialism.

The Nixon-Voorhis campaign of 1946 came just at a moment when Uncle Joe's valiant Mother Russia, erstwhile utopia of the twenties and thirties, began to seem something quite different. Sensible American Communists of the earlier thirties (including

Whittaker Chambers) had repudiated the Party after the news of Stalin's show trials and mass murders began to seep out.

Postwar America struggled to ascertain what the new game was and what its rules were. Should Communists be allowed to use American rules (the Bill of Rights, the court system) to subvert and defeat America? How should Americans fight back? Politicians could use such issues as cover for the pursuit of their own ambitions.

The United States stood in a new relation to the world: The oceans no longer quite moated sanctuary America. After the war, the United States was at the same time (1) the preeminent power among the nations of the world, and (2) unprecedentedly vulnerable. America alone possessed the secrets of nuclear weapons, and yet America felt, as never before, at risk before the possibility that some power elsewhere might steal the secret—a thief taking fire from the American gods—and turn America's own terrible knowledge into the instrument of its own destruction. America, in effect, became terrified of itself, or of what it knew how to do: make world-destroying new weapons that carried in them an implication of the forbidden. Had not Americans themselves stolen this apocalyptic fire from God? That was the true new moral frontier that had been crossed.

Commentators in the years since have often spoken of one event or another as the "end of American innocence." The true end of American innocence occurred just after 8:00 A.M. local time on August 8, 1945, at Hiroshima. After that moment, America was no longer innocent—was un-innocent, had, as Robert Oppenheimer said, "known sin." The story of 1948, especially, is the story of America's attempt to come to terms with its new moral state.

But America fiercely resisted the idea of its un-innocence, of its sinfulness. Such a notion was dangerous to the American idea itself, to American exceptionalism, and to the entire rationale for the world war just won. If America was not essentially innocent, then it was something else. The thought of American sinfulness opened a Pandora's box of inadmissible speculation—raised the possibility, in fact, that America might even be capable of doing evil.

In some ways, the convulsions set off by the rise of anti-communism after World War II—including the Hiss case and Joe McCarthy's pageants—were a symptom of the American innocence attempting to defend itself, not entirely against Stalin's Soviet Russia (a fierce and real enough enemy) but also against self-knowledge, an unbearable moral insight.

In making issues of the New Deal, Big Labor, and Communist subversion, Nixon merely aligned himself with a Republican strategy all around the country. The nation was not wrong to worry about Stalin and communism. Nor was it untrue that the New Deal and Big Labor had been infiltrated by Communism. Many good Democrats, including Melvyn Douglas (husband of Helen Gahagan Douglas), Ronald Reagan, and other future members of the liberal Americans for Democratic Action, were fighting hard to expel Communists from the Democratic Party and from the labor unions (for Reagan, it was the Screen Actors' Guild, of which he became president). The Republican strategy was to make all Democrats seem as pink as possible—dupes, at best, of their own previous idealism, and, at worst, members of a Fifth Column burrowing away in the woodwork of the American Dream.

On March 6, 1946, Winston Churchill had delivered his Iron Curtain speech in Fulton, Missouri. By June, the Soviets had rejected the so-called Baruch Plan for international control of atomic energy; to most Americans this meant that a dangerous Soviet Union was now bent on acquiring its own atomic weapons. By September, the Gallup poll found that relations with the Soviet Union had replaced labor turmoil as the voters' first worry.

The Republican National Chairman, B. Carroll Reece of Tennessee, attacked the national CIO-PAC as "the spearhead of Red reactionism." He announced that the 1946 elections were a "fight basically between Communism and Republicanism." He said the Democrats had been taken over by "a radical group devoted to Sovietizing the United States." Pushing the theme to scurrilous extremes, he claimed that the Democrats hoped to establish, as in the Soviet Union, a "one-party system and a police state." Even Robert Taft of Ohio, the conscience of the Republican Party (and later one of John F. Kennedy's subjects in *Profiles in Courage* for his stand against the trial of Nazi war criminals at Nuremberg) charged that the Democratic Party was "divided between Communism and Americanism." A Republican Party campaign pamphlet showed a Democratic donkey wearing a turban emblazoned with the hammer and sickle of the Soviet flag.

Nixon saw what might be done with a specific application of the theme of anti-communism in 1946—by making an issue of Voorhis's support by a political action committee tied to big labor. Nixon had a debater's and lawyer's gift for spotting weak spots in the enemy's fortifications, and he surprised Voorhis by slipping a knife in, as a man shucking oysters places the tip of the blade at just the right spot near the hinge of the shell . . . and pops it open.

The mistake of Nixon's enemies was usually complacency; they did not foresee an opponent whose mind did not sleep, but rather, watched them always and struck while they were dozing.

That was what happened to Jerry Voorhis. He did not foresee Nixon. He could not have. Voorhis was a decent, honorable, effective congressman, by any account—including Richard Nixon's. As Nixon told Stewart Alsop, years later: "I don't suppose there was scarcely ever a man with higher ideals than Jerry Voorhis, or better motivated than Jerry Voorhis."

Was Richard Nixon a nice Quaker boy? Or was he what Herblock and his many other enemies believed—a man working as close to the borderline of evil as any American politician can work while remaining inside the American system?

Throughout his career, Nixon drew energy from the resource of his resentment: Some core of grievance made him alert and cunning and aggressive and ambitious. He had a good lawyer's instincts for the manipulation of truth in the cause of a client (which meant—as a politician on the make—himself) and the working lawyer's dispassionate amorality. He found it in himself to be cunningly unscrupulous because he had persuaded himself that playing rough was all right in a fair fight, and he seems to have justified a certain amount in his own mind by referring rough play on his part to a deprived childhood, to an Orthogonian lack of privilege that made it all right to try to get some of his own back by seizing advantages that had been unjustly bestowed upon the Franklins and their kind—for example, Jerry Voorhis and, later, Jack Kennedy. Nixon was bruised, early in life, and it marked him. It was his lifelong sense of grievance and disadvantage that gave Nixon the indispensable justification for unscrupulous behavior, including that of Watergate. Nixon thought he had ground to make up. The techniques thus justified were found to be effective and, as a result, they became habitual—the aggressively spun half-truths, the protests of disinterested probity, the somewhat plastic indignation, all these became his political style. If a pitcher can get more onto a curve ball by scuffing the rawhide slightly, perhaps it is all in the game.

JOHNSON AT BAY

In December 1945, the first Christmas that Harry Truman was in the White House, Lyndon Johnson sent the president a Texas-grown turkey, along with an effusive and fulsome letter of tribute. Truman said thanks. But no more than that.

Johnson's political ambition had often collaborated with his psychological need to seek out surrogate fathers. Franklin Roosevelt had been one of them—a mentor, a sponsor, a protector. The day that FDR died, Johnson said tearfully: "He was just like a daddy to me, always." Johnson's Texas friend and adviser Alvin Wirtz was another father. And so was House Speaker Sam Rayburn, a bachelor who had taken to spending his lonely Sundays at the Johnson apartment in Washington, reading the papers, talking politics, enjoying Lady Bird's home-cooked meals. Rayburn had become a member of the family.

Now Johnson was not as close to Rayburn as before; they had fallen out after LBJ committed an act of minor political treachery. But, more important, Johnson's presidential father, Roosevelt, was dead. Harry Truman had neither the temperament nor the inclination to become Lyndon Johnson's father figure. Truman had a daughter, Margaret, and he needed no other offspring. Truman had little patience with complex emotional manipulations; he did not believe that private lives and public lives should be mixed up with one another, and he didn't much like Johnson anyway.

The war had changed America. Johnson had been something of a wunderkind of the New Deal. Now, in his late thirties, he felt tired and stale. So did the New Deal. The war had stimulated new energies and rearranged the terms of the American drama: Truman was appointing moderate or conservative Democrats to government jobs, replacing some of the "intellectual" or "nonpolitical" liberals who, at their worst, as one Truman aide said, represented the "crackpots and lunatic fringe." Truman considered himself a "legatee of the New Deal . . . a liberal of sorts," but there had come an atmospheric change.

Johnson's political ambition (like that of Richard Nixon and John Kennedy) always superseded ideology. He responded to the new political world of postwar America with complex course corrections. In some respects he remained liberal. In 1946, he was one of only eighty-one House members to vote against continued funding for the House Un-American Activities Committee. He favored the Bernard Baruch plan to put the atomic bomb under UN-supervised international control. He remained in favor of government activism in some areas, especially where it benefited his Texas constituents—employment, housing, farm electrification, road building, conservation, hospital construction.

But in 1947, Johnson voted for the Taft-Hartley Act, which banned the closed shop, allowed employers to sue unions for broken contracts or damages inflicted during strikes, and authorized a government-imposed cooling off period of eighty days for strikes that might endanger the national welfare. He also voted to override Harry Truman's veto.

Unions for twelve years had enjoyed the protections of the pro-labor Wagner Act. Now their massive wave of postwar strikes had combined with anxieties about inflation and even about communism and Communist influence in the unions to produce a more conservative mood in America—and in Texas. In 1946, Texas voters had installed a right-to-work, law-and-order conservative Democrat named Beaufort Jester as governor.

Jester also moved to rally other Southern governors in opposing Truman's civil rights programs. In 1948, Truman asked Congress for federal legislation against lynching, and in favor of repealing the discriminatory poll tax and setting up a Fair

Employment Practices Commission. Johnson—the man who in the sixties did more than any other, except Martin Luther King Jr., to help end legal racial discrimination in America—now signed up with his Southern states rights colleagues in opposing Truman on racial matters.

Johnson would repeatedly display this gift for tactical atavism. An actor gives his best performance when he believes in the part and throws himself into it. Johnson, a brilliant mimic, could, it seems, make the believing and feeling part of his mind fall for the role that his thinking mind deemed necessary to advance his political career and, in the longer term, his larger agenda, which, he thought, would atone for whatever sins he may have had to commit along the way. It was clear to Johnson that his political future, as a governor, or a U.S. senator, and even beyond, depended for the moment upon his making himself acceptable to Texas businessmen and to the state's new mood of conservatism.

In 1946, Johnson thought about running for governor, but early straw polls raised doubts about whether he could win. He decided not to risk it. Sick with flu, and then pneumonia, Johnson wanted an easy run for reelection to his House seat. Instead, he found himself facing Hardy Hollers, a forty-five-year-old attorney and former army colonel, a onetime JAG lawyer who had helped Supreme Court Justice Robert Jackson prepare cases for the Nuremberg trials. It was a fairly dirty campaign. Hollers accused Johnson of corruption—of making money for himself and his friends through the abuse of his congressional office. As the historian Robert Dallek observed, "Some of Hollers's suspicions were justified." But Johnson beat back the assault. He brought in the cowboy star Gene Autry to sing his signature tune, "I'm Back in the Saddle Again"—an early use of celebrity magic in political campaigning. He had a four-piece band called Johnson's Hill Billy Boys sing of his incorruptibility: "For he's one guy / No one can buy." He used humor to neutralize Hollers's charges and to spin them away. "This mudslinging and mire reminds me of a story," he would tell his audiences. "One fellow would say to another, 'Say, did you hear about Smith making $100,000 on wheat?' The other said, 'Yes and no.' The first asked, 'What do you mean, yes and no?' 'Well,' said the second, 'It's true and it isn't true. His name wasn't Smith, it was Jones. It wasn't wheat, it was rye. It wasn't $100,000, it was just $10. And he didn't make it, he lost it.'" And the people would roar with laughter.

It was a telling piece of legerdemain that, amazingly enough, managed to leave the impression that Lyndon Johnson was not a perpetrator of corruption but, rather, a victim of it. Johnson was not "Smith" but "Jones." Profit was loss. Among other things, the Smith and Jones story calibrated the distance between the now prospering Lyndon Johnson (who had made a lot more than Smith's $100,000 by this time) and the failed father who haunted him, Sam Ealy Johnson, who had lost a great deal more than Jones's $10. In the subtle theater of his own conscience, Johnson identified himself with his own father's failure—took on its dramatic context even as he belittled the loss as a mere matter of $10—to neutralize the fact of his own enrichment through corruption.

Johnson easily beat Hollers in the Democratic primary in July, carrying all ten counties in the district. But the massive Republican wins in the November 1946 elections (which sent Nixon and Kennedy to Congress for the first time) pretty much ratified the end of the New Deal as the dominant American political force. Johnson was moving right along, which meant moving right. When he gave an interview to the Associated Press in the spring of 1947, he said, "The term 'New Dealer' is a misnomer." He said he still supported water power, rural electrification, and all-weather roads. "But I believe in free enterprise, and I don't believe in the government doing anything that the people can do privately."

Still, Johnson was an internationalist. He supported the Truman Doctrine (the United States would go to the aid of nations threatened by Communist aggression) and helped push the appropriation through the House, over the opposition of the isolationist bloc.

In a speech to the House, Johnson declared:

> Whether Communist or fascist, or simply a pistol-packing racketeer, the one thing a bully fully understands is force, and the one thing he fears is courage . . . I disavow the demagoguery of a jingo. I repudiate the tactics of a warmonger. I want peace. But human experience teaches me that if I let a bully of my community make me travel back streets to avoid a fight, I merely postpone the evil day. Soon he will try to chase me out of my house. We have fought two world wars because of our failure to take a position in time.

That was Johnson's succinct summary of Munich Logic, which in time became his rationale for going into Vietnam. By the time Johnson left the White House in 1969, the lesson of Munich (don't appease aggressors) had become the almost entirely opposite lesson of Vietnam—beware of Munich's leading you into a Third World quagmire.

Personally, Johnson felt that his time was running out. He would be forty in 1948. The Johnsons tended to die early, of heart disease—his father at sixty, his Uncle George at fifty-seven, his Uncle Tom (after two heart attacks) at sixty-five. John Kennedy kept up the façade of vigor even while he concealed menacing illnesses, but Johnson liked to parade his forebodings; his self-pity had an aspect of Shakespearean woe: "I'm not gonna live to be but sixty," he would tell his friends.

Some of them suggested that he might stay in the House and eventually inherit his friend Sam Rayburn's office of Speaker. "Too slow. Too slow," Johnson would respond.

But a Senate seat would be open, if Johnson had the courage to run for it, risking his safe place in the House. Texas's cornball isolationist embarrassment Pappy O'Daniel would be leaving the Senate.

Johnson agonized over the decision. He toyed with the idea of getting out of Washington, and out of politics, and going back to Texas to teach while his wife ran the radio station in Austin. He told supporters that he would announce his retirement early in 1948.

On January 1, 1948, during a game break in the Cotton Bowl, Coke Stevenson announced that he would run for the Senate seat.

But Johnson delayed his Senate decision for months. Coke Stevenson was well known all over Texas. Johnson was little known outside his congressional district. Polls showed the impeccably conservative Stevenson ahead of the old New Dealer Johnson by about four to one. After another conservative, George E. B. Peddy of Houston, entered the race, the polls still had Stevenson beating Johnson by three to one—some progress, but not enough.

As late as May 1948, the conflicting monsters of Johnson's ambitions and his insecurities still wrestled with one another— the two contestants being fairly evenly matched. On May 11, he assembled staff and friends in his backyard in Austin for a marathon discussion of the Senate race. Johnson's ferocious insecurities prevailed. Everyone finally went to bed.

But at last, with more encouragement, especially from Texas newspaper editors pledging their support, Johnson announced that he was in. On May 22, dressed all in white, Johnson stood on the bandstand in Woolridge Park in Austin. He tossed his Stetson into the air and announced, "I throw my hat in the ring." A witness said, "It was the corniest thing I ever saw."

Indecision yielded now to an indignant sense of entitlement. Johnson told a news conference that he would have won a special election for a vacant Senate seat seven years earlier, except that his opponent, Pappy O'Daniel, had cheated, "finding" just enough very late and very crooked votes to edge Johnson out. A certain amount of flim-flam, taradiddle, and highway robbery were the norms of Texas politics, and part of Johnson's regret about his lost 1941 Senate election amounted to chagrin at his innocence in not arranging enough vote-theft in his own behalf to offset the O'Daniel thieveries. He vowed that it would not happen again.

Robert Caro's dense and vibrant biography of Lyndon Johnson tells the story of the Johnson-Stevenson race in 1948 as an epic clash of characters, and even of different epochs. Laconic self-made Coke Stevenson stood for the old Texas virtues—reliability, competence, a certain courteous but immobile rectitude of character, a manly distaste for excesses of emotion or rhetoric. Johnson, on the other hand, staged a campaign of a kind that Texas had not seen before—outrageously cynical, entertaining, innovative. Against Coke's immobile rectitude, Lyndon pitted his own highly mobile improvisations.

THE AMERICAN SCENE

WASHINGTON

WASHINGTON WAS LAID OUT along the lines of eighteenth-century French rationalism—Pierre L'Enfant's radiant avenues spoking out, in a sunburst of diagonals, across rectilinear streets gridded by alphabet (east to west) and numbers (north to south).

A premeditated city: The marble dimension of Washington was given over to mall and monuments, arranged across inhuman distances (a salute to the wide open spaces between the Mississippi River and the Rockies). The city lay low to the Earth. The skyline, except for the Washington Monument and the great white dome of the Capitol on the Hill, was unobtrusive, almost below the tree line. One was aware of large sky above, which gave the city an august, abstract quality.

No buildings (except the Washington Monument) rose higher than thirteen floors. Without high-pressure hoses, nineteenth-century fire companies could not pump water to reach any higher. The ban on taller buildings was later formalized for aesthetic and civic reasons: It meant that no other enterprises (office buildings, apartment towers, for example) could overshadow the Capitol, the White House, the monuments. Washington had its visual priority. Government was the reason the city had been created. It was a company town. By 1948, the city's skyline was hardly taller than when Abraham Lincoln stood in his bedroom in the White House and looked across the Potomac at the Confederacy and worried that Lee was coming.

The federal scale was sweeping, imperial. The effect, if you stood on the mall looking at the distant rectangular escarpments of bureaucracy—the massifs of the Department of Commerce, the Department of Agriculture, the Department of the Interior—was one of a great emptiness of light and air, expanses of threadbare grass, a ceremonial prairie across which bands of tourists might make their way like pioneers, small on the landscape, in an ambivalence of piety and agoraphobia.

In 1948, the Mall and other stretches were littered by ugly remnant one-story "temporary" buildings, a shanty-town of beaverboard erected to give office space to the overflow of bureaucracy brought into Washington by the New Deal and the war. By L'Enfant's Enlightenment standards, the "temps" were squalid; they slapped a look of makeshift army barracks onto his city so carefully arranged. Richard Nixon had labored in a "temp" on Independence Avenue when he came to Washington early in the war to work for the Office of Price Administration, sending out letters to rap the knuckles of businessmen if they charged too much for such items as rubber tires. When Nixon arrived in Congress in 1947, a woman who had worked with him at OPA wrote a letter of congratulations about his election and his just-born baby daughter Julie: "Everything in your lot seems to be too wonderful for words—but you deserve it—a far cry from those dog-days in Temporary Building D."

For all the dominance of sky in Washington's government neighborhoods, the light elsewhere in the city was mitigated and scattered, in a profuse and leafy Southern way, by elms, sycamores, oaks, lindens, willows, gingkos, hornbeams, basswood, dogwood, cherry, locust, beeches, black walnuts, cottonwoods, catapas, birches, chestnuts, and persimmons. Washington was the world's best-shaded city.

Peter the Great staked out St. Petersburg in the boggy delta of the Neva. Washington, D.C., was a geographical compromise imposed upon a cypress swamp. The capital was not an organic growth, but an idea stenciled on landscape. The scale and design of the city, which was an official hallucination and projection of the republic, more a hope than a going concern, tended therefore toward the grandiose and the abstract: A future idea embarrassed by present reality, it was, as John Dos Passos wrote, "a vastly overgrown small Southern town in a stagnant hollow between the Potomac River and Anacostia Creek." A WPA *Guide to Washington,* published in 1942, noted that "beneath the National Archives Building huge pumps operate to safeguard the foundation from waters of the old [now subterranean] Tiber Creek."

In the late forties, Washington seemed a cross between Ancient Rome, and Athens, Georgia—the headquarters of postwar world power, it is true, but provincial, oddly unsophisticated, and surrounded, not, as now, by endless suburbs and satellite cities, but by Maryland and Virginia countryside that was abruptly and surprisingly rural, with that sense of sultry, vaguely menacing remoteness one sometimes feels at night deep in the Mississippi or Alabama countryside.

John Kennedy would joke that Washington was a city of Southern efficiency and Northern charm. That was an elegant variation on what almost all politicians said about the city. They professed an aversion to Washington—a political reflex to reassure the people at home that their elected representative had not gone native on them. Politicians talked of the city, for constituent consumption, as if it were Sodom and Gomorrah—a preposterous idea, especially in 1948, when Washington's provincialism was in full flower. Even during the Kennedy administration, which congratulated itself on bringing youthful cosmopolitan vitality to the capital (New Frontiersmen doing the twist in the White House or, after a few drinks on summer nights, throwing one another into Bobby and Ethel Kennedy's swimming pool at Hickory Hill), the columnist Russell Baker, who understood the city perfectly, wrote: "Of course it isn't any fun. It's the dullest capital in Christendom."

Civil servants, a more or less fixed population, laid upon the city their instincts of punctuality, their orderly in-box/out-box decorum, their habit of eight hours' sleep. At the same time, the politicians, who were transients by definition, believed that to prolong their tenure in Washington they must act as if they hated the city and the odious things going on there: They must act as if they had not succumbed to its temptations. In 1948, the range of fleshly temptation and sinful pleasure that the city offered was narrow—as the range of hidden opportunities for corrupt money and power was wide.

When John Kennedy, Richard Nixon, and Lyndon Johnson were young men in Washington, there were no nightclubs (except the forlorn Blue Mirror downtown), and only a handful of decent restaurants: Duke Zeibert's, on M Street NW, for example, and the Old Angler Inn west of the city, on the C & O barge canal, and the splendid Hall's down near the river in the "colored" ghetto in Southwest Washington, a restaurant that had a long black walnut bar and lustrous nudes reclining on the wall behind it, and a shiny tin spittoon-gutter with running water in it along the bar at the customers' feet (a touch of weird and ingenious luxe to address the disgusting and all-but-vanished American habit of chewing tobacco and spitting the juices any which way, like a drunk cowboy spraying shots from a revolver). Classic Old South white-haired Negro waiters brought Chesapeake oysters and deviled crabs. Southwest Washington in those days, before urban renewal, was a jumbled Southern shantytown. White folks went there to eat at Hall's.

The tinny National Symphony played in Constitution Hall. The National Theater on Pennsylvania Avenue (around the corner from the Treasury Department, the theater an island of lonely festivity in the surrounding darkness of deserted downtown Washington) offered shows that (if one was lucky) were trying out for Broadway or (if one was not lucky) for earnest cultural exchange companies—troupes of folk dancers from Bulgaria. The Washington Senators baseball team played at ramshackle wooden Griffith Stadium on Florida Avenue, and usually finished near the bottom of the American League.

Congressman Kennedy fled town when he could. He was mostly camping out there. He bombarded his father's New York office with telegrams requesting that they get him tickets for Broadway shows; he was the only one of the three future presidents who had an active interest in musicals and movies. For Johnson and Nixon, politics was entertainment enough. Who needed theaters in a town where the machinations of power and the secrets thereof were a continuously unfolding drama?

The Kennedy Center would come later, eight years after President Kennedy was assassinated, and even that worthy gesture of federal patronage seemed slightly misbegotten, its Kultur mainly ceremonial, symbolic, done to prove that the capital of American power had grown up and knew how to be civilized—not to prove that the men in Washington who had the power loved Mozart, or wished to gratify aesthetic longings; the Kennedy Center, stranded among freeways, smacked of Brasilia. It was not as tastelessly grand and alien and sinister, however, as the Watergate complex nearby, just up the river, where Nixon's unraveling would begin one night, years later, when he thought he had everything. Men wore hats and double-breasted suits. Neither men nor women in Washington dressed with much style, by New York standards, because dressing plainly, without flash, was part of the city's dynamic of public-servant self-effacement. But the ex-haberdasher Harry Truman looked trim and chic for a Missouri farm boy, and in the Senate, you saw now and then a regional flamboyance (wing collars on old Senator Hoey of North Carolina, for example) and, in the hot Washington summers, an opulence of creamy white linen Palm Beach suits that gave the senators the look of Sidney Greenstreet in *Casablanca*.

It was a well-upholstered era, a generation before the onset of exercise and low-fat diets and the vanities that would keep older men aspiring to preserve the illusion of youth into middle age. Men past the age of forty in Washington in 1948 had begun, as a matter of course, to thicken—on a diet of deviled eggs and roast beef and whisky—to the heft of walruses and rhinoceroses. Younger men, back from the war, were sleeker animals.

In the class of '46 in the House, for example, there was Florida Congressman George Smathers, who would become a friend of both Kennedy and Nixon, and, for Kennedy, a longstanding companion in womanizing. Smathers, tall, dark, and lean, much oiled in his black hair, looked like a corrupted movie star—like a Robert Taylor playing a professional gambler. Smathers was almost too beautifully suited, and wore round-collared shirts fastened with a gold pin under the knot of the Countess Mara silk tie.

Clark Clifford, Truman's young special assistant at the White House, dressed elegantly. But the sartorial masterpiece was Dean Acheson, who would take over as secretary of state from George Marshall at the start of 1949. Republicans mocked Acheson for his flawless English tailoring and his jauntily upswept little robin's-wings moustache and his suffer-no-fools High Church Episcopalian hauteur.

When Kennedy came to work in Congress at the beginning of 1947, he looked and dressed like a skinny, sloppy kid (sometimes mistaken at the Capitol for an elevator operator), and by 1948, he remained half-man, half-adolescent, and dressed the part; it was in 1948, however, that he made a transition from a shirttail-flapping Mucker from Choate to an emaciated grownup wearing off-the-rack single-breasted suits.

Nixon dressed like an earnest Rotarian, in the dark colors and manly conservative cuts that would be his public costume throughout his public life—even, famously, when he walked alone on the beach in Florida or California. Kennedy walked in the surf wearing rolled up khaki trousers and a shirt with shirt-tail flapping. Nixon wore business shoes and a starched shirt and creased suit trousers hiked up above his belly, to the altitude of an Empire gown.

Johnson was the best turned out of the three, the smoothest and flashiest. He wore custom-made monogrammed shirts with French cuffs, and gold cufflinks, and Countess Mara ties (an exorbitant $20 each, as compared to $4 or $5 at most for a standard tie from Rogers Peet or Best & Co. or Lewis and Thos. Saltz on F Street, where the well-dressed Washington man bought his clothes).

Kennedy held himself gracefully, gingerly, his athlete's flow of motion made mysteriously brittle and wary by spasms of secret pain. His body concealed illnesses that often betrayed him and threatened his life. He had learned to live with them, however; his mind and body were integrated.

In Nixon, on the other hand, there seemed a certain disconnection of a highly active mind from a merely utilitarian body. His discomfited body would contradict his mental motions—as if his mind and body were Siamese twins that disliked one another and had different lifestyles and appetites and different ideas of how to have a good time. His smile would go out of kilter with the moment and with the thought that even at that instant was being formed by his lips.

Nixon's body lacked muscle tone, and looked oddly dressed when wearing anything except a suit. In the Nixon Library in Yorba Linda, there is an Acme Roto Service photograph of Nixon from early 1947, when he first came to Congress. The caption reads: "Among the many new faces in Washington is the youthful but rugged countenance of Richard Milhous Nixon of California . . . a tall, husky ex-football player and OPA attorney."

Such manly PR was the sort of thing that would be sent out as a matter of course by a congressman's office. Nixon had tried bravely to be a football player at Whittier College, but like, say, Humphrey Bogart or Bob Hope or other men of his generation and body type, he seemed to have no muscle tone beyond what was required to fill a suit; his gait, like Hope's (without the jauntiness), was curiously hinged at the knees and hips, a sort of utilitarian glide (like that of a glider sofa on a forties front porch). The walking legs were somehow disengaged from the upper body, which did not swing, but floated on its own.

The caption's word "husky" suggested a physicality in Nixon that simply did not exist. He was a mental presence—eyes, voice, brain incessantly at work. His body seemed to have a curious irrelevance. Critics over the years interpreted Nixon's squirming manner as a sign of his covertness, but it seems, on the contrary, that his darting eyes and the notorious lack of synchronization between eyes and smile signaled not covertness but rather the reverse, an unusual transparency of character—Nixon's inability to conceal the motions of his busy, dogged, never-resting brain.

Johnson, no football player, either—and, according to his biographer Robert Caro, something of a physical coward in his younger days—was famously the most physical of men in other ways. John Kennedy did not like to be touched, especially by men. He had an intriguing remoteness of manner—the charm of something withheld, a reticence. Johnson, however, embraced people and kneaded their muscles with his enormous hands and all but ingested them as they talked.

Johnson ended his presidency by being entangled, like Laocoon, by the serpents of war, serpents of history. But if you watched him in those early days, twenty years earlier, working the halls of the Capitol, you would have said that the true Laocoon was the poor man Johnson was talking to, and that Lyndon's two ensnaring arms were the snakes that Poseidon had sent. Johnson was a primitive and infuriating force. If God had an id, that was where Lyndon Johnson came from.

WASHINGTON WAS A CITY FOR MEN, for drinking and politics and power. Men controlled all three of those. If a woman wanted a drink at the National Press Club she was obliged to take it in a small lounge off the lobby, because the men's bar was off limits.

The lounge was known ruefully to the women who went there for a drink as the Tampax Room.

If you took a lover, and you were smart and discreet, you went out of town—probably to New York, or at least to Baltimore; in any event, taking a lover seemed a waste of time, a distraction from the Washington game that mattered. In 1948, a woman was having an affair with a senator and checked in, of all places, at the Hay-Adams Hotel, in the middle of the afternoon, for a couple of hours; that was adultery as a form of exhibitionism, of ostentation. They were showing off. The most powerful people in Washington walked in and out of the Hay Adams on Lafayette Square every day.

Sexual anecdote among men might be a deflected badinage the point of which was not really sex, but power. There was an anecdote about Nicholas Longworth, the former Speaker of the House. Longworth, who had gone almost totally bald at an early age, was lounging in a leather chair in the Capitol when another member ran his hand over Longworth's bare scalp and said, "Nice and smooth. Feels just like my wife's bottom." Longworth ran his own hand over his head and said, "Yes, so it does."

Longworth's own wife was Teddy Roosevelt's daughter, Alice Roosevelt Longworth, an aging fixture in Washington by 1948, cherished for her astringency. "If you don't have anything nice to say about someone, come sit next to me," said the needlework on Alice's sofa cushion. Her heterodoxy was calculated and somewhat tiresome—a sort of safe naughtiness in what was mostly a crushingly orthodox town. Alice Longworth was talking of conventional politics and power, not sex, when she wrote: "Anyway, it is always an entertaining spectacle . . . the show is there for us, and we might as well get what entertainment we may out of it."

Humor focused on power, pomposity, corruption, hypocrisy—dramas of political temptation satirized. What other subject would interest Washington? The CBS Radio commentator Elmer Davis reported on a New Jersey senator's dilemma over a bill that would be good for the American military effort in World War II but might harm New Jersey's interests. The senator announced he felt "torn" about the bill and would consult his conscience. Elmer Davis reported on the air: "Senator H. Alexander Smith of New Jersey spent the day wrestling with his conscience. He won."

Everyone knew everyone. The politicians and journalists certainly knew one another—in that sense, it was still what Henry James called "the city of conversation," although not many of the conversations in Harry Truman's Washington sounded particularly Jamesian.

BRUMIDI'S FRESCOES
AND FILM NOIR

THE MYTHS THAT WE HAVE of Kennedy, Johnson, and Nixon, the impressions that the three men have made upon the American imagination, emerge from the collective memory's mixed media—iconic television clips, still photographs, magazine articles, memoirs, docudrama adulterations of the kind that, say, Oliver Stone makes, and oral transmission from those who lived through their time. Modern historical memory tends to be sensational, depressive, debunking—that is, it tends, as time goes on, not to glorify historical figures but to expose them, to belittle them with demystifying revelations.

The lives of Kennedy, Johnson, and Nixon mark an American turning point. Before them, an American tendency toward glorification. After them, an American appetite for demonization.

In the mid-1850s, the Italian immigrant fresco artist Constantino Brumidi worked toward glorification.

Constantino Brumidi presided over the patriotic murals and frieze work and decorative design of the U.S. Capitol. He was a burly, humorous man of five feet five inches with beard and beetling eyebrows and blue-gray eyes, nearly fifty years old when he arrived in the United States in 1853. He came as a refugee from political turmoil in Italy, where he supported the unsuccessful movement to depose Pope Pius IX as the temporal power in Rome and to establish a republic. Brumidi was imprisoned. The pope commuted his eighteen-year sentence on condition that the artist emigrate to America.

Trained at Rome's Accademia di San Luca, Brumidi was one of the leading Italian artists of his generation. He had been a student for fourteen years, during which he mastered geometry, history, and mythology as well as drawing, painting, and classical sculpture. A study of Brumidi's work on the U.S. Capitol aligns 1) Raphael's Alba Madonna, painted in 1511, with 2) Brumidi's Raphaelesque figure of Prudence, painted on the ceiling of the Throne Room in the Palazzo Torlonia in Rome, done before Brumidi's emigration to America, and 3) a similarly Raphaelesque *tondo* (circular painting) of a female figure called Legislation, done in the 1850s in the President's Room of the U.S. Capitol. In design and style, Brumidi's figure of Legislation traces straight back to Raphael—an attractive ancestor, to be sure, but a foreign one.

Brumidi was a magician, an illusionist, a master of old Roman tricks of perspective—for example, of ways of painting a flat surface of friezes (as he would do around the Rotunda of the Capitol) in such a way that they looked exactly, from a distance, like three-dimensional sculpture.

In the mid-1850s, the Know-Nothings turned on Brumidi.

The nativist xenophobia of the American Party, which was the Know-Nothings' formal name, had come to a boil. Fifty-one members of the House identified themselves as Know-Nothings. As they walked through the still uncompleted U.S. Capitol, they recoiled at Brumidi's brilliant, bustling, gaudy work: un-American work.

What bothered nativist critics was the idea of models and moral atmospheres imported from the sort of corrupt or defunct traditions that America had been founded to escape—ideas from the Golden House of Nero, from the murals of pre-apocalyptic Pompeii and Herculaneum, from the décor of the Medicis.

One of the ideas that Brumidi brought to America was the indispensable technique of "real fresco"—in which paint is applied directly to the wet surface or wall or ceiling. No other artist in America was trained to do that difficult work. Brumidi described the technique:

Fresco derives its name from fresh mortar, and is the immediate and rapid application of mineral colors, diluted in water, to the fresh mortar just put upon the wall, thereby the colors are absorbed by the mortar during its freshness, and repeating this process in sections day by day, till the entire picture will be completed. This superior method is much admired in the celebrated works of old masters, and is proper for historical subjects, or Classical ornamentations, like the Loggie of Raffael at the Vatican.

The U.S. Capitol would become the major American building decorated in true fresco.

The technical difficulties were considerable. The artist had to work rapidly, as the mortar (or plaster) was drying. He painted section by section, each day's completed work being called a "giornata." The complete picture had to be planned out, giornata by giornata, so that it would work exactly with its architectural context, without visible discrepancies of color and line from one segment to another. Many of Brumidi's frescoes were painted on groined or barrelled vaults, a task that involved a masterly skill at perspective.

Brumidi's great challenge would be the vast masterpiece that he performed at the canopy of the interior dome of the Capitol, *The Apotheosis of Washington,* a vision of George Washington's ascent into heaven that Brumidi, sitting on a scaffold 180 feet above the floor of the Rotunda, was working on in April 1865, when Lee surrendered to Grant at Appomattox and Lincoln was assassinated. Brumidi pictured the female representation of armored Freedom, sword in hand, vanquishing various evil figures, including Discord, who holds two lighted torches in hand and to whom Brumidi gave the face of Jefferson Davis. Before the Southern states seceded and he became president of the Confederate States of America, Davis had been the U.S. secretary of war, and, as the Capitol was being constructed by the Army Corps of

Engineers, had been the man who approved Brumidi's appointment to execute the art work and had passed judgment on all the artist's earlier paintings in the Capitol.

America repeatedly reworks primal themes—among them the struggle between who's in and who's out. That push-and-pull reproduces, on one hand, the tension between an expanding pluralistic democracy, and, on the other, the cohesions of American tribalism. The anti-immigrant, anti-Catholic American Party was the spiritual ancestor of the House Un-American Activities Committee.

A tribal hatred and suspicion of strangers is as old as human nature; it is also an old American habit: Thomas Jefferson once said "The yeomanry of the United States are not the canaille [scum] of Paris." Theodore Roosevelt, as New York City police commissioner, would speak of Irish immigrants as if they were lawless bacteria—wretched refuse indeed.

Halfway in time between Thomas Jefferson and Teddy Roosevelt, the Know-Nothings aimed their alarm mostly at the potato famine Irish flooding into America. Nativists feared the immigrants' political power, which many Protestants believed would be directed by the Catholic Church and the pope. The alien inundation included political refugees pouring in from Germany and Italy after the upheavals of 1848. The American Party proposed, among other things, that newcomers should have to wait for twenty-one years to be granted citizenship, instead of the usual five.

It seemed to the Know-Nothings—who would have leverage in voting appropriations for work on the Capitol—to be an outrage that a foreigner, an Italian Catholic, should be imported to impose an overripe, un-American style upon the temple of the American legislative branch. The *New York Express* complained that few native-born American artists had been put to work on the Capitol; the paper listed the names of seventy-four artists and claimed that only twelve "could be pleaded as Americans." The

New York Tribune wrote: "The best artists of the country, with scarcely an exception, have offered their services and asked to be employed upon the Capitol. Without an exception their applications have been rejected, and the work of decoration is going rapidly forward under the direction of an Italian whose reputation is little more than that of a skillful scene painter, and who employs under him a crowd of sixty or seventy foreign painters, chiefly Italians and Frenchmen."

Years later, Brumidi would be called "the Michelangelo of the Capitol." But in 1859, a select committee of the House complained that the sacred Capitol was being decorated by foreigners and claimed to find "nothing in the design and execution of the ornamental work of the Capitol, thus far, which represents our own country." The committee said that "a plain coat or two of white-wash" would be preferable as a temporary finish to the "tawdry and exuberant ornament with which many of the rooms are being crowded."

On George Washington's birthday in 1860—as the Southern states were speeding toward secession—the United States Arts Commission issued a report that complained about the art of "an effete and decayed race, which in no way represents us" on the walls of the Capitol. The commission attacked Brumidi directly: "It is not enough that the artist select an American subject for his work. He must also be imbued with a high sense of the nature of the institutions of the country, and should have a certain assimilation of its habits and manners."

The commission spoke for a prejudice that recoiled from the alien Mediterranean incursion—even if the sources were classical: "We are shown in the Capitol a room in the style of the 'Loggie of Raphael' [in the Vatican]; another in that of Pompeii; a third after the manner of the Baths of Titus; and even in the rooms where American subjects have been attempted, they are so foreign in treatment, so overlaid and subordinated by symbols and impertinent ornaments, that we hardly recognize them."

Brumidi's colors, said the report, were "gaudy, inharmonious," and "unsuited to the hall of deliberation."

The commission recommended that the Capitol's corridors—which Brumidi was busy covering with an astonishing display of murals, lunettes, and wondrous proliferations of squirrels, mice, pelicans, bats, and other decorations—should be "painted in flat colors."

But history moved on. The Civil War was coming. The Know-Nothing Party passed its moment, and the nation became less preoccupied with the threat of immigration than with the issues of slavery and secession. Many of those 1848 immigrants would become cannon fodder at Antietam and Gettysburg and Cold Harbor—would be assimilated by fire into the country they had chosen. In the draft riots of 1863, it would be the immigrant Irish against the blacks. "Native" and "alien," "authentic" and "foreign" were moveable, relative labels. Mathematicians speak of a point of inflection at which concave turns into convex: At an inflection point of American experience, foreigner turns into native, invader becomes defender. The arrival of a new enemy may make the old enemy a friend and ally, a member of the American family. At some point, Brumidi's work became an American tradition.

The Arts Commission was abolished on June 20, 1860, having lost its political support and the moral energy of its nativist argument. The Italian immigrant Brumidi went on with his work at the Capitol.

Homer described Hephaestus fashioning the shield of Achilles as a magnificently detailed living and dramatic panorama—two noble cities, the king's estate, fields, vineyards, thriving life. In the domes and vaults, on the walls and columns of the Capitol, Brumidi set about fashioning an Achilles shield, a panorama of American origin myths—Columbus making landfall in the New World, DeSoto's explorations, the Boston Massacre, the Battle of Lexington, the winter at Valley Forge, the Storming of Stony Point—and of the heroes (Washington, Jefferson, Franklin) and driving American abstractions (Commerce, Science, War, Liberty, Religion).

Brumidi signed his individual paintings "C. Brumidi, American citizen." He idealized his new homeland and its history in a deeply felt way that now may cause political correctness to avert its gaze. His version of the American drama told the story of virtuous, enlightened (white) civilization discovering a savage wilderness, settling it, cultivating the land, and bestowing upon it the blessings of law, science, commerce, justice: White marble America, George Washington a god and saint, the Founders as archangels, brainy and estimable.

Immigrants tend to be such good American mythmakers because their minds, like fresco mortar, are fresh and receptive, their grateful imaginations not yet inhibited or jaded by too much knowledge and experience of the subject. If they are not yet disillusioned, then they may, for just that reason, develop a genius for illusion. Ignorance stimulates invention. So does hope.

Artists invent what they do not yet quite know. The artist's mind fills in the blanks, invents a world it has caught first only by intuition: creates a home made of dreams, preconceptions, ideals, and a greenhorn's misunderstandings. Sometimes, even in such misunderstandings, the greenhorn will catch the essence.

Brumidi brought the artistic traditions and techniques, the colors, the aesthetics, groupings, ideas, symbols, and styles of centuries of classical and Renaissance art. American history and American characters transformed such traditions into a distinctly American thing, the Capitol. The Italian immigrant's mind, his images, were absorbed at the highest level into the American civic myth-system.

America was wet and fresh: Upon its surface the fancies and dreams and stories were daubed, and the colored images dried and became permanent expressions of the new home. Creation meant assimilation. Art validated citizenship: The artist bestowed, like a ritual offering, a dowry, what he had been and what he knew, in exchange for citizenship, the right to become something new in a new land.

Politics and government by the same process offered the wet fresh surface to which Kennedy, Johnson, and Nixon brought versions of America that originated in different places, had different colorations, different stories to tell, different ideals and heroes.

The murals of Kennedy's mind displayed a pageant of apparent contradiction—working-class South Boston Irish ward politics in the Honey Fitz tradition, crossed somewhat weirdly with an anglophile nostalgia for the atmosphere of Lord Melbourne and the Whig aristocracy, and, in the private dimensions, a sneaking identification with the lifestyles of people like Frank Sinatra and the Rat Pack. Kennedy managed to integrate the first two elements (Boston pols and Whig aristocrats) into a coherent political self, but the Sinatra side of his nature was his Mr. Hyde, a sexuality that came out when the moon was full.

Lyndon Johnson brought to Washington a distinctive Texas version of the American myth—the manly Lone Star virtues put to work in an interesting way, at first, in scenes of New Deal paternalistic compassion and conscience. Then, after the war, the Texan acquired a harder, more venal glint in his eye, and in his nostrils the smell of oil and money and a certain sybaritic possibility that would take a cowboy from the homespun virtues of the Texas Republic to custom-made silk shirts with monograms and hand-made Tony Lama boots that were comfortable in deep carpets, not in mesquite and manure. The old Texas virtues, the old moral fossil fuels, had been a cartoon of the hard-bitten frontier American virtues (Kit Carson said: "The cowards never started and the weak died on the way"). By 1948, they had been refined into sleek power, and the big money that made political engines purr.

As for Richard Nixon, the lunettes and friezes of his mind might have been painted by Norman Rockwell. Nixon had Rockwell's taste for sentimental anecdote and, at his best, a likeable middle-class decency and absence of pretension. Nixon lacked Norman Rockwell's sense of humor, however, his playful dimension. He lacked Rockwell's sly, knowing affection for people. Rockwell's America was happy. Nixon's was anxious. Nixon's mind saw a Norman Rockwell America all right, but the distinctive Rockwell virtues were missing. The resulting tableau was somewhat flat and square. If the picture lacked the Rockwell virtues, however, it grew interesting where it was darkened by the Nixon flaws. The Nixon version of America was smudged by anger, cunning, ambition, resentment, accusation, fear—by mysterious shades of loss. Nixon's Rotarian sentimentality was an enameled shell that concealed, in perfect dark, his secret.

Washington itself, the city, was, in a different way, a masterpiece of refulgence and concealment. The large black population of Washington lived lives essentially invisible to white society, negligible: the black city was the shadow of the white city. It is true that late in his business of decorating the Capitol, during the period of Reconstruction after the Civil War, Brumidi painted a lunette of the Boston Massacre in which he made the central figure the escaped slave Crispus Attucks. Attucks is raising a wooden club and clutching the barrel of a British redcoat's musket, an instant before he will be shot dead; the first martyr for American freedom was a black man whom America had enslaved.

But aside from Attucks' haloed image in a picture over a doorway, few Blacks were to be seen in the government temples of Washington, except for those working as janitors and serving people—certainly not congressmen, senators, cabinet secretaries, or their aides. Ralph Bunche, a light-skinned African American, refused Harry Truman's offer to make him assistant secretary of state because housing in Washington was so segregated. Blacks and whites lived in virtual apartheid. Bunche's greatest accomplishment would be achieved not in his own country but in the Middle East where, as successor to Count Folke Bernadotte, the

United Nations negotiator who was assassinated in September 1948, Bunche mediated an armistice in the first Arab-Israeli war.

Bunche's career was a commentary on the inside/outside theme of American tribalism. Inside America, Bunche was outside. Outside America, he was inside. At home, he was a Negro, subject to the usual humiliations of segregated housing, washrooms, restaurants, swimming pools, and seating on public buses. Abroad, Bunche was a man of distinction, of honor and accomplishment.

Yet the honor abroad did change his status at home, and even served to embarrass white racism a little. Or—to put it ruthlessly—it served to make Bunche, as it were, an honorary white man. Just as money may be laundered by sending it abroad, so Bunche's negritude was, for American purposes, decontaminated by his United Nations service elsewhere in the world. After the Middle Eastern armistice, Bunche received a tickertape parade up Broadway in New York, a hero's welcome home. Los Angeles declared a "Ralph Bunche Day." In 1950, he received the Nobel Peace Prize, an honor amounting to sanctification—the elevation of the man to a status somewhere above race, an apotheosis erasing Bunche's stigma as the descendant of slaves just as, in Brumidi's rendering, Washington's apotheosis lifted him up into nacreous clouds, far above Mount Vernon, far above the morally troubling detail that his estate was worked by slaves.

It was a small measure of Bunche's status as a member of the establishment elite that in early August 1948, when he was the number two man in the UN Trusteeship Department, he was one of the first to send a letter of support and consolation to Alger Hiss. Bunche was Inside with Hiss. Whittaker Chambers was Outside.

The politics of 1948 had an edginess like that of film noir—an amoral air and sense of venturing into new territory where anything can happen. Postwar power played sometimes in that ominous, shadowed lighting—the atmosphere of things not quite seen, of faces unreadable: of secrets. Raymond Borde and Étienne Chaumeton, the film historians, applied five adjectives to film noir: oneiric, strange, erotic, ambivalent, and cruel. "Erotic" did not apply to the politics of 1948, but the other adjectives did.

Film noir, Borde and Chaumeton wrote, is a "film of death" in which the fair fight gives way to the settling of scores; the "hero" is not Superman, the ideal hero, pure of motive, but rather a figure morally smudged, ambivalent, selfish in a way Superman could never be. World War II and its aftermath gave many Americans a sense that they had become strangers to themselves. Film noir registered that sense of emotional estrangement that could set off an unwonted ruthlessness, or disable faculties of human sympathy and forgiveness.

In such films as *Double Indemnity,* in *The Postman Always Rings Twice,* in *The Blue Dahlia*, wives and husbands turn viciously upon one another. In *The Blue Dahlia,* as in *The Best Years of Our Lives,* a hero returns from the war and finds that his wife has been drinking and playing around with other men: All the films feature betrayal, secret lives, unreadable motives, and hidden selves. The essential perception is that people are not as they seem, but may conceal a capacity for viciousness, even for evil, that the prewar, conventional American mind, which practiced a religion of sentimentality, did not suspect.

In Carol Reed's 1949 film *The Third Man,* Orson Welles plays Harry Lime, good old Harry Lime, friend of Holly Martins (Joseph Cotton), the naïve author of pulp Westerns who stands for the sentimental America that has not quite come to grips with the evil possibilities of the world. Good old Harry turns out to be a racketeer who, in the ruins of the war in Vienna, has made an evil fortune. Among other things, he sells watered-down penicillin that either kills children or mentally maims them. In the famous Ferris wheel scene, Welles urbanely mocks sentimental morality and order: The violent amoral Borgias produced Michelangelo. The orderly moral Swiss produced the cuckoo clock.

Welles improvised the cuckoo clock speech. The movie's script, however, was written by Graham Greene, who in the years to come began to detest what he saw as an obdurate, grotesque American innocence, a Wilsonian sentimentality turned corporate/imperialist and armed with nuclear weapons. In *The Quiet American* in 1954, Graham Greene wrote that the Americans' "innocence"—a complicated word suggesting, in Greene's use of it, a culpable moral stupidity—made them "the most dangerous people in the world."

Greene's novel appeared the year that Viet Minh besieged the French garrison at Dienbienphu, in the last battle of the long French colonial experience in Indochina. At the time of the siege, in the spring of 1954, the Eisenhower White House debated whether the United States ought to intervene to help the French. Vice President Nixon was among those who entertained the possibility that the United States might use tactical nuclear weapons to relieve the garrison. Eisenhower rejected the idea.

But the Cold War abhorred a vacuum. Once the French were gone, and Eisenhower was gone, John Kennedy's military advisers and Green Berets seeped back into Indochina through a kind of a capillary attraction, and set in motion the fatal escalation-by-retaliation that swept Lyndon Johnson's Gulf of Tonkin resolution through Congress in 1964 and eventually turned the handful of advisers into 600,000 American soldiers (so many of them the babies who were born in 1948 and 1949) and turned Vietnam into the swamp that would suck Lyndon Johnson under and, in its backblast—Watergate—blow Richard Nixon out of the White House.

The long pursuit of Lime through the sewers of Vienna was the perfect postwar metaphor: Below the surfaces of things, beneath the streets of the everyday ran secret, invisible, systematic, shadowy rivers of filth. Ran fugitives, ran evil designs. This was the skull beneath the skin, the crawling hidden amoral life that appeared when an American lifted the rock of normality and morality and looked underneath. Kennedy started his presidency by complying with the secret Bay of Pigs design; toward the end of his presidency, he complied with the secret plot to overthrow Diem. Kennedy concealed so much that it remains a question to this day what secret business finally murdered him in Dallas. He had learned secrecy from his father, who taught his boys never to leave a paper trail. Kennedy as president worked instinctively through back channels, by informal calls to unexpected sources in the middle levels of government.

The films noirs were vicious dreams, just as suspicions are vicious dreams. It was an age of deep suspicion. Nixon was the quintessential film noir politician. He was the perfect politician for black-and-white film. If little in Nixon's life suggested eroticism—Nixon was the quintessential antilover as John Kennedy was at the time a somewhat adolescent playboy and dreamboat—it might also be said that Humphrey Bogart (whose snarling self-absorption and five o'clock shadow, in the *Maltese Falcon* and other films, had a Nixonesque quality) was also unpersuasive as a lover. (When Bogart kissed a woman, his lips were not sensual but curiously tentative and maladroit—he had nerve damage in his upper lip; when he kissed a woman, he looked like a horse eating an apple.)

What was Nixonian in the eroticism of film noir was the ulterior quality—the element of calculation and incipient betrayal, as if sex were a façade concealing something more sinister, a play for power. The eroticism of film noir was never straightforwardly sensual—sexual—but drew its excitement precisely from that air of ulterior motive, the allure of what was hidden, perverse. Sex was only a kind of misdirection, a false scent. Sex concealed a darker purpose. The pleasure came not from sex itself but more likely from the exertion of power, the satisfactions of cruelty, or the recondite thrills of ambush and viciousness—an uglier game altogether.

ELLIS ISLAND, THE FRONTIER, AND
THE TAFT-HARTLEY ACT

THE BIRTHPLACES—and the gravesites—of John Kennedy, Lyndon Johnson, and Richard Nixon are widely scattered across America: Kennedy born in Brookline, Massachusetts and buried in Arlington National Cemetery; Johnson born and buried in the Hill Country of Texas; Nixon laid to rest in Yorba Linda, California, outside Los Angeles, just yards from where he was born. The places, like the men, represent an American triangulation—three lines of meaning, three geographical personalities and histories.

The meanings can be approached by looking at basic poles of American experience: Ellis Island and the Frontier. Of course, neither Ellis Island nor the Frontier exists anymore in a physical sense, and yet the two persist as states of mind, as presences in the American imagination, as value systems. They are two extremes of the American story.

Americans tend to be attracted, like iron filings, to one or the other of the national narratives, with its attendant attitudes and sympathies.

America is a large, complicated country, with cultural admixtures that every year make it less susceptible to generalization. But it remains useful to study the interplay between Ellis Island and the Frontier—useful to measure the political distance between them, and the frequent hostility between them as organizing metaphors.

George W. Bush, to an unusual degree, thinks of himself as part of the frontier story, the cowboy story that sees itself as self-reliant, competent, individualist, freedom-loving, morally autonomous, and responsible. Ronald Reagan belonged distinctly to the same point of view. He played the role. Like George W. Bush, Reagan owned a ranch. He wore cowboy clothes—cowboy boots, blue jeans, an enormous silver buckle on his belt, a cowboy hat, his eyes crinkling and squinting into the distance. In the Oval Office he displayed a dozen Frederick Remington sculptures of cowboys and Indians and bucking broncos.

The Ellis Island mentality is that of the communitarian sentimentalist. If the geography of the frontier involves big skies, untrammeled space and freedom, the Ellis Island story enacts itself in cities; its emphasis is human and sympathetic. Ellis Island is ethnic, crowded, urban, multilingual, gregarious, and noisy, alive with distinctive cooking smells and Old Country customs. The frontier is spacious, physically demanding, silent. It values freedom and autonomy and personal responsibility.

So Americans have a vivid sense of a choice between the Ellis Island sympathy-for-the-underdog sentimentality of the Democrats and the bracing cowboy dream of the Republicans. The Frontier tends to vote Republican. Ellis Island tends to vote Democratic. The Frontier tends to support the American right to bear firearms. Ellis Island, which sees guns in a dangerous, urban, criminal context, tends to support gun control. The Frontier tends to favor capital punishment. Ellis Island does not. The Frontier tends to mistrust welfare and social engineering—even though so many cattle ranchers and others of Frontier mentality living in the western United States take enormous sums in subsidies from the government. Ellis Island likes government, and people like the American Irish found their start to power in American life by organizing themselves into political machines designed to control and exploit the government.

Ellis Island and the Frontier collided in 1947 over the Taft-Hartley Bill—a measure that was designed, in spirit, to strike a blow for Frontier values of individualism and free choice against the Ellis Island ethics of collective solidarity.

The bill, as formulated in the House by Representative Fred Hartley, of New Jersey was tough. It banned industry-wide bargaining, the closed shop, jurisdictional and sympathy strikes, mass picketing, strikes by government workers, and Communist officers in unions.

In 1947, the Republicans, after so many years of the New Deal, when they were in opposition, had control of Congress again. In a swing of the pendulum back toward management and business, much of the nation was preoccupied by the question of whether labor had too many rights now. A new law was needed to replace the leftish, pro-labor Wagner Act of 1935. Hence Taft-Hartley. The motif of the moment said that the New Deal, in all ways, had gone too far. The idea of the Frontier resisted big government and big labor as forces that stifled the individual; Ellis Island embraced both, as forces that protected the individual. The Frontier saw the closed shop and other instruments of Big Labor as corrupt, socialistic, and inimical to freedom. Ellis Island saw them as bulwarks against corrupt, overbearing capitalism and as necessary means to social justice and worker security.

John Kennedy and Richard Nixon, both freshmen, had been assigned to the House Committee on Education and Labor. It was the debate over Taft-Hartley that would bring the two of them together to debate at a public forum in McKeesport, Pennsylvania. Nixon favored Taft-Hartley. Kennedy opposed the bill, a stand that placed him squarely in opposition to his father and became a marker in Jack's gradual process of detaching himself from his father's generally more conservative views.

As for Lyndon Johnson, he would use the Taft-Hartley Act—in an ingenious ploy that mocked the truth but made splendid theater—as an instrument with which to defeat Coke Stevenson in the Texas senatorial race. Johnson's political sleight-of-hand in the Stevenson race—proclaiming the conservative Stevenson to be a leftist in bed with Big Labor, and repeating the charge over and over until it acquired a life of its own—was reminiscent of Nixon's misdirections in the Jerry Voorhis race in California two years earlier, and even more outrageous.

Between the extremes of Frontier and Ellis Island, Kennedy located himself somewhere a little to the left of the Frontier individualism that his father had adapted to his freewheeling purposes on Wall Street and in Hollywood.

Nixon located himself farther to the right, on what might be called the Chamber of Commerce Frontier. Ellis Island was quite a distance from the Whittier grocery store, and from the entrepreneurial capitalism and the trim Lawrence Welk-Mantovani America where Nixon felt at home.

One of the things that made Lyndon Johnson so interesting and complicated was the fact that he so thoroughly, and conflictedly, embodied both the frontier and Ellis Island—and tried to enact both—in the Great Society and in Vietnam. Perhaps it was this duality in Lyndon Johnson that brought him down. As a son of the Hill Country of Texas, with its lingering folklore of the Alamo and of long-ago massacres under the Comanche moon, Lyndon Johnson was also a New Deal Democrat with all the activist-government Ellis Island instincts. And so, as a result of the interplay of Ellis and the Frontier, he tried to bomb Ho Chi Minh into submission while at the same time offering to turn Vietnam into a Great Society, full of New Deal projects, if only Uncle Ho would listen to reason.

Johnson mobilized his gifts as a shapeshifter to occupy the moral ground of the Frontier and of Ellis Island simultaneously—and (in a display of Machiavellian skill) managed to make the public think that his opponent, Coke Stevenson, who was the very essence of the frontier, had unaccountably passed through the Looking Glass into the mentality of Ellis Island. Johnson played a dangerous game—bait-and-switch—with the sacred moral heirlooms of the Texas frontier. But it worked. Johnson contrived to turn the cowboy hero Stevenson into an agent of

Ellis Island, and to make himself, the erstwhile New Dealer Johnson, by inference, the champion of frontier individualism.

———

THE 1974 MOVIE *Blazing Saddles* is Ellis Island's travesty of the frontier story. Mel Brooks (an urban Jewish wise guy from the Ellis Island branch of comedy, by way of the Catskills) satirized the mythic American west as the home of bigotries almost endearingly moronic ("rural idiocy," as Lenin said), the empty, windswept home of brain-damaged American *canaille*. Everyone in the inbred town of Red Rock seems to be named Johnson—Gabby Johnson, Howard Johnson, and so on. At a meeting in the local church bearded Gabby Johnson stands in his pew and delivers a spittle-spraying and intensely felt, incomprehensible line of nonsense. Howard Johnson earnestly thanks Gabby Johnson for "that example of authentic frontier gibberish." The church scene parodies a similar meeting in the Gary Cooper movie *High Noon*, when the townspeople gather to debate how—or whether—to help out Cooper, the town's retiring marshal, as he faces Frank Miller and his gang, who are returning to kill Cooper. In *High Noon,* Cooper represents the embattled frontier virtues at their moment of crisis, when the community, the respectable shopkeepers and professionals of the town, abandon their frontier courage and opt for softer solutions (nonconfrontation, temporizing, hoping the problem will go away): If there were some federal government official to whom they could appeal to avoid having to act themselves, they would rush to file the papers. By inference, the Ellis Island solution (if this were high noon in Boston or New York) would be for the local party machine either to pay off the Frank Miller gang or to meet them at the train and beat them senseless and send them on to the next town.

But Gary Cooper represents the frontier individual who is taking responsibility for facing danger because there is no one else to face it and subdue it. The mythic masculine Texas ideal had it that a man should be taciturn, courageous, restrained until unconscionably provoked, chivalrous (indeed shy with women), and, above all, honest.

Which version of the story was more accurate—the Gary Cooper, or the Mel Brooks? In the Texas Senate race in 1948, Coke Stevenson played Gary Cooper. Lyndon Johnson's manipulations of rural voters' credulity had in them somewhere the Mel Brooks imp. Lyndon Johnson knew how to talk to all the other Johnsons.

A case can be made that in 1948 (and at other times as well), Lyndon Johnson displayed the opposite of those frontier qualities: that he showed himself to be garrulous, pusillanimous, unrestrained in gratuitous attack, unchivalrous (indeed, abusive) to women, especially to his long-suffering wife, and dishonest in his political manipulations. It was as if Lyndon Johnson went about redefining Texan manliness as a different kind of ruthlessness altogether.

In time, Kennedy, Johnson and Nixon would all three become, for the men of the baby boom generation (their children, more or less) interestingly variant models of American manhood. But each would be a flawed model. And after Kennedy's death, the sum of the egregious faults of the remaining two, Johnson and Nixon—especially Vietnam and Watergate and the massive official lies that attended both—would become the new generation's justification for rejecting the authority of the older generation. Only early death, it may be, spared Kennedy the humiliation that descended upon the two who survived.

Or would Kennedy have found a way through, and succeeded where Johnson and Nixon failed?

CHAPTER TWO

FAMILIES

THE JOHNSONS OF TEXAS

LYNDON JOHNSON ONCE BRAGGED: "Listen, goddammit. My ancestors were teachers and lawyers and college presidents and governors when the Kennedys in this country were still tending bar."

It was true enough. But the families' trajectories were heading in opposite directions. The Kennedys and the Fitzgeralds were rising in the world and making their way into the wealthy ruling classes; simultaneously, the Johnsons and the Buntons and the Baineses were falling and failing. In the 1920s, when Joseph P. Kennedy was swashbuckling on Wall Street, churning stocks and building the family fortune, Lyndon Johnson's father and model in all things, Samuel Ealy Johnson Jr., lost almost all he had to a failed cotton crop and floods and heat in the Texas Hill Country. He sold the family ranch. He fell $40,000 into debt, money that he could never repay and that his son Lyndon, himself straitened, would have to make good later when the old man died in 1937.

Sam Johnson, who had once driven the biggest, most expensive car in Hill County, who was given to strutting around in high-priced polished boots and Stetson hats, and who sat as an honored member of the Texas State Legislature in Austin, now found merchants in Johnson City writing "Please!" on his monthly bills, and finally cutting off the Johnson family's credit entirely, so that Sam would have to find merchants in other towns to give him credit. Before long, they, too, cut him off.

Lyndon and his siblings would sometimes come home from school to find there was no food in the house. Their father, formerly a preening, expansive, gregarious man, a story-teller and joker and big drinker-with-the-boys in Austin, would now return to the house in Johnson City, where he had moved the family when they sold the ranch, and stalk past the children in a black rage, slam the door, and stay in his bedroom for hours. He got sick with an undefined draining illness. The real malady was failure and shame. His face broke out in boils. He gave up his seat in the legislature, and he took the only jobs he could find—first as a two-dollar-a-day part-time game warden, and after that, as a foreman on a highway maintenance crew, working outdoors in the vast Texas emptiness in searing heat or bitter cold.

Variations on the Book of Job play regularly in Texas—sudden big money from cattle or oil may vanish overnight, victim of biblically bad weather and a Texas tendency to bet double or nothing on next year's weather, or expensive drilling that comes up dry. John Connally, Lyndon Johnson's early confederate and protégé and later governor of Texas, wounded in November 1963 with Kennedy in Dallas, and Richard Nixon's Secretary of the Treasury (whom Nixon had hoped would succeed him as president), went bankrupt in the 1980s because of bad investments and had to sell his house and furniture at auction. Boom and bust.

One day, when he was in the Senate, Lyndon Johnson was walking in the streets of Johnson City and saw a shabbily dressed man he recognized as an estimable figure from long ago. Johnson treated him kindly and remarked later that only about a quarter of an inch of happenstance had separated him from that man. It was in 1936, toward the end of Sam Johnson's life, that Robert Frost wrote a sardonic poem called "Provide, Provide:" "Too many fall from great and good / for you to doubt the likelihood." And this: "No memory of having starred / Atones for later disregard, / or keeps the end from being hard." And so: "Provide, provide."

Sam Johnson never recovered his fortunes. The sharp break in his life, between what he had been, and what his family had been in former days, and what he had become—that crack became a conspicuous fault line in Lyndon Johnson's own nature. It helped to explain some of his double-minded, contradictory character—of his energies as New Deal-Great Society Alldaddy benefactor on the one hand, and, on the other, the "provide, provide" of his personal greed and corruption; his decades-long alliances with such big-money Texans as the Brown Brothers, the contractors whose firm, Brown and Root, had poured so much money into his early campaigns, and especially into the 1948 Senate race, and would years later become the principal defense contractor in Vietnam, reaping multimillion-dollar projects such as the giant U.S. base at Danang. The extravagantly humane and feeling neo-Populist idealist who helped to electrify the remote night-black Texas countryside, and later on as president conceived of the War on Poverty, was morally counterweighted by his other self, his venal twin, who knew how to work out of sight to turn political power into the sort of cash that could not be washed away as his father's cotton crop, so painfully planted in the inhospitable hardpan along the Pedernales, had been carried off, again and again, by savage flash "gullywashers."

A day or two after Sam Johnson's funeral, a friend of Lyndon's found him sitting in a "half-dark office," rubbing his forehead and weeping, and repeating, "I'll never get all my debts paid." By the time he took the oath of office as president, aboard Air Force One in Dallas after Kennedy was shot, Johnson had become the richest man ever to assume the office—with more personal wealth (estimated at $14 million) than even Joe Kennedy's boy Jack.

Lyndon Johnson had been finally exhausted by elemental wars going on inside him all his life—mostly simply, it might be said, the struggle between his generosity and his greed, between the urgings of his heart and the urgings of his heartlessness. Johnson presided over the only war that America had ever lost. In some twisted or deflected sense, Vietnam had become an external expression of the unresolveable conflicts in Johnson himself: At the very least it may be said that he conducted the war badly because of his own disabling ambivalences: He fought with conditional ruthlessness, always pulling the punch, assembling massive military strength in a tiny rice-growing land and then so circumscribing that American might with his strictures and ambivalences and target-picking micro-management that he in effect unmanned the men he had sent to battle, and turned the war into a drama of his own dilemmas and interrupted dreams.

Explaining history as the pageant of great men's neuroses is an invitation to fatuousness. On the other hand, who would deny that the history of the 1960s, and of the Vietnam War, was deeply influenced by Lyndon Johnson's character? Or, for that matter, that the fate of Richard Nixon's presidency resulted from the indelible and unique peculiarities of Nixon's character?

And so when LBJ died in 1973, he left a fortune to Lady Bird and his daughters. But the political legacy was as problematic as Sam Johnson's: a war that was a mess (which Richard Nixon would have to clean up, one way or another), an accumulation of bad debts on his grandiose unfulfilled Great Society, a shattered Democratic Party that he had turned against itself and that had in 1972 nominated George McGovern, the bitter enemy of the Vietnam War. McGovern would be crushed by Nixon in the greatest landslide until then in American history.

Johnson had insulated himself handsomely (and sometimes illegally, corruptly) against his father's penury, but he had in another sense recapitulated his disgrace.

Probably Johnson never read Robert Frost's poem. It was part of his rebellion against his parents and against their failures that he would never read books—ever. Throughout his political career, he got his information in other ways, from the news media, on the telephone, talking to other people, other politicians mostly, listening to them: absorbing and studying their living and useable and malleable information, the stuff of politics and public life. What good were books—the coffins of embalmed ideas, the insubstantial feckless realm of the "Harvards," or the fairyland of his beloved but ineffectual mother? Rebekah Baines

Johnson had been a dreaming, poetic creature who escaped into books and ultimately could not cope with harsh Hill Country life or with the shame of hollowed-out threadbare gentility; his father had been a bragging, big-front populist idealist gone to seed, a man who failed to provide. All hat, no cattle. What was more humiliating than braggadocio brought low?

In the years between 1867 and 1870, the Johnson brothers, Sam and Tom, drove cattle up the Chisholm Trail from their 320-acre ranch on the Pedernales River to the railhead at Abilene, Kansas—an arduous drive of five weeks and six hundred miles, along the route that the fictional Matt and Tom took in Kennedy's favorite movie, *Red River.* The Johnsons ran into most of the troubles that the movie portrayed—stampedes, rainstorms, outlaws—though they did not have to cope with the Ahab obsessions of Matt Dunson. The Johnsons were hardy characters, prototypes for Howard Hawkes's or John Ford's Westerns. During the Civil War, Sam Johnson, Lyndon's grandfather, had ridden with the 26th Texas Cavalry and had his horse shot out from under him by Union artillery at the battle of Pleasant Hill, northwest of Natchitoches. He had fought in the western Louisiana parishes along the Red River and, after the war, gone out to the Hill Country to take up cattle ranching with his older brother.

In 1870, the Johnson brothers drove 7,000 head of cattle to Abilene and rode back to the Hill Country with $100,000 in gold coins in their saddlebags. They bought more land, thousands of acres, and the next year drove 10,000 cattle up to Abilene. But big profits had attracted competitors, and suddenly so many cattlemen were driving their herds to market (a total of some 700,000 head that year) that the price collapsed. The Johnsons had bought most of their cows on credit, and had to sell them at a considerable loss.

The manically exaggerated highs and lows of Texas life turned suddenly against them. The summer of 1872 brought a devastating drought. Comanches raided their ranch and made off with

$20,000 worth of horses. Unable to pay their debts, they sold most of the land they had bought with the big money of the previous five years. Shirtsleeves to shirtsleeves, the American story.

When Lyndon Johnson bragged about the college presidents and governors in his family, he was referring mostly to the Bunton side—the forebears of Sam Ealy Johnson's bride Eliza Bunton, who was eighteen when she married Sam in 1867 and moved to the Pedernales. As with the Nixon family story, there would be a persistent theme that the women married beneath themselves. As the more refined Hannah Milhous had descended slightly in the social order to marry the streetcar man Frank Nixon, so Eliza Bunton seemed to be making a step down when she married Sam Ealy Johnson. And similarly Rebekah Baines, Lyndon Johnson's mother, seemed to be settling for something beneath the life she had been used to as a girl when she married Sam Johnson's son, Sam Ealy Johnson Jr.

Eliza Bunton's ancestors had served in the Scottish Parliament, had migrated to North Carolina in the middle of the eighteenth century, and had served in the Revolutionary War. One became a congressman from Kentucky, another the governor of the state. John Wheeler Bunton came to Texas from Tennessee in 1833, joined in the 1835 siege of San Antonio, signed the Texas Declaration of Independence, and served on the committee that wrote the new republic's constitution. He won election to the congress of the Texas Republic, and he wrote the bill that established the Texas Rangers.

Eliza Bunton was a beautiful young woman with "patrician bearing, high-bred features, raven hair, piercing black eyes, and magnolia-white skin." She became in memory a frontier heroine—a prototype of the splendid Texas ideal woman, durable, resourceful, brave, strong. She went along with Sam on the cattle drives to Abilene. She endured the difficult life of the Hill Country, where a woman had to haul water and firewood, cook, wash, make soap, mend, and can fruits and vegetables in a round of days, bitterly cold in winter, oppressively hot in summer, that mercilessly aged most ranch women and left them exhausted by thirty-five. Comanche raiding parties still hit remote ranches from time to time. In Blanco County in the summer of 1869, a young couple named Tom and Eliza Felps were dragged off by Comanches, stripped naked, scalped alive, and killed. Sam Johnson was in the posse that rode out after the Indians—unsuccessfully.

Once when Sam was away from the ranch, Eliza Bunton Johnson spotted Comanches riding through the mesquite toward the house. She took her daughter, Mary, into the cellar beneath a trap door and used a stick pushed through a crack in the floor to pull a braided rug over the hiding place. She tied a dirty diaper over her daughter's mouth to keep her quiet. The Comanches ransacked the house, stole horses from the barn, and then rode off. Eliza and Mary stayed in the cellar until Sam came home in the evening.

There was in Ancient Greece—and there has always been in human nature—the idea of a previous and now inaccessible golden age of heroes and wealth from which the present is inevitably a falling off, a disappointment, a banality, and a kind of shame. The American West, and especially Texas, has always cherished similar origin myths. There is an ideal remembered youth (whatever the actuality was) that grows more radiant as it recedes in time. The old glory is superseded by harder times; the present is not worthy of the past.

The Buntons's heroic frontier past and the Johnsons's cattle drives up the Chisholm Trail had made them heroes. Lyndon Johnson as a child would listen for hours while his grandfather told him stories about those days. And within the span of his young life, Lyndon saw the pattern of the fall from grace recapitulated in his father's story. Sam Johnson Jr., LBJ's father, seemed to young Lyndon to be the ideal of Texas manhood, a popular and important man, a legislator. And then when things turned bad and the cotton crop failed and there was no money in the house and his father turned up drunk and uncommunicative and bitter, Lyndon Johnson had to watch the abrupt descent from grace and favor. In the myth, Daedalus watched his son Icarus fall from the sky. Now, in Texas, the son watched his father fall. Sam Johnson plunged from the ideal into failure. Few things are harder on a boy than the sight of his father humiliated.

The transaction left a permanent mark on Lyndon Johnson. John Kennedy had the opposite problem. He had an overbearingly successful father: Joseph P. Kennedy had created, almost *ex nihilo,* a golden age for himself and his family. His son Jack had to struggle to escape the shadow of his father's success. Sam Johnson's son Lyndon had to struggle to escape the shadow of his father's failure.

Lyndon Johnson's humane generosity and his coldly ungenerous voracity for money sprang from the same source in his past— from his father's failure, from the shame thereof. In his abundant and even elemental humanity, Johnson sympathized with those who were poor because he understood above all the humiliation and helplessness of poverty. In his personal greed, Johnson desperately wished to see to it that he would never fall as his father had fallen.

Two basic and contrary patterns are at work in the way people look at the idea of progress. One is the Ancient Greek conception of a golden age past. The other is the West's idea, since the Enlightenment, that the past is a kind of ignorant darkness and the present represents the ever-advancing progress of human knowledge and understanding as they approach some future perfection.

America has generally worked as a partnership between the two concepts—the mythology of the Founders and the Constitution and Lincoln's "mystic chords of memory" dynamically twinned with the idea of an ever-brightening progressive future.

It is interesting that it was in the era of the three presidents, Kennedy, Johnson, and Nixon, that amid the crises of the Vietnam War, the civil rights movement, and women's liberation, many Americans repudiated its supposedly heroic and glorious golden past. The myth of the West was bunk. The real heroes were those Comanches, not the genocidal whites who had come to steal the Native Americans' lands and kill off their buffalo. John Wayne (who played the Johnson brothers and other men like them in the movie versions of the myths) was the sort of monster of machismo whose sham heroics in *The Sands of Iwo Jima* had been playing in the minds of naïve American boys when they went off to Vietnam to murder peasants.

It was in the presidencies of the three that the American myth pivoted on its axis until the side that had been bathed in sunlight became dark.

THE KENNEDYS: JOHN BUCHAN AND
A STRANGE IRISH ANGLOPHILIA

IN HIS BOOK OF RECOLLECTIONS, *Conversations with Kennedy,* Ben Bradlee recalled his friend Jack's comment when Nixon's *Six Crises* appeared in 1962: "I can't stand the way he puts everything in Tricia's mouth. It makes me sick. He's a cheap bastard; that's all there is to it."

Twelve years earlier, Jack Kennedy had personally delivered a $1,000 campaign contribution from Joe Kennedy to the Nixon race against Helen Gahagan Douglas. John Kennedy told a Nixon aide, "My father wanted to help out . . . . It isn't going to break my heart if you can turn the Senate's loss in Hollywood's gain."

But in 1960, Kennedy delivered his famous verdict on Nixon: "No class."

It was an interesting choice of words, given the Kennedy family's long struggle to transcend the class of Paddy-off-the-boat immigrant Irish (laborers, coopers, barkeeps, braying ward heelers, and East Boston stage Irishmen) and win social acceptance in Brahmin Boston; given Joe Kennedy's vigorous and piratical Gatsby act to lift the tribe up to plutocratic and even ambassadorial rank, lifting them so high that Joe Kennedy saw his eldest daughter, Kathleen, marry into the British aristocracy. Some class.

"No class," in the way Kennedy meant it, of course, signified a stylistic judgment. It meant no instinctive good taste, no sense of appropriate behavior, no individual elan. (If that was his judgment on Nixon's behavior, there would surely be something pungent for him to say about Lyndon Johnson's barnyard exhibitionism, his fondness for urinating and defecating in front of an audience, for example.)

It is worth lingering on Kennedy's idea of "no class." It was clear what Kennedy meant. At the time the remark was reported, it seemed that, in those offhand two words, Kennedy had succinctly described the world of difference between the two men. The phrase caught the shuddering distaste that many felt for Nixon; there was a touch of Franklin snobbery about an uncouth Orthogonian, of course. But Kennedy's phrase also appealed to the idea of the natural aristocracy of the graceful. Classy behavior was not necessarily Franklin behavior, rich behavior; it meant behaving like a mensch, with grace and, when necessary, with self-effacement.

One can argue comparative "class." Both John Kennedy and his father (from whom Jack learned so much) treated their wives cruelly. To humiliate one's wife so relentlessly is surely not evidence of "class."

Thurston Clarke, in *Ask Not,* his study of John Kennedy's inaugural speech, wrote: "How a man who spoke and wrote so eloquently about integrity and morality (and who would say in his inaugural address that 'a good conscience' was 'our only sure reward') could have had so little conscience about his sexual behavior is a question that still mystifies those who thought they knew him. One possible answer is to be found in a passage he wrote in one of his notebooks shortly before being elected president. He considered it so insightful that he included it alongside quotations from Churchill, Lincoln, and Webster." Kennedy wrote that: To be a positive force for public good, a politician needed "a solid moral code governing his public actions." Clarke commented, "The word public was key, implying as it did that a politician's private actions and morals were irrelevant to his ability to promote the public good."

Perhaps it was only in posthumous revelation that John Kennedy's public self was reunited with his private self, and even then the resulting whole man, private and public, does not quite seem to make sense. For Richard Nixon and Lyndon Johnson, the reunion of public self and private self seems to have occurred—despite their best efforts at concealment—during their presidencies, in the working out of their deepest private character through the exercise of the ultimate public office. The fates of both their presidencies, that is, were determined to a large extent by the emergence, through the office, of their private traits of character. But for John Kennedy, assassination intervened before his private character emerged—as it surely would have—to set its mark upon his presidency and his place in history.

John Kennedy seemed a double-faced young man—Tom Sawyer alternating with Lord Byron. He appeared to be fascinated by Byron, by his darker urgings, by his struggle between irony and romanticism, by the club foot that some biographers have taken to be a wound associated in Kennedy's mind with his own physical ailments.

But throughout his life, Kennedy's mind seemed to be working at a reconciliation of opposites, and his partial and temporary identification with Byron (a juvenile role model) pointed toward a much deeper interest in William Lamb, Lord Melbourne—the man who was scandalously cuckolded by Lord Byron before going on to become the young Queen Victoria's prime minister and close friend.

Lord Melbourne represented a late, mellow flowering of the Whig aristocracy in its transition from its natural home in the eighteenth century to the very different empire of Queen Victoria. Lord David Cecil, a British historian and a member of Kick's set in London, published, in 1939, a biography of Melbourne that became one of Kennedy's favorite books. Cecil's *Melbourne* is a wonderfully lively, elegantly written portrait of a man and an age and a class that held much attraction for Kennedy. Kennedy would not have been interested, for more than a moment, in seeing himself in the Byron model. The example of Melbourne would have been more to his taste—and seemed closer to his own experience.

John Kennedy was a second son who entered politics only after his older brother, Joe, heir to their father's dynastic ambitions, died over the English Channel in 1944. Likewise, William Lamb, born in 1779, was the second son born to Lord and Lady Melbourne. William's older brother, Peniston, heir to the title, died of consumption in 1805, making William heir to a peerage and a large fortune, and sending him into politics. As David Cecil wrote: "For William [his older brother's death] was momentous. . . . As a younger son, there was no practical reason—if he had ever felt the inclination—why he should not break away from conventional existence and devote himself to that life of thought and writing in which he could most fully express himself."

Before Joe Junior's death, before his father tapped him to take over as heir to the family's makeshift Irish-American peerage, John Kennedy had vaguely anticipated a life of thought and writing, perhaps as a journalist or a college professor. Young Joe's death changed all that.

Cecil continued: "But future peers in that day were not free. They were integral and active parts of the great machine of aristocratic government and social life; to them, almost as much as to a royal prince, was allotted a ready-made role, function, responsibilities."

That was in some sense John Kennedy's fate as well. His father, the redoubtable founder, grandson of a County Wexford immigrant and cooper on the Boston docks, planted in America his own vigorous seedpod of a new aristocracy and laid down the rules of role and responsibility and succession that were, in their way, as rigid as those evolved over centuries by the British ruling classes that had been the conquering masters of the Kennedys' ancestral Ireland. In the Kennedy family's attitude toward the English one saw occasional contempt and even condescension. But for Kathleen, the pattern was like that of converts to Catholicism who become more Catholic than the pope; the Irish Kathleen became Marchioness of Devonshire. Jack responded with instinctive warmth to the English ruling classes; in later years, some of his closest friends were members of the British ruling class, among them Alec Douglas-Home and Harold Macmillan.

When his older brother died, William Lamb took it for granted that, like other eldest sons, he must now go into the House of Commons. After Joe Junior's death, John Kennedy took it for granted that he would have to go into the House of Representatives. (His father, the impresario, the stage manager and financial backer of Jack's political career, at first wanted him to run for lieutenant governor of Massachusetts in 1946, but the Ambassador became convinced that James Michael Curley's old House seat from the Eleventh District would be a better bet, and a more reliable launching pad for a future president of the United States.)

Cecil wrote of Melbourne: "He was a skeptic in thought; in practice a hedonist." It is a succinct description of John Kennedy's thought and practice for all his adult life.

Further, Cecil says of Melbourne: "His detachment and his curiosity, his honesty and his perceptiveness, his sense of reality and his power of generalization—all these mingled together to make his mind of the same type, if not of the same high quality as that of Montaigne or Sir Thomas Browne."

The "type" of their minds—Kennedy's and Melbourne's—was urbane and undogmatic. They were "foxes," as opposed to "hedgehogs," in Sir Isaiah Berlin's useful distinction. Both Lord Melbourne and John Kennedy shuddered at any expression of the doctrinaire or fanatical. Melbourne was horrified by the rickburning, rioting insurrections during his term as Home Secretary in 1829–1830. Kennedy, rational above all, was even slightly appalled by his mother's rigid Catholicism.

Both were tall, handsome men. Melbourne came from an aristocratic eighteenth-century world filled with intense recreational amours. Cecil writes of the young Melbourne: "His animal nature and his taste for women's society united to make him amorous, and natural tendency had been encouraged by the tradition of his home. Already, we gather, he had sown some wild oats. Like the other young men of his circle he thought chastity a dangerous state, and he seems early to have taken practical steps to avoid incurring the risks attendant to it." Kennedy was of course encouraged in sexual ventures by his father's relentless priapism.

Cecil said of the Whigs: "They were not spiritual. Their education did not encourage them to be . . . they found this world too absorbing to concern themselves much with the next."

They were no better at self-control than, in certain matters anyway, the Kennedys were. "Good living gave them zest; wealth gave them opportunity; and they threw themselves into their pleasures with animal recklessness at once terrifying and exhilarating to a modern reader."

The Whigs seem to have been cheerfully unconcerned about some of the consequences: "The historian grows quite giddy," says Cecil, "as he tries to disentangle the complications of heredity consequent on the free and easy habits of the English aristocracy. The Harley family, children of the Countess of Oxford, were known as the Harleian Miscellany on account of the variety of fathers alleged to be responsible for their existence. The Duke of Devonshire had three children by the Duchess, and two by Lady Elizabeth Foster, the Duchess one by Lord Grey; and most of them were brought up together in Devonshire House, each set of children with a surname of its own."

Lord Byron, whatever his flashes of genius as a poet, was a somewhat ridiculous human being; he had an air of vulgarity about him, a gift of meretricious self-dramatization that Cecil emphasizes with sneering delicacy. Lady Caroline Lamb, Melbourne's wife and Byron's partner in a scandalous affair, was herself given to displays of a somewhat tacky narcissism that mortified Melbourne and would have repelled John Kennedy—

although Kennedy would doubtless have enjoyed one of the spectacles at Devonshire House, where "scandal had it that Caroline was once carried in concealed under a silver dish cover, from which she emerged on the dinner table stark naked, to the consternation of the company."

Both Kennedy and Melbourne were worldly men who appreciated characters like Lady Caroline and Lord Byron as theater; but their intelligence was always slightly amazed and affronted by stupidity.

The world that Joseph P. Kennedy created for his family aspired to the self-assurance and invulnerability of the eighteenth-century Whig aristocracy: "The Whig nobles were never provincial and never uncouth. They had that effortless knowledge of the world that comes only to those who from childhood have been accustomed to move in a complex society, that delightful unassertive confidence possible only to people who never have had cause to doubt their social position."

This is the American irony. The upstart Irish Joe Kennedy had to fight ruthlessly for position in Boston against the Brahmins. He carried a resentment of them throughout his life. Joe Kennedy's triumph was to build a world for Jack and his other children that simulated, indeed outdid, the Brahmins in wealth and power and privilege. Jack had money, attended the best schools, and, above all, enjoyed the atmosphere of position and power and self-confidence and familiarity with great events of the world. So Cecil's Whig effortlessness of attitude did come to Jack as a birthright—arriviste it may have been, but bought and paid for.

Joe Kennedy made his money, piratically enough, and in a classic rags-to-riches-to-culture-and-philanthropy-and-social-register pattern that for the Kennedys was fiercely concentrated into two generations (it took the Rockefellers three, and they never made it to the White House), and he catapulted at least two of his children back a century or two into the civilization of the English ruling classes. Kathleen married Billy Hartington, heir to that same Devonshire House where Caroline Lamb supposedly popped up naked on a silver serving tray. And Jack had about him, consciously and unconsciously, many of the airs and assumptions—the mental and moral style—of Melbourne's great family Whigs.

Furthermore, Joe Kennedy built his own country club. His children and Hyannisport and the entire mystic construct of the Kennedys were his country club, and membership in the club could not have been more exclusive. Membership was restricted to his own genes. That was Joe Kennedy's answer to the Brahmin society and the clubs that had snubbed him: He would found a society of his own flesh and blood and install it in the impregnable fortress of his money; he would rule there like a warlord, and could, if necessary, tell even a demigod like Franklin Roosevelt to go to hell.

Jack Kennedy shared much of Melbourne's innocence of the harsher realities of the world—poverty, for example. Melbourne, who read widely in the classics, in theology, and philosophy, looked over a couple of pages of Charles Dickens's *Oliver Twist* and threw it aside as being disagreeable. Melbourne was terrified of revolution. He said *Oliver Twist* was "all among workhouses and pickpockets and coffinmakers. I do not like those things. I wish to avoid them. I do not like them in reality and therefore do not like to see them represented." Kennedy, brought up rich and privileged, given a Harvard education and a trust fund and a *pater ex machina* worth $400 million, was shockingly ignorant of conditions among the American poor; he was moved and appalled when, campaigning in West Virginia during the primary in 1960, he saw an Appalachian hunger and squalor whose existence he had not quite suspected in the country that had been so generous to the Kennedys.

Melbourne loved life. So did John Kennedy. Both were amused by people, and interested in them. Both found arrogance and pretension to be ridiculous. Melbourne, who had a gift for aphorism (as Kennedy did), was fond of quoting the line "To those who think, life is a comedy, to those who feel, a tragedy." The distinction was congenial to Kennedy as well, who, as one of the thinking category, was inclined to regard life as comic enough, even though from childhood on Kennedy had been given enough pain and illness to have turned a man of different temperament into a sour hypochondriac. His death in 1963 set off waves of tragic feeling that washed over the rest of the decade and beyond; Kennedy would have been appalled and amused by some of the excesses of grief and memorializing, and the torrents of mawkish prose that his death elicited.

Another of John Kennedy's favorite books was *Pilgrim's Way,* John Buchan's "essay in recollection," published in 1940, just after Buchan's death. Buchan (Lord Tweedsmuir) in his book gave the young congressman a civilized, idealized, Anglicized version of Joseph P. Kennedy.

Buchan, who died just as he completed *Pilgrim's Way,* was a Scottish Calvinist minister's son. He had led a varied and accomplished life that combined thought and action, literature and politics. Author of *The Thirty-Nine Steps* and *Greenmantle,* Buchan invented the modern spy thriller. He wrote some one hundred books, including biographies, romances, children's books, poetry, and screenplays. Simultaneously, he conducted an abundant parallel life in politics, as a member of Parliament, confidant of prime ministers, and, at the end of his career, as governor-general of Canada. He wrote: "Politics is still the greatest and most honorable adventure." His ideal was a combined life of thought and action.

Buchan lost a brother, killed at the Battle of the Somme in 1916, in the World War I, as Kennedy had lost Joe in World War II. Buchan suffered from painful, debilitating ulcers, just as Kennedy endured his variety of chronic illnesses. Buchan was a great reader, as was Kennedy. And, like Kennedy, Buchan located his spiritual home somewhere in the eighteenth century. The two shared a swashbuckling spirit of pre-modernism, an adventurousness born on the sunnier slopes of imperial optimism. Buchan wrote that when young, "a worthy life seemed to me to be a series of efforts to conquer intractable matter, to achieve something difficult and perhaps dangerous." He spoke of his "high destiny," of life "compounded of both heavenly and hellish elements, with infinite possibilities of sorrow and joy." He had a secret terror of what he called "cockney suburbanism."

In 1948, when his fellow veterans were eager to settle down and raise a family in a little patch of the great new American suburbanism, John Kennedy was of Buchan's mind. Buchan's high rhetoric about destiny and adventure would be echoed decades later in Kennedy's inaugural address.

Buchan was one of the Border Scots, of whom he wrote: "They lacked the dourness of the conventional Scot, having a quick eye for comedy, and, being in themselves wholly secure, they were aristocrats with the fine manners of the aristocracy." Kennedy had a quick eye for comedy. His father had raised him in a secure world, and, although the other Kennedys' conduct in general was more exuberant and raucous than "fine," Jack Kennedy's polished and essentially kindly manners—cool, but elegant and generous—aspired to the Buchan ideal.

Buchan wrote of his "dislike of grandiose mechanical systems, and a distrust of generalities"—traits he shared with Kennedy, who, like Buchan, was "critical of a superfluity of dogmas." Buchan and Kennedy would have agreed in their pre-modernist romanticism: "The conception of mankind, current in some quarters, as a herd of guzzling, lecherous little mammals seemed to me the last impiety."

In 1948, T. S. Eliot won the Nobel Prize. The prize committee praised *The Waste Land*: "The melancholy and somber rhapsody aims at describing the aridity and impotence of modern civilization. . . . The *horror vacui* of modern man in a modern secularized world, without order, meaning, here stands out with poignant sincerity."

John Buchan hated Eliot. He wrote that after World War I, "the interpreting class plumed themselves wearily on being hollow men living in a waste land. 'A man may dwell so long upon a thought,' Halifax wrote, 'that it may take him prisoner.'" Buchan dismissed Eliot and his kind: "They had no philosophy, if Plato's definition in the Theaetetus be right—'the mood of the philosopher is wonder: there is no other source of philosophy than this'—for wonder involves some vigor of spirit. They would admit no absolute values, being by profession atomizers, engaged in reducing the laborious structure of civilized life to a whirling nebula." Post–World War intellectuals like Eliot, Buchan thought, "found themselves living among the fears and uncertainties of the Middle Ages, without the support of the mediaeval faith." Eliot and his kind, said Buchan, were "a haunted race, who seemed to labor under perpetual fear." (Eliot ultimately agreed with Buchan, for he did himself embrace a medieval faith.) Fear seemed detestable to Buchan. Courage, on the other hand, was the virtue that Kennedy admired most—the one that he proclaimed in *Profiles in Courage.*

In many ways, Kennedy was not, essentially, a modern man. He took over the White House in 1961 as the youthful, vigorous torch bearer of a "new generation" ("born in this century," etc., as he said in his inaugural address), replacing the elderly Dwight Eisenhower. Yet Kennedy, like Buchan, came from an earlier time. If he was born in the twentieth century, he had skipped, or rejected, much of its cultural meaning, including Eliot. The Catholic Church rejected the anomie and accidie and fragmentation of so much twentieth-century culture as being secular or spiritually destructive, or something worse. Joseph P. Kennedy was either contemptuous of such culture or did not understand it. The Church, his father, and his temperament tended to steer

John Kennedy away from modernism's creeds of anxiety and despair and meaninglessness.

What Kennedy took from Buchan was panache—attitude and coloration, a polished masculine style of engagement and thought. In *Pilgrim's Way,* in telling the stories of his friends who died in World War I, Buchan even prefigured Kennedy's drama of dashing youth and early death.

Buchan wrote of his friend from Oxford, Raymond Asquith, son of the prime minister: "For the chosen few, like Raymond, there is no disillusionment. They march into life with a boyish grace, and their high noon keeps all the freshness of the morning. Certainly to his cradle the good fairies brought every dower. They gave him great beauty of person; the gift of winning speech; a mind that mastered readily whatever it cared to master . . . a magic to draw friends to him; a heart as tender as it was brave. One gift only was withheld from him—length of years."

Raymond Asquith died, like Buchan's brother, at the Somme, at the age of thirty-seven. His Grenadier Guards division advanced from Ginchy to Lesboeufs. Their flanks were enfiladed. And so, in Buchan's term, Raymond "fell."

Buchan wrote of Asquith's death in the sort of Camelot prose that attended Kennedy's own burial under the Eternal Flame at Arlington: "He loved his youth, and his youth has become eternal. Debonair and brilliant and brave, he is now part of that immortal England which knows not age or weariness or defeat."

Raymond Asquith died—fell—in the appalling and futile slaughter of one of the bloodiest battles in history. Buchan's glorification of his memory—brilliant youth struck down before his time, the Lycidas note—may have reverberated in a complicated way in Kennedy's mind in the years just after his own war, in which he had himself been briefly given up for dead, and had been decorated for a somewhat less than glorious episode in which he allowed his PT boat to be sliced in half.

After the assassination, Kennedy's retainers Kenneth O'Donnell and Dave Powers published a book of their memories of JFK. They called it *Johnny We Hardly Knew Ye.* The title came from an old Irish song, and if the readers of O'Donnell and Powers's fondly elegiac reminiscences of JFK—full of charm and wit and blarney in the slightly mawkish stories-at-the-wake style of Honey Fitz or James Michael Curley—had recalled the actual lyrics of the song, they might have recoiled, and thought, especially in the wake of Dallas, that the reference was far too savage.

"Johnny I Hardly Knew Ye" is a brutal, graphic antiwar tract. The narrative of the song is that "Johnny" has returned from war alive, but so shot up and so maimed as to be unrecognizable. In the astonishing payoff stanza: "You haven't an arm and you haven't a leg, / You're an eyeless, noseless, chickenless egg, / You'll have to be put in a bowl to beg, / Johnny I hardly knew you."

The Clancy Brothers sing it in the rousing saloon style of such IRA anthems as "The Rising of the Moon," but the message of "Johnny I hardly Knew Ye" might have been used by the IRA to dissuade Irish boys from going off to fight in the British army.

It was important to the message that Johnny should not die a martyr in battle, but rather should come back from the fight in a condition inglorious and repellent and loathsome and horribly stripped of the manhood that he presumably went into battle to prove.

Johnny's fate is entirely different from the beautiful and glorious martyrdom of "young Roddy McCauley"—who "goes to die on the Bridge of Tuam today." That spectacle would inspire youth to sacrifice: "When we stepped out in the narrow street / smiling proud and young / around the neck, around the neck, the golden ringlets hung / there was never a tear in his blue eyes / but sad and bright were they. . . ."

There hung about the fate of John Kennedy something of the music of young Roddy McCauley—the handsome hero, proud and young, bright of eye, never a tear. . . . Mocking death. That

was the American adaptation, post-Camelot, of the Irish nation-
alist hero-lore, a kind of iconography.

"Roddy" is the bright mythic self. "Johnny" is the savage, debunking inner truth—the countertheme.

Kennedy was not maimed in battle, like "Johnny." But he carried around in his body, out of sight, an array of debilitations
that from time to time rose up and nearly killed him and
brought priests around to administer the last rites.

Self and antiself played metaphysical tag. The Kennedys were
brilliant at the stagecraft of the "Roddy" version. "Roddy" was
the public relations of heroism. But "Johnny" was always there,
like a dangerous inner logic, like an embarrassing relative in the
house—like (although it is brutal to say it) his sister Rosemary,
whom the family hid away.

Kennedy's death in Dallas smacked of Roddy McCauley at his
most gallant, and the funeral ceremonies (the riderless horse and
so on) ratified the idea. The title of a movie that came out after
the assassination caught the Roddy McCauley spirit perfectly. It
was called *Years of Lightning, Day of Drums.* Everyone wept when
they saw it.

Poetry and political rhetoric work at pipe dreams, and some
say that impoverished subject peoples—as the Irish were for centuries—develop a gift for that sort of thing, for using words to
conjure glories that oppressive reality has denied them.

It must have been a strange psychological transaction for
Kennedy—to have survived and risen from the dead after he had
been thought lost in the Pacific, but then to survive his rival
older brother's death as well, one for which the younger brother
might secretly blame himself: A contradicting windshear of public triumph and secret guilt might assault the young man who
had come through all that.

And then, of course, there came Kick's death. Fate declared
open season on bright young Kennedys—except that Jack, for
now, survived. A young man in that position does not know

whether he is a favorite of the gods, or whether there has simply been an oversight in his case. Either possibility might encourage recklessness: If he is the gods' favorite, then ordinary rules don't apply to him, and no retribution can touch him; if there has merely been some mistake, then better to take advantage of it before the gods get wise and call in the debt. John Kennedy may have been acting on both assumptions at once. On November 22, 1963, it seemed that the second premise was the operative one, and the debt was called.

John Kennedy grew up in the insulated world that his father had created—a sort of enchanted island of governesses and sailing lessons and private schools and the insularity of his unusually bright and boisterous tribe. Buchan, describing his own youth, wrote: "It was a secure and comfortable world, that close of Victoria's reign before the disillusion and change of the South African War. Peace brooded over the land, and we should not have believed a prophet had he told us that most of our group would fall in battle."

Pilgrim's Way offered Kennedy a gallery of portraits of heroes and role models at the moment when he was emerging from his father's shadow and forming a character and political will of his own.

Buchan's rhetoric has the scent and color of Sir Walter Scott: "His like had left their bones in farther spaces than any race on earth, and from their uncharted wanderings our empire was born. . . . In a pedestrian world he held to the old cavalier grace, and wherever romance called he followed with careless gallantry." Buchan projected upon the young heroes his wistful, sometimes mawkish sense of what they might have been and might have done—and of course, John Kennedy's death gained drama and poignancy from the same projection.

Saul Bellow said that the experience of fame was like touching the naked electricity of a high voltage cable—or like a religious zealot handling snakes. Triumphant boyish dreams might come with an agonist underside, a torment of physical suffering and a sexual counterpoint—for Kennedy, priapism. The boy-hero Charles Lindbergh would eventually evolve to his own grownup squalors of alleged anti-Semitism and bigamy; and the media mob that had made him a world hero in 1927 turned cannibal on him a few years later when his baby was kidnapped and killed. John Kennedy would eventually be struck down by the high-risk voltage of fame and power.

The cross-fertilizations of media (truth miscegenating with fiction in the most lascivious way) were baffling in all of these careers. A very young Lowell Thomas "discovered" Lawrence of Arabia and "made him into one of the world's first film stars." Thomas had been "pointed toward the Middle East by Britain's information director, John Buchan, author of the novel *Greenmantle* (1916), in which a young Oxford scholar leads a Moslem uprising against the Ottoman Empire," David Fromkin observed. Buchan based that hero of *Greenmantle* on another of his colorful friends from Oxford, Aubrey Herbert.

Lawrence believed that "history is but a series of accepted lies." And so Lowell Thomas, a prototype docudrama journalist, collaborated with Lawrence in turning the "Arab Revolt" (in actuality a confused and historically negligible business) into one of the great romances of the twentieth century, eventually to be aggrandised by David Lean in the film *Lawrence of Arabia,* with the five-foot-four-inch Lawrence of actuality played onscreen by the six-foot-three-inch actor Peter O'Toole.

David Fromkin wrote: "Lawrence, with his romantic fantasies, and Lowell Thomas, with his hyperbole and ballyhoo, together concocted a story that took the world by storm. Using photos as lantern slides as he narrated, Thomas created a show that toured the globe and broke entertainment-business records. In London alone, a million people came to see it."

It is possible that Kennedy operated on the principle that pleasure stimulated his mind. At any rate, it made him forget his pain. Perhaps sex, was merely preventive medicine: Kennedy told Harold Macmillan that he had to have sex at least once a day; otherwise he suffered severe headaches. Sex was apotropaic: It warded off the evil eye, it warded off death, or at least cheated death a little. If Lawrence's love of pain had a Puritan twist, Kennedy's love of sex may have been his pagan thumb in the eye of his mother's Catholic pietism.

A vexed-mother story appears, with local variations, in all these men's narratives—in Lyndon Johnson's, in Richard Nixon's, in John Kennedy's—and in Lawrence's. Lawrence's sexual puritanism shaded into masochism. He wrote of his highly religious mother: "I have a terror of her knowing anything about my feelings, or convictions, or way of life. If she knew, they would be damaged: violated: no longer mine. . . . Knowledge of her will prevent my ever making any woman a mother."

Kennedy would have responded to something that Lawrence wrote: "The War was good, by drawing over our depths that hot surface wish to do or win something." Kennedy had been raised in a family that almost frenetically concealed—suppressed—the energies of its depths, and that had been taught by their father, the *Primum Mobile* of their universe, to "wish to do or win something." Doing something, winning something, was the tribal meaning, and without it, one was, in the father's eyes, a waste.

Joe Kennedy had the mind of a sort of gangster Rotarian; its creed was *mens sana in corpore sano.* Yet John Kennedy, like T. E. Lawrence, had a powerful shadow self—*mens morbida in corpore morbido.* In 1948, when Kennedy thought long and distractedly about his dead sister and dead brother, and asked such friends as George Smathers what they thought would be the best way to die, he would have sympathized with Lawrence's moods: "Oh, Lord, I am so tired!" Lawrence said. "I want so much to lie down, to sleep and die. Die is best because there is no reveille." Buchan remarked: "To use a phrase of his own, he was done with trying to blow up trains and bridges, and was thinking of the Well at

the World's End." Kennedy in 1948 had a romance with the
Well. He had either to yield to his morbidity or else be, in effect,
reborn into the next stage of his life.

His father's driving control—the most important and distinctive force in John Kennedy's formation as a man—had now, inevitably, necessarily, belatedly, begun to be counterproductive,
and possibly sinister in a new way. John Kennedy was a man now
past the age of thirty. He was Prince Hal, growing older. His father had become Coriolanus. Joe Kennedy had lost much of his
public authority. Joe Kennedy, still coarse and goatish, made
passes at his son's women and his daughters' schoolmates; but he
had retracted himself from public life. But unlike King Lear (the
other unhappy Shakesperean model that suggests itself), he re-
tained both the money of his kingdom and his sanity.

John Kennedy would find in John Buchan a paternal model
that would help him to fashion an autonomous self. Buchan's
world—peopled by such perished heroes as Raymond Asquith
and T. E. Lawrence—possessed (to use Emerson's phrase) an
"alienated majesty." It was a better and more heroic world than
his own father's sometimes squalid and often barely legal world
of shrewd moneymaking. Henry Luce used to complain that nov-
elists never wrote heroic stories about businessmen; men like Joe
Kennedy, if they turned up in novels at all, would be villains,
and that seemed to Luce an affront to what he saw as the heroic
story of American enterprise.

The Buchan world possessed nobility, and the immigrant Irish
Kennedys—however much they had prospered in Wall Street or
Hollywood or the whisky trade—aspired to nobility: both to the
literal titles and the abstract virtue. It was as if John Kennedy
sought to reverse the film of the family story—or to take the
treasures that Joe Kennedy had accumulated (grubbing in the
markets with the ruthlessly ignoble) and carry them back to a
state of heroic nobility that would amount, after all, to a restoration of heroes to their ancient, better selves.

And so if *Red River* gave John Kennedy a raw Western version of the father-son myth, Buchan's *Pilgrim's Way* looked back in the other direction to a more polished and chivalric model—gave Kennedy some glimpses of what his own, heroic self might amount to.

THE NIXONS OF CALIFORNIA

HANNAH NIXON HAD TOLD Richard he could have no secrets from her; she knew what he was thinking. That was what Sunday school teachers said about God: He knows your thoughts, you can hide nothing from Him. Don't try. When Nixon called his mother a saint, he was suggesting—remembering—not only her patient self-abnegations as mother and nurse and comforter but also her almost dangerous clairvoyance, her omniscience. It cannot have been easy for a bright, dutiful boy to live up to a mother endowed with at least some of the powers of God.

His father, Frank Nixon, was God the thunderer. Hannah was God in a quieter and more effective form. Hannah said later, "I tried not to yell at my children. It does something to a child." She did not raise her voice. But as Richard remembered, "She could be immensely effective with that voice." He once recalled a time when Arthur had been caught smoking behind the house in 1923:

> And my mother had known about it, and so I went and talked to Arthur about it to ask him whether he had and I remember he said to me . . . "if mother knows, tell her to give me a spanking," he said. "Don't let her talk to me . . . I just can't stand it, to have her talk to me." And so we always, in that family, in our family, we would always prefer . . . my mother used to say later on that she never gave any one of us a spanking. I'm not so sure, she might have, but I do know that we dreaded far more than my father's hand, her tongue. Not that it was very sharp, but she would just sit down and she would talk very, very quietly and when you got through, you had been through an emotional experience.

When Nixon was very young in Yorba Linda, in 1916 or so, Hannah Nixon hired a young Quaker woman named Mary Guptill to help care for Richard and his two brothers. Guptill remembered "a quiet, little round-faced boy with large, dark eyes," who often played contentedly alone. "He was not as outreaching as many children are," Guptill recalled. "He lived more within himself." Guptill thought Richard, the second son, was the least noticeable of the children, "kind of in between" the baby Donald, whom she found "very easy to enjoy and love," and an older Harold whose illnesses had aroused this parents' continuing concern.

Nixon's biographer Roger Morris commented that the Nixon children "seemed to have no particular toys or pets, and few playmates at hand. When Hannah took Richard to visit a friend in Whittier, an older girl who watched him on the visits said, 'The first thing that little tyke wanted to do was to hightail it upstairs and play with my dolls. He liked to play with them better than I did.'"

One glimpses in Nixon, for a moment, an unexpected maternal tenderness. It manifested itself after his beautiful and doll-like and doomed baby brother Arthur was born.

Family and friends would remember Harold or Don Nixon with the normal flow of human warmth and affection. A schoolmate said of Harold, who was himself doomed to die of tuberculosis at an early age: "He was a leader, but not a serious kind of person. He liked to play and roughhouse and things like that." But they seemed to recall only Richard's "seriousness." Virginia Shaw, a neighbor in Yorba Linda, remarked: "I actually never can recall him laughing and having fun, too much except whooping it up when we were playing boats or playing cars. The older brother, Harold . . . was just full of fun." But Richard seemed, even as a child, to watch the world across a certain distance. He possessed an animal's acute sense of critical distance—of surrounding himself with invisible boundaries, the violation of which caused him discomfort and confusion.

But with the baby Arthur, Nixon seems to have experienced a clear, untroubled emotional connection. He wrote later: "The first two or three years of my baby brother's life are rather indistinct in my memory, for I was engrossed in the first years of my grammar school education." As years passed, some thought that Arthur seemed to have Richard's temperament. "He was rather quiet and sort of a loner," Nixon's Aunt Olive said later. "[Arthur] wasn't gregarious like Harold and Don . . . he was keen enough and smart enough but he played by himself." Some photographs taken at a birthday party in the spring when Arthur was seven show him standing apart from the other children, as Richard often did.

Only a few months later, Arthur began to have headaches and indigestion. He could not eat, and became habitually sleepy. Hannah Nixon called a doctor, who tested the boy and found tubercular encephalitis. Nixon recorded in his memoirs that his father came down the stairs from the boys' room after one of the tests with tears streaming down his face. Richard had never seen Frank Nixon cry before. His father said: "The doctors are afraid the little darling is going to die."

Writing about it many years later, Nixon remembered that Arthur rallied briefly and asked for one of his favorite dishes—tomato gravy over toast. Donald and Richard brought it to him, and watched him eat.

Donald and Richard were hurriedly packed off to their aunt Carrie Wildermuth's house in Fullerton. Two days later, as he was saying good night to his mother, Arthur told her, "I wish you had another baby." She asked why. He said, "So you would stay home and wouldn't be in the store." Arthur said his bedtime prayers: "If I should die before I wake, I pray the Lord my soul to take."

Later that night, their Aunt Carrie woke Don and Richard in Fullerton and rushed them home to East Whittier. But Arthur was already dead when they arrived.

"Richard slipped into a big chair," his mother remembered later, "and sat staring into space, silent and dry-eyed in the undemonstrative way in which, because of the choked, deep feeling, he was always to face tragedy." He did weep later, however. They buried Arthur in a family plot in Whittier Heights. Nixon wrote: "For weeks after Arthur's funeral, there was not a day that I did not think about him and cry. For the first time I learned what death was like and what it meant." Richard was twelve.

What did Hannah Nixon herself feel when she used that vivid phrase about Richard's "choked, deep feeling?" Did she have some sense of what it was that had "choked" him? The answer to that question remained a central mystery of Nixon's character; he probably did not know the answer himself. Did Hannah choke him with her steely passivities, her saintly, long-suffering expectations—a form of coercion that was more powerful and punishing than Frank Nixon's strap? "Choked" was an odd, alarming, almost violent word for a mother to use. At the far end of her statement is another powerful word, "tragedy." In a healthier emotional physics, a tragedy such as a child's death sets off a normally expressed and understandable grief, just as a good joke causes laughter and a child's birthday party tends to cause children to enjoy themselves by playing together, or, for that matter, fighting together, but nonetheless being together. But there was, as the mother said in a perfect choice of imagery, something choked in Richard, something obscurely strangled. It was a side of him, a wing of the house that was sealed off and could not be entered by anyone except himself. Sometimes not even by himself.

What was the key? Or who?

It is possible that the boy was simply like that, and that the distinctive line (of privacy, loneliness, of "choked, deep feeling") running through Nixon's life from Yorba Linda to the White House and back to his simple grave at the Nixon Library quite simply defined . . . *him,* and that that self would have been more or less the same regardless of what Hannah or Frank had been like, what kind of parents they had been, regardless of the family's financial circumstances, and regardless of what medical disasters had, or had not, been visited upon the Nixons. Biographers politically hostile to Nixon have frequently made their attack upon him from an oblique private angle, marching with flashlights up the dark corridors.

Nixon was by heritage and inclination, it seems, an intensely private and disciplined and self-conscious man. He held himself back physically from other people (unlike Lyndon Johnson). He had a fastidiousness, a bodily reticence. As a boy he asked his mother to smell his breath before he went off to school. He may have felt that he might harbor the dirty private secret of bad breath and must not disclose it to anyone else. He was fastidious not only about himself but about others. He complained that the other children sometimes smelled, especially those from the poor farm families outside of town.

THE SHIP BRINGING Nixon back from the war docked at San Diego on July 17, 1944.

He had looked forward to the moment for a long time. He had written to Pat from Bougainville about the homecoming he dreamed of: "Whether it's the lobby of the Grand Central or the Saint Francis bar—I'm going to walk right up to you and kiss you—but good! Will you mind such a public demonstration?"

Pat flew down from San Francisco, where she had been working while Dick was overseas. Pat Nixon was a strong, self-sufficient woman and she had somewhat savored her independence while

Dick was away. Her last letter to him before he came home was a sort of warning: "I will have to admit that I am pretty self-reliant and if I didn't love you I would feel very differently. In fact, these many months you have been away have been full of interest, and had I not missed you so much and had I been footloose, could have been extremely happy. So, Sweet, you'll always have to love me lots, and never let me change my feelings for you."

Pat Nixon was born in a mining shack in the frontier copper town of Ely, Nevada, and spent the years of her childhood in a tiny two-bedroom white-frame bungalow (for a family of six), with no plumbing or electricity, on a dusty, windswept ten-acre "ranch" in Artesia, California, nine miles south of downtown Whittier. Her father, Will Ryan, a knockabout Irish American from Connecticut who was forty-six when Pat (who was actually christened "Thelma") was born, and had spent years banging around the world as a whaler, prospector, miner, and what one account called a "luckless speculator," now struggled to support the family by trucking small crops of cabbage and cauliflower, pimiento peppers, beets, corn, and tomatoes eighteen miles into downtown Los Angeles in a trailer behind a Model T Ford.

Nixon pursued Pat with humiliating doggedness for two years before she agreed to marry him. He was twenty-seven in 1940. She was twenty-eight. He loved her. For much of their courtship—he pursuing, she pursued and somewhat irritable about it—she forbade him to speak of love or marriage. He tried to obey. But in February 1940, on the second anniversary of their meeting (in a little theater production in Whittier of a play called *The Dark Tower*), he wrote an adoring letter to her that recalled their meeting. He was the "funny guy" who "gets the same thrill when you say you'll go someplace with him." Then, though she had asked him not to speak of it, he ended with a declaration of his love, couched tenderly in Quaker plain speech: "And when the winds blow and the rains fall and the sun shines through the clouds, as it is now, he still resolves as he did then, that nothing so fine ever happened to him or anyone else as falling in love with Thee—my dearest heart. Love, Dick."

He proposed to her one March evening, two months later, in her Oldsmobile as they sat parked on a rocky promontory looking out over the Pacific, near a seaside town called San Clemente.

Pat Ryan finally said yes. "Even as she consented," her daughter Julie wrote, "she was not sure she wanted to marry. She was twenty-eight years old and had been independent for a long time."

They drove immediately to Whittier and woke up his parents to tell them the news. Frank was exuberant. Hannah said little. Pat recalled that their reaction "broke the romantic spell of the evening." Pat and Dick disagreed over the engagement and wedding rings. Pat wanted a simple, wide gold band. Dick wanted to buy diamonds. He did so, spending $300. She was annoyed and grudgingly accepted them.

He wrote her an extravagant letter, addressed to "Dearest Heart":

From the first days I knew you, you were destined to be a great lady—You have always had that extra something which takes people out of the mediocre class. And now, dear heart, I want to work with you toward the destiny you are bound to fulfill.

As I have told you many times—living together will make us both grow—and by reason of it we shall realize our dreams. You are a great inspiration to me, and though you don't believe it yet, I someday shall return some of the benefit you have conferred on me.

It is our job to go forth together and accomplish great ends and we shall do it too.

The private document, couched in such public rhetoric, sounds strangely, poignantly, like a political love letter. A man who, in the transports of young love, tells his bride that "it is our job to go forth and accomplish great ends and we shall do it too" has picked a curious occasion on which to rehearse his inaugural address.

As sometimes happens in contemplating Nixon, one glimpses for an instant a sweet, touching human emotion, a need, and then finds it mitigated (almost ruined) by an almost inexplicable falseness. Here, in a love letter to his bride, of all places, Nixon in his ardor falls back upon political boilerplate.

A familiar speculation: The deeper wells of Nixon's emotional nature were from time to time so occluded that little genuine, nourishing, healthy feeling—love, for example—could pass through from Nixon's true self to others, even to Pat. The letter he wrote to her on the eve of their wedding about destiny and inspiration and the rest seemed one of those Nixonian moments when his partially disabled emotional capacity deflected him, as it were, from the private track to the public track. Even—or especially—on such an important emotional moment love defaulted to declamation, to the safe vocabularies and dynamics of political ideals.

One of the keys to Nixon's performance over many years may lie in this transaction. Nixon's was a perennially staged personality. He played roles. He became acutely uncomfortable when he was not playing a role, when he was uncertain what the role was or what demeanor was required of him. That was the reason he was maladroit at improvising small talk. As a bridegroom-to-be, he addressed his bride as if he were competing again in the *Los Angeles Times* oratorical contest on the glories of the U.S. Constitution.

Dick and Pat were married in a Quaker service at the Mission Inn in Riverside—a small wedding because Pat did not want to burden her brothers with the expense of a large one, and she did not want the Nixons to pay. The ceremony took place in the hotel's "Presidential Suite," because, Pat said, it was the smallest and least expensive to rent for the afternoon. They went to Mexico for their honeymoon, driving in Pat's Oldsmobile and eating out of cans they had brought from the Nixon grocery store. Their friends as a wedding prank had removed all the labels from the cans, so Pat and Dick were left to open the cans at random and accept whatever chance gave them to eat: spaghetti for breakfast, pineapples for dinner.

The two most important women in Nixon's life, his mother and his wife, both possessed the combination of strength and self-abnegation that Nixon (and others) described as saintly. Both nursed dying tubercular patients (Hannah, her son Harold and the others in Prescott; Pat, her father), selflessly boiling dishes, sanitizing bedsheets, disposing of the ubiquitous, disgusting sputum cups.

In the studio portrait that Pat sent to Dick (at his repeated urging) in the Pacific in 1944, her eyes are deeply charged with an ineffable pain. Pat Ryan was a lovely young woman, but it is possible that what Dick Nixon recognized in her when he fell so spontaneously and deeply in love was a quality of understanding and suffering in her eyes that took him a long way back. Nixon referred to her in early love letter as "you with the sad but lovely smile."

THE WORLD SCENE

FROM SOCIETY OF NECESSITY TO
SOCIETY OF CHOICE

THE COMMUNIST SAID, "Comrades!"

The voice on the loudspeaker in the supermarket said, "Shoppers!"

The first would address a society of necessity. The second would speak to a society of choice.

Both terms of address would be abstractions—coercive categories. The individual (the housewife in Minsk, the accountant in Wichita) would vanish into the socioeconomic classification.

The "comrade"—or *tovarisch,* the heavy term of officially affectionate solidarity—had no choice. Not to be a comrade is to be an enemy of the people.

The "shopper" would have nothing but choice, by definition: What defined a shopper was the shopper's choice between, let us say, Super Chunk Skippy Peanut Butter and Creamy Smooth Peter Pan Peanut Butter.

But the shopper has no choice except to make a choice.

Choice, to be sure, is freedom—freedom of choice—but there does come a moment in advanced material societies when what had seemed to be a wonderful freedom of choice would begin to look like no choice at all: a globalized coercion toward standard and not very interesting products franchised and distributed worldwide, accompanied by a concomitant die-off of the local, the distinctive, the tasty. The British journalist-moralist Malcolm Muggeridge would say: "What will make historians laugh at us is how we express our decadence in terms of freedom." What we would get was not even the decadence of multiplicity but rather only the proliferating lifelessness of the standard.

This began in 1948.

As the baby boom grew up they would become the shoppers. As they reached the age of financial discretion, many of them would conceive of themselves, at first, in the sixties, as idealists. But in a sense, their ideals—at any rate, their opposition to the war in Vietnam (which was a self-interested idealism that faded instantly when Richard Nixon ended the draft in 1973) and their ideals of race and gender equality—were misdirections of history, not quite the point, even though those apparent passions, along with sex and drugs and freedom, received the most attention from the press. But the real meaning of the sixties and of the ascendancy of the boomers was dispassionately economic: That demographic wave eventually swelled to become the energy of globalization.

The birth of the American suburbs—the first Levittown opened in October 1948, to the relief and delight of thousands of veterans who had been bunking with relatives and friends—and the automobile culture, and the entire American consumer civilization, a vast new society of choice, unprecedented in the world, represented a transformative moment in the history of the world.

It represented the birth of the idea of freedom as freedom of material choice; and it brought Thomas Jefferson's phrase about the pursuit of happiness down to the concrete, to a multiplicity of specific choices in the world of discretionary consumerism: What opened now for the first time was the door to a world in which the consumer could travel anywhere, consume (a happy word with an ominous shadow) any one of multiple products (cars, cigarettes, toothpastes, hair tonics, mattresses, beers, and so on.) Tide, the first laundry detergent, made its appearance in 1948. So did television on a mass consumer scale; television offered, in a new metaphysical way, a new multiplicity of realities—even if its realities for the moment came in a grainy black-and-white fed onto a twelve-inch screen.

Here was the birth of the idea of life as a drama of choice rather than of necessity. In Ancient Rome the Emperor Nero entered his Golden House for the first time. He inspected the statue of himself, 120 feet high. He saw the enclosed lake surrounded by buildings that were designed to represent the cities of the empire. He admired the pillared façade that stretched for a mile, the dining rooms paved with porphyry, the ceilings of gold and fretted ivory inlaid with jewels. "At last," he said, "I am beginning to live like a human being."

Nero had entered his McMansion. What was available 2,000 years ago only to the Roman emperor (he paid the price when his armies revolted and the Senate condemned him to death) would in the fullness of time become a widely distributed dazzlement of home furnishings and multiplicities of freedom of travel and information and death-cheating medical technique.

America as a society of choice was born out of the necessities of economic depression and world war. When the American economy, revived and focused by the demands of war, converted after 1945 from war production to consumer goods, there opened the cornucopia of expanding choice.

THE DIFFERENCE BETWEEN those two conditions—the dynamics of choice against the imperatives of necessity—explains a certain amount about the world today. To say that the world faces conflicts of civilization is true; but the essence of the conflict lies deeper, in the profligate energies of societies of choice confronting the radical indignation of societies of necessity. It is a war almost of one physical dimension against another; the conflict represents a dangerous event of nature, like the meeting of mutually intolerable or intolerant forces that resolve their differences in earthquakes or hurricanes.

At what was called "the Cornfield Conference" of Indiana Re-publicans at the farm of manufacturer Homer Capehart in 1938, Capehart declared that "Republicanism is Americanism. Only employment in private industry is American." It was impossible, he said, to live under two systems, the American system and the New Deal experiment. By 1948, Capehart would be an influen-tial Republican senator from Indiana.

Capehart was the inventor and manufacturer of the mass pro-duction jukebox, first as a Capehart Orchestrope, and later as the Wurlitzer jukebox, a brightly lit pay-by-the-song public phono-graph (for bars, cafes, and diners) that brought to listeners, for a nickel a song, an on-demand choice of music. The Capehart and Wurlitzer were in a sense way ahead of radio because the choice of song, on demand, was at the discretion of the listener for a price. Radio has its own schedule and the listener must conform to it. The jukebox (which eventually came to be a gaudy bub-bling thing—Capehart did not want it to look like a casket laid on end) was a big step forward in the discretionary aspect of the pursuit of happiness. It was democratic in that it was in a public place and, when one person paid, all could listen; the payer chose, but all would listen.

The society of necessity in the first place does not regard pop-ular music as a necessity—and certainly not a multiplicity of choices of popular music. The jukebox brought discretionary, if evanescent, pleasure and a direct economic transaction: Put money in, the box plays.

That was the essence of the society of choice: discretion, evanescence, direct economic cause-and-effect. Pleasure follows payment. The money causes a magic reflex of music.

What was new was not that one paid for goods but rather that the American civic religion (life, liberty, and the pursuit of hap-piness) worked through technology and industry to produce a machinery through which it could enact the ideal of freedom. The multiplicity of choices on the jukebox (the choices were initially limited to ten, but eventually in the forties increased to many times that) was not unlike the multiplicity of choices available through the automobile and through the American highway system. Catalogs and chain stores offered the same consumer freedom through multiplicity of choice—so that where the society of necessity would offer, by definition, only necessities, and usually only a few of those, the society of choice offered not only necessities but nonnecessities, and plenty of choices among those—different brands, different styles, different cuts.

Agricultural societies tend to be societies of necessity: Industrial societies tend to be societies of choice, because the industries' imperative and raison d'être is to produce in ever widening variety and profusion, products to "satisfy" popular "demand."

Autonomous agricultural societies are tied to seasons and to place—the necessities to be provided in the rhythms of crops and so on. Societies of choice have not only industrialized but have evolved beyond the manufacture of basics to the production of the vast imaginative array of discretionary items whose marketing depends on advertising that will either 1) persuade buyers that they need the product even if the buyer is not quite aware of how badly he needs it; and 2) give prospective buyers an intimation of the pleasure that awaits when they have bought the car, the bottle of whisky, the suit, and so on.

The turnaround from society of necessity to society of choice was especially dramatic after about fifteen years of depression and world war because America was filled with pent-up desires, deferred pleasures, and an entirely new dimension of anxieties, the Communist and nuclear kind. So the famous American Pursuit of Happiness became especially intense in the years after the war—the years of political initiation for Nixon, Kennedy, and Johnson.

MARSHALL

AS MUCH AS ANY MAN, George Marshall saved world democracy at the moment of its greatest danger. He assumed his duties as U.S. Army chief of staff on September 1, 1939, the day that Hitler marched into Poland. He began with an absurdly ill-equipped army of 174,000 men, ranking nineteenth in the world behind such nations as Bulgaria and Portugal, and turned it into a global fighting force of 10 million, an army without which the Allies could not have defeated Nazi Germany and Japan. Ulysses Grant was the first master of industrial warfare. Marshall was the first genius of bureaucratic warfare. Not martial flamboyance but logistics saved the world in 1939–1945.

George Marshall is half forgotten now, or four-fifths forgotten, as he knew he would be. There was a moment around Thanksgiving of 1943 that might have propelled Marshall into higher historical orbit. Franklin Roosevelt, on his way to meet Stalin in Tehran, needed to settle upon the general who would lead the Allied invasion of France and the reconquest of Europe. Everyone assumed that Army Chief of Staff George Marshall would get the job he had magnificently earned—the most important battle-field assignment in the history of warfare.

Roosevelt, during a layover in Tunis, discussed the question with Dwight Eisenhower, who was then the American com-mander in London. As they flew over the Tunisian battlefields of the Third Punic War, the president thought out loud: "Ike, you and I know who was chief of staff during the last years of the Civil War but practically no one else knows, although the names of the field generals—Grant, of course, and Lee and Jackson, Sherman, Sheridan and the others—every schoolboy knows them. I hate to think that fifty years from now practically nobody will know who George Marshall was. That is why I want George to have the big command. He is entitled to establish his place in history as a great general."

Eisenhower listened in silence. He, of course, wanted to command the invasion, but like everyone else assumed the job would go to Marshall. In the days that followed, FDR tried to get Marshall to state a preference, in effect to make the decision for him. If Marshall had asked for the command, it might have been his. He said simply that he would do what the president wanted him to do. He told Harry Hopkins that Roosevelt "need have no fears regarding my personal reaction."

Days later, in Cairo, FDR made his decision. He reasoned that no one else could deal with Congress as effectively as Marshall— no other soldier would have Marshall's moral authority and credibility. No one else knew the world military situation so well; if Eisenhower came to Washington as chief of staff, he would be familiar with Europe but not with the Pacific or with the China-Burma-India theaters. And so, as the Cairo Conference ended, Roosevelt told Marshall: "I feel I could not sleep at night with you out of the country."

It was done. Marshall accepted the decision without question or comment. Both Roosevelt and Marshall were correct in predicting that being kept at his desk in the War Department would deprive Marshall of the honor in history that he deserved.

History is not fair. Marshall was a greater man than Dwight Eisenhower, but it was Ike who went to the White House for eight years. Marshall was a greater general, and a better man, than Douglas MacArthur. Yet MacArthur, by turns brilliant (as at Inchon, the stroke that turned the Korean War around, for a little while) and by turns bogus, theatrical, and petty, lives on more vividly in whatever remains of American historical memory. MacArthur had flashes of genius as a soldier; his natural gift was for publicity.

Marshall possessed an instinct for publicity, but it was tactical and never intended for self-promotion. He was uncorrupted. Despite the offer of seven-figure publishers' advances, Marshall refused to write his memoirs; he said that to do so would require him to tell the full story, honestly, and that such truth-telling would sometimes wound old colleagues. He honored his obligation to the historical record by conducting long interviews with his superb biographer, Forrest Pogue, whose four-volume life is probably the fullest accounting Marshall will receive.

Colin Powell and Norman Schwarzkopf, heroes of the first Iraq War, made millions for their memoirs. Marshall belonged to a pre-television, almost Plutarchan order. In some ways, the burden that he bore was greater than that of Churchill or Roosevelt, because Marshall was the man who turned policy, mere ideas, into men and steel, into facts. He was held more mercilessly than the others to the standard of reality. When World War II ended, Churchill, who worked closely with Marshall and often quarreled with him over Allied strategy, said of the Chief of Staff, "This was the noblest Roman of them all."

Franklin Roosevelt's presidential career fell into two acts: the Great Depression and World War II. Marshall played his two acts in the opposite order, from war to peace—first as the organizer of global battle, then as a preeminent statesman of the postwar period.

Marshall's two great acts intersected in June 1947. Harvard University's President James B. Conant presented to George Catlett Marshall a doctor of laws degree, honoris causa. The honor, Conant told the audience of 8,000 in Harvard Yard, went to "an American to whom Freedom owes an enduring debt of gratitude, a soldier and statesman whose ability and character brook only one comparison in the history of this nation." The comparison was, of course, to George Washington.

By June 1947, the relief attending victory two years earlier had been lost in new anxieties. Churchill, deposed as prime minister and leading the loyal opposition, asked: "What is Europe now? It is a rubble heap, a charnel house, a breeding ground of pestilence and hate." The wartime alliance with the Soviet Union had all but disintegrated; the threat of Communist regimes in Western Europe and the Mediterranean was real. In 1947, Marshall had a new assignment: secretary of state.

Marshall mistrusted eloquence; he said that he was bad with words, and in any event thought an officer should express himself through his deeds. Marshall looked out at Harvard Yard, adjusted his reading glasses, and began: "I need not tell you that the world situation is very serious . . ."

With that, Marshall set forth the outline of the European Recovery Act—the Marshall Plan. As the Cold War began, he set in motion the program that would save Western Europe from economic and political chaos, and from the totalitarianism that overtook mainland China and the East Bloc countries.

DEAN ACHESON PRAISED General George Marshall's greatness, his "grandeur and completeness of character."

Who would apply those words—greatness, grandeur, completeness of character—to Richard Nixon, John Kennedy, or Lyndon Johnson?

But Acheson set a high standard. Which presidents would have measured up to it?

Washington, surely. Jefferson, perhaps—though something in him (if only the slaveowner) was evasive and inconsistent and morally incomplete. Lincoln had grandeur certainly, and a tragic completeness that might be said to have been accomplished, finally, at Ford's Theater. Franklin Roosevelt exhibited grandeur, and a mysterious, inaccessible completeness of character—although his great skill as an actor, staging grandeur as a performance, was itself part of the effect of grandeur. And, as his enemies noticed, Roosevelt lied a great deal. He was a magician, Prospero. The great saint of Depression and world war—or, as his enemies, Joe Kennedy among them, came to think, a devious and stagey cripple.

But what other presidents met the Marshall test? Not Eisenhower the president; Eisenhower the soldier had the grandeur and completeness of his military triumph in invading Europe and defeating Hitler (from the west).

Not Truman. Not Woodrow Wilson, whose grand vision ended badly. Not Teddy Roosevelt, really: TR had great energy and imperial brass, but Mark Twain had a point when he said he detected the glint of lunacy in Teddy. George Marshall, on the other hand, was close to being the sanest man who ever lived.

Reagan? His admirers saw grandeur and completeness. His critics saw emptiness. But Reagan came close to the Marshall standard. He was in a sense the last of America's thoroughly public men, the last of the public man as all performance and façade: He predated the notion that the private man was the important thing and that the discrepancy between his private life and public façade was the measure of his corruption and hypocrisy.

Nixon did not remotely exhibit grandeur in a personal sense, although his geopolitical vision came to be large and historic. His character—flawed, angry, paranoid, intensely neurotic—had no completeness.

Kennedy's life, with its personal imperfections, was cut off by an assassin and was therefore by definition incomplete, or did not evolve to what it might have become. The course of Kennedy's presidency changed him, matured him: But the process was cut short in Dallas.

Johnson was larger than life, and if that was grandeur, it was the grandeur of a chaotic, chthonic kind, id-driven, filled with fierce energies. Grandeur, however, in the sense that Acheson applied the word to Marshall, suggests a certain serenity and loftiness; Johnson was neither serene nor lofty.

None of the three was a great man. All three had great qualities, and great moments.

Nixon had China. Johnson had the Civil Rights Acts.
Kennedy had his inaugural address (a great promise, an indelible
moment) and his American University speech on the test ban
treaty; he handled the Cuban missile crisis well, but, in those
thirteen days, was perhaps more lucky than great.

It was difficult for a politician to rise to the George Marshall
standard. Grandeur may not be available to politicians working
in the heat of democratic politics. Grandeur implies a certain distance. Marshall had the distance and authority of military rank.
Marshall's character was formed under military discipline, under
clear lines of authority and settled, agreed-upon rules of command and obedience and advancement. In politics, there are almost no rules of any kind; in fact, Nixon, Kennedy, and Johnson
achieved their political ambitions, to a degree, by lies and distor-
tions that would not have been tolerated in a military career.

When George Marshall tried to function as a politician—on
his mission to try to sort out China in 1946–1947, for example—he failed. In fact, the young John Kennedy (echoing Henry
Luce and others in the conservative China lobby) blamed Marshall for the "loss" of China.

Marshall told the story of standing at the dock in Hoboken,
New Jersey, in 1917, and watching American soldiers embarking for France. Captain Marshall commented to a colonel beside
him: "The men look very solemn." The colonel replied: "Of
course they are. We are watching the harvest of death."

By 1917, no intelligent soldier had illusions about the war
that was devouring an entire generation of Europe's young men.
In one day, July 1, 1916, at the Battle of the Somme, England
squandered 60,000, some 2,000 more than the Americans lost in
twelve years in Indochina.

Woodrow Wilson, reelected in 1916 on a promise of keeping
the America out of the war (as Franklin Roosevelt promised to

do in 1940 and as Lyndon Johnson promised in 1964), sent American forces to France under General John J. Pershing, who was fresh from chasing Pancho Villa in Mexico the year before.

Marshall, with a temporary promotion to major, took over as the First Division's operations officer, training and organizing the inexperienced American troops at Gondrecourt in Lorraine. He saw combat briefly as an observer along General Henri Philippe Petain's Verdun front (Marshall got caught in the open under fire, then entangled in barbed wire and left part of his pants on the wire as he scrambled back to the trenches.) Made temporary chief of staff of the First Division, Marshall had a memorable encounter with Pershing. General Pershing exploded at Marshall's commander, General William L. Sibert. Marshall in turn lost his temper (anger was the one vice that Marshall always had to struggle to control) and blistered Pershing with a furious monologue. Marshall's fellow officers predicted that his career was finished. Instead, Pershing decided that he had found an officer who would tell him the truth.

Marshall hoped for a troop command. Douglas MacArthur, a month younger than Marshall, was already a full colonel and chief of staff of the Forty-second Division. Marshall, however, was judged too valuable as a staff officer. He was transferred to Pershing's headquarters at Chaumont. Ludendorff's spring 1918 offensive had failed. Marshall was ordered to plan the American part in a general Allied counterattack against the Germans.

Marshall's later story in World War II—too valuable for combat, condemned against his wishes to function as a sort of military desk wizard—was prefigured in the St. Mihiel and Meuse-Argonne campaigns. Marshall, rising rapidly and now promoted to colonel, organized the movement of 600,000 American troops and 900,000 tons of supplies and ammunition from the St. Mihiel sector to the Meuse-Argonne battlefield, all moving by night, in secret, without detection by the Germans. It was the largest and most complicated logistical undertaking of the war. Marshall accomplished it magnificently.

The Meuse-Argonne operation in the fall of 1918 was a kind of localized rehearsal for the global task that Marshall accomplished in World War II. It called into play Marshall's remarkable gift of dispassionate concentration upon the task at hand. His second wife, Katherine Tupper Marshall, years after his first wife's death—observed his behavior during the first bleak months of 1942, when the Allies were being thrown back on almost all fronts around the world. She said, "It was as though he lived outside of himself and George Marshall was someone he was constantly appraising, advising, and training to meet a situation."

Neither the Meuse-Argonne campaign nor the logistics of America's global war succeeded simply because Marshall had character. He possessed an extraordinary intellect, a magnificent memory, and what might be called a kinetic military imagination—a genius for seeing the dynamic interaction of facts in rapid motion through time, his designs a watchworks operating by his intricately syncopated instinct. Ulysses Grant in the midst of battle exhibited something of the same deft, fluid clarity.

Marshall's epigrams were delivered in plain style. As chief of staff, he told his aides: "Don't be a deep feeler and a poor thinker." His focused, analytical intelligence would be on display when he testified before congressional committees or gave occasional press conferences during World War II. Sometimes he would invite forty or fifty correspondents into his office, listen to a long series of questions from them, and then, without notes, deliver a half-hour monologue in which he answered each question in turn (facing the correspondent directly as he answered that correspondents question) and at the same time wove all the answers into an overall coherent picture.

After World War I, America, of course, demobilized, turning away in horror and relief from foreign nightmares and relying upon its vast Atlantic and Pacific moats. Marshall returned to America as personal aide to Pershing, who in some ways became Marshall's military role model. Like Marshall, Pershing expected frank, direct, and even critical advice. His five years with Army Chief of Staff Pershing gave Marshall an education in the political realities of soldiering in a democracy and dealing with world leaders, even when they are mediocrities like Warren Harding.

But Marshall, sufficiently horrified by the carnage of the war, now faced again a soldier's frustration with peacetime. He was stuck with the permanent rank of major. The nation heedlessly downsized its army to virtually symbolic proportions. Marshall, after five years with Pershing, became assistant commandant of the Infantry School at Fort Benning, Georgia, and there set about training young officers in the lessons of firepower and maneuverability to form the basis for the new army. Tactics could no longer be static. He sought to train officers for the opening campaign of a war, as Marshall biographer Edward Cray said, "that first aggressive thrust by an enemy increasingly motorized, with aircraft rather than cavalry to scout ahead. Then there were no settled lines, no well mapped trenches, no elaborate telephone networks." In one lecture, Marshall said, "Picture the opening campaign of a war. It is a cloud of uncertainties, haste, rapid movements, congestion on the roads, strange terrain, lack of ammunition and supplies at the right place at the right moment, failures of communications, terrific tests of endurance, and misunderstandings in direct proportion to the inexperience of the officers and the aggressive action of the enemy. Add to this . . . fast flying planes, fast moving tanks, armored cars . . ."

It was in his five years at Benning, during what became known in the army as the "Benning Revolution," that Marshall began accumulating the roster of names—kept in his own first-class memory or else in the fabled "black book" that officers thought he maintained—upon which Marshall later drew to put together American military leadership in World War II. Lieutenant Colonel Joseph Stillwell and Major Omar Bradley were among Marshall's instructors at Benning. It was at Benning, too, that Marshall developed the reputation—later a sometimes rueful army legend—for his ruthlessness in judging officers and sacking even the most experienced men in favor of junior officers who, in Marshall's judgment, could lead the new army.

At one point, Pershing asked Marshall to review a draft of his memoirs. Marshall advised Pershing: "I suggest you point out the real difficulty (with the American Expeditionary Force), which was a collection of old officers at the head of every (American) division, who had ceased mental development years before." It was on his trip to Washington to read the Pershing memoirs that Marshall met for the first time a promising young officer, Major Dwight Eisenhower, who had edited the revision.

The 1930s were difficult for Marshall. He was in his fifties now, still a colonel, and worried that he might even face forced retirement without getting his star. The army's atherosclerotic system had reasserted itself. Marshall confessed to Pershing: "I'm fast getting too old to have any future of importance in the army." But finally, in November 1936, he made brigadier.

Marshall went to Washington to become assistant army chief of staff to General Malin Craig. By now, history was boiling along like one of the dark-cloud montages tumbling in time-lapse photography across a movie screen. From Tokyo to Berlin, from Moscow to Chungking to London and Washington and New York, the world situation deteriorated. Stalin, Hitler, Mussolini, Roosevelt, Chiang, Mao, all were making their preliminary moves. The Italian invasion of Ethiopia dramatized the weakness of the League of Nations and was a prelude to larger tragedies. The struggle for China had become a triangular war among Chiang, Mao, and the invading Japanese. In the Soviet Union, Stalin had launched the show trials that would end in the imprisonment or execution of millions of the USSR's party functionaries, bureaucrats, poets, military officers, scientists, and scholars—a social and cultural apocalypse.

And in March 1936, Hitler had moved unopposed into the demilitarized Rhineland. Germany sealed alliances with Italy and with Japan, and established Francisco Franco in power in Spain.

When Marshall reported for duty at the War Department in Washington, Chief of Staff Craig, an old friend from World War I, greeted him by saying, "Thank God, George, you have come to hold up my trembling hands."

The world began its rapid tumble into World War II. On March 15, 1939, Hitler marched into the remains of Czechoslovakia.

Today, World War II and its aftermath seem a Jurassic age, a remote time when giants roamed the Earth perpetrating primitive deeds (fascism, global conquest, holocaust, and the nuclear awakening that was the wars last act). The cast of characters (Hitler, Stalin, Churchill, Roosevelt, Mussolini, Mao) has an earthshaking, mythic quality. Out of the origin myth, Hitler became the baseline for discussion of evil, as Munich became the cautionary model of appeasement.

In that light, George Marshall becomes the paradigm of a certain kind of American virtue, now all but extinct. Marshall lingers in memory with a wistful poignance—a kind of reproach.

SCIENCE AND DISCOVERIES

THE *SATURDAY EVENING POST* still gave Americans a Norman Rockwell version of themselves as an essentially loveable and virtuous people, capable of small follies, but kindly, humorous: a sweet people. The first programs on the new medium of television worked the same vein. But the war had delivered the nation into a new dimension that was heady, miraculous, and disquicting: hopeful and horrible and, it seemed from time to time, weirdly heartless. A new territory.

The war—as war always is—had been a violent exploration of the possibilities of human behavior. Technology, for good and ill, had expanded the possibilities in the direction of apocalypse, at Hiroshima, for example, and at Auschwitz.

And now at home, the exploration of the possibilities of human nature, and of technology, proceeded. The themes of an old American sentimentality and a new American ruthlessness—scientific or psuedo-scientific—were interbraided, and they posed the question that Americans always ask about themselves,: "Are we a good people or a bad people?"

In 1948, Alfred Kinsey published his unprecedentedly candid research on Americans' sexual behavior. Kinsey fed his research results into computers so that sexuality became measurable and quantifiable, and therefore objectified. Before that, sex had been an area of darkness, or reticence, certainly not discussed in anything like the way it is now. *Time* reported: "One Kinsey researcher found 1,000 wives who were virgins and had no idea why their marriages had been childless."(Their husbands were also perplexed.)

Sex was a subject attended by immense superstition. Masturbation was the practice of degenerates. French kissing caused pregnancy and venereal disease. "What is perhaps hardest to grasp," wrote William Manchester, "is the conviction of powerful social institutions that they had a sacred obligation to propagate these private terrors." Both church and secular leaders believed that only children scared stiff could be counted on to approach the altar as virgins. All of this was predicated on the assumption that the system worked—that boys who had been properly reared "saved themselves" for well-bred girls who had remained "pure"—hence white for brides and that after marriage and until death they remained faithful to one another. Male homosexuals, usually called fairies or perverts, were considered indistinguishable from the criminally insane. Even among sophisticates such practices as pederasty, fellatio, cunnilingus and sodomy with barnyard quadrupeds were presumed to exist only in fantasy and locker room jokes."

Kinsey's report revealed that the reality of sexual practice contradicted the approved models of behavior:

- Eighty-five percent of married men had engaged in sexual intercourse before marriage.
- The average groom had experienced 1,500 orgasms before his wedding day.
- Fifty percent of American husbands had committed adultery.
- Fifty percent of American females "were nonvirgins, if single, or had been nonvirgins before marriage."
- Two out of three single women had engaged in premarital sex of some kind.
- Ninety-five percent of males were sexually active before their fifteenth birthday, and maximum activity occurred at sixteen or seventeen.
- By the age of forty, more than one wife in every four (26 percent, or over 7 million) had committed adultery at least once. Kinsey thought the figure might be much

higher—women tended to conceal adultery. The instance of adultery increased as the marriage lengthened.

- One male in three, and one female in seven, had some adolescent homosexual experience.
- Ten percent of the male population was "more or less exclusively homosexual" for at least three years between the ages of sixteen and fifty-five.
- Four percent (2,600,000) of American men were "exclusively homosexual throughout their lives, after the onset of adolescence."
- One in six American farm boys had copulated with farm animals.
- Nearly 70 percent of men had had relations with prostitutes by the age of thirty-five.

And so on.

John Kennedy presumably was not startled by the Kinsey report. There is no record of Richard Nixon's reaction. The rest of the country was fascinated and sometimes horrified, and in any event confirmed in its impression that America had pushed on into a new dimension. The *New Yorker* published a cartoon depicting one proper matron asking another: "Is there a Mrs. Kinsey?" The real Mrs. Kinsey was said to have remarked, "I hardly see him at all at night since he took up sex."

If the primary message of the Kinsey Report was that nothing is sacred, then the secondary message was that nothing is profane either. Oppenheimer said that with the detonation of nuclear weapons, the scientists had "known sin." Was sex still a sin? Had sex become innocent, or a matter of moral indifference, in the same time frame when science had fallen from the state of grace and learned to commit transgressions of biblical significance, as if the sin of Eden (disobedience presumably enacted through an act of sex) were now redefined as the sin of presumption enacted through an act of annihilating violence.

Was science naturally sinful, or redemptive?

In 1948, the Nobel Prize in Physiology went to the Swiss chemist Paul Hermann Muller for his work in developing the "miracle" compound DDT, which seemed at the time to give promise of delivering the world from typhus and malaria. The Nobel citation said: "Dr. Paul Muller . . . the man of natural science must include certain qualities which he has in common with the saints, especially those cast in the mold of St. Francis: patience, persistence, singleness of mind and purpose, a profound feeling for the mystery of life, combined with an acute sense of its realities. Fortunate you, Dr. Muller, have not carried the Franciscan virtues so far that you would not harm even a fly. . . . You have found [a combination] which killed, not flies alone, but also many other kinds of vermin. . . . In the mind of the layman, you stand out as a benefactor of mankind."

Fourteen years later, when Kennedy was in the White House, the *New Yorker* would begin the serialization of Rachel Carson's *Silent Spring,* a jeremiad that described how DDT flowed into the food chain, destroyed insect and bird life, and caused cancer and genetic damage in humans. Kennedy ordered his Science Advisory Committee to examine the issues Carson had raised. The report vindicated Carson and DDT was eventually banned, under Richard Nixon. But that argument goes on. Many today assert that DDT is essential to prevent millions of deaths-by-malaria, especially in the Third World.

The Nobel Prize for Physics went to the Englishman Patrick Blackett for his work in nuclear physics and cosmic radiation. He turned his acceptance speech, in December 1948, into something of a jeremiad himself: "Now we find ourselves surrounded by rumors and threats of a third world war—a war which, if it comes, will be made more terrible than the last through the wonderful discoveries in atomic physics. . . . Pure science has proved the most dangerous of pursuits. . . . The world today is facing the great problem of how to avoid a catastrophe made pos-

sible by the work of so many Nobel Prizemen in physics." Blackett looked forward to the "future occasion when the United Nations finally consign the world's store of atomic bombs to the
depths of the ocean."

CHAPTER THREE

EARLY
1948

LYNDON FOR SALE

WHEN JOHNSON RAN FOR REELECTION to the House in 1946, his opponent, Hardy Hollers, accused him of using his public office to enrich himself. The charge followed Johnson for the rest of his career. It gained an impression of plausibility if one considered that in the late 1930s, the idealistic young New Dealer despaired of being able to pay off his dead father's accumulated debts, and ten years later bragged to friends that he had become a millionaire. There was a narrative line suggesting that Johnson's tactical drift to the right in politics during the forties, especially after the war, had been accompanied by an upward mobility in his fortunes—and that the two were related. Hollers called Johnson "an errand boy for war-rich contractors." He said, "If the United States Attorney was on the job, Lyndon Johnson would be in the federal penitentiary instead of in Congress. Will Lyndon Johnson explain how the charter for KTBC [the radio station in Austin], owned by Mrs. Johnson, was obtained? Will Lyndon Johnson explain . . . his mushrooming personal fortune?"

One day Johnson asked a supporter why, considering all that he had done for the people there over the years, he was not more loved in his district. The friend replied, "That's simple. You got rich in office." Johnson jumped to his feet and stalked out of the office.

Lady Bird Johnson called the 1946 campaign "a watershed. It was the first time we had ugly things said about us. We ceased to be young shining knight." The charges of corruption were difficult to prove. Evidence of political influence bought and sold tended to be circumstantial. Post hoc, ergo propter hoc did not necessarily stand up in a court of law; the fact that Johnson sat on the House Naval Affairs Committee and that his almost bottomlessly generous political supporters, George and Herman Brown, of Brown & Root, received the contract to build the Corpus Christi Naval Base, along with many other defense contracts, did not prove that payoffs had been exchanged.

It was the first time that the connection between Johnson and the Brown brothers came into the public discussion. Brown & Root had abundantly bankrolled Johnson's unsuccessful 1941 Senate race against Pappy O'Daniel, and had remained doggedly generous ever since; Johnson was the firm's key to defense contracts. The relationship would continue all the way through the Vietnam War, when Brown & Root received contracts worth hundreds of millions of dollars to build massive American installations.

The 1948 Senate race only deepened the Brown brothers' commitment to Johnson. They had narrowly escaped indictment on federal income tax charges "for their financing of Lyndon Johnson's first senatorial campaign, largely (perhaps only)," writes Robert Caro, "because they had a friend in power in Washington. In this second campaign, they had multiplied their illegalities and if Lyndon Johnson lost, who would be their friend in power?" The Brown brothers' attorney said later that if Coke Stevenson had become senator, "he would have run them out of Washington. He would say, if anyone wanted to give them a contract, 'They are personally objectionable to me.' The Browns had to win this. They *had* to win this. Stevenson was a man of vengeance."

And so throughout the 1948 Senate campaign, cash poured in to Johnson's campaign—not only from the Browns but from big corporate and oil donors, among them Wesley West in Houston and Sid Richardson and Clint Murchison. John Connally, asked how much money came in, smiled and said, "A hell of a lot. I'd go get it. Walter [Jenkins, another Johnson aide] would get it. Woody would go get it." One night, Connally took a private plane on such an errand, from Austin and Houston, and returned with $50,000 in hundred dollar bills in a brown paper bag.

When gentlemen agree, there is no need to conspire. There is such a thing as government among friends. Lady Bird's radio station in Austin prospered. The FCC was good to KTBC, and Johnson helped his friends on the FCC. Johnson went to New York and asked William Paley to make KTBC a CBS network affiliate, and Paley agreed. Did it matter that Johnson was a congressman whose powerful friends included Sam Rayburn? The other Austin radio station, KNOW, had been trying for years to secure a CBS affiliation, and the network always refused on the grounds that the network already had an affiliate, KTSA in San Antonio, which could be heard in Austin.

It seemed to pay for local businessmen to advertise on Lady Bird's station. Those "who wanted to obtain—or keep—contracts with the Army camps near Austin, or with the huge Bergstrom Air Force Base, got the idea, which was soon being openly discussed in the Austin business community." One businessman said, "Everybody knew that a good way to get Lyndon to help you with government contracts was to advertise over his radio station."

Johnson insisted to the end of his life that his government service and the family's financial fortunes were entirely separate. "All that is owned by Mrs. Johnson," he would say, referring to the LBJ company and associated business enterprises. "I don't have any interest in government-regulated industries of any kind and never have had."

Journalistic inquiries into the Johnson fortune over the years tended to end inconclusively—admitting that the businesses were indeed in Lady Bird's name, even though under Texas law the spouse of the owner was entitled to half the income from such holdings. If there was corruption in the accumulation of the Johnson fortune, it was either a matter of hard work and luck, as the Johnsons insisted, or else of arrangements so artfully interwoven into the fabric of relations among politics and business and government regulation that they were either concealed, or, technically, legal. The truth is that hard work and luck and a good deal of reciprocal favor-trading went into making Johnson a very wealthy man, a prosperous rancher and businessman in the Hill Country where once his impoverished father had had to drive from town to town to find a store that would give him credit.

YOUNG, OBSCURE AND
ORTHOGONIAN

Roy Day, one of the California Republicans who recruited Lieutenant Commander Richard Nixon to run for congress in 1946, introduced his earnest wunderkind at a Lincoln's Day dinner in Pomona: "The man I now present to you could very well go all the way to the Presidency of the United States." Another of his backers told guests just after the election: "You fellows right here will be guests of Dick Nixon's in the White House someday." Nixon would confide a similar fantasy.

Privately, Day told Nixon to give up the loud neckties he liked to wear, and to look people in the eye when he talked to them, "or they won't think you are telling them the truth."

Pat and Dick had met as actor and actress in the little theater in Whittier, and in this first postwar suburban act of the great drama that now began, which took them to the White House— and moved them forcibly out of it, at last—they came onstage as a couple almost too perfectly typical of the American middle class of that moment; or, more precisely, too perfectly typical of the idea and self-image of the young American middle class as, emerging from the backstory of Depression and world war, it proceeded with its version of the Dream.

Nixon was installed in Washington in a freshman's attic office in the remoter reaches of the Old House Office Building, and in the postwar housing shortage, he and Pat, now with their baby, Tricia, found a modest apartment across the Potomac in the new Park Fairfax development in Arlington, where Washington was just beginning its massive suburban sprawl. They were well enough off, having their wartime savings of $10,000 in government bonds, another $3,000 in savings, $14,000 in life insurance, a new car, and Dick's $15,000 a year salary as a congressman. Pat submerged her strong, once-independent personality in the hidden domestic dimension, in the raw relative isolation of northern Virginia woodland, now cleared and bulldozed for housing projects and the coming shopping malls.

Nixon left the Park Fairfax early and stayed at the Capitol late. He applied himself to his ambitions, and he moved rapidly. Like Lyndon Johnson, he had few interests outside of politics and his own career.

As a freshman, Nixon of course had no seniority, and yet he managed to secure a choice seat on the House Education and Labor Committee, which would play an important role in the anti-union drama of the Taft-Hartley Act. And he landed on the House Un-American Activities Committee, which would, before his first term was over, make Nixon a national figure.

In his memoirs, Nixon claimed that he only reluctantly accepted the new Republican Speaker Joe Martin's request that he go on the Un-American Activities Committee. He wrote of "the committee's dubious reputation." But his aide at the time, Bill Arnold, said later that Nixon had sought the job, with "characteristic prescience."

For a freshman congressman, Nixon was skilled, focused, surefooted. He was a natural. He virtually jumped the queue of power to insert himself in the forefront of the drafting of the Taft-Hartley legislation, "so intimately in the later stages that congressional aides, if not their jealous employers, thought Richard Nixon 'a principal architect' of the ultimate legislation."

In the midst of House debate on the bill, bitterly opposed by Democrats and their allies in organized labor, Nixon took the floor to offer an eloquent extended metaphor that compared Taft-Hartley to the Magna Carta, as a "bill of rights" that would curb the "barons of union labor." Later his lawyerly defense of the bill, inserted into the Congressional Record, would become the talking paper for Republicans around the country defending Taft-Hartley against its critics. Nixon had been in Congress only a few months.

THE NOTION OF A "real Nixon" is a subjective idea, or a politically colored conceit that necessarily depends on the eye of the beholder. As with Orson Welles's Charles Foster Kane, observers have wanted for years to believe that there existed some recondite "Rosebud," a key to the code of Citizen Nixon's character.

There was the quest for the Real Nixon. There also developed a somewhat silly journalistic habit of proclaiming, every few years, a "New Nixon," as if he had abandoned an old (sinful) self and taken up residence in a refurbished and more virtuous identity. There was a procession of New Nixons down the years—each one thought for a little while to be a more civilized and more statesmanlike version, but then each, in turn, disappointing. In a subconscious cultural way, the idea of a procession of New Nixons owed something to the patterned sequence of new cars that emerged in the postwar period: A bright new Ford or Studebaker or Dodge or Chrysler would sparkle forth in the fall, advertised with much excitement in the pages of *Life* or *Colliers* or the *Saturday Evening Post*. And then, betimes, that vivid new model would become familiar and begin to lose its novelty, and eventually a superseding version—a rebirth of the idea!—would come forth. This pattern of planned obsolescence was, and is, critical to the forward motion of a dynamic consumer economy. The washing detergent Tide must, after a time, become "New Improved Tide," and so on. Part of the secret of Richard Nixon's longevity as a political product lay in his artful sequencing of himself, in the way he refreshed his own identity from time to time. In the media's eyes he was first rehabilitated (after the

Douglas campaign and the Checkers fund crisis) when as vice president he seemed to have attained a new "maturity" and mellowness. He had a long fight during the sixties to recover from the 1960 defeat and from the debacle of the "last press conference" in 1962; but by 1967 and 1968, he was another New Nixon. The opening to China represented perhaps the disclosure of the ultimate good New Nixon—the high-water mark of New Nixons: Here sat the old anti-Communist HUAC gutter-fighter (as his enemies described him) exchanging pleasantries with Chou En' Lai and Mao Tse-Tung—a radical redesign. Watergate, in turn, disclosed the ultimate bad New Nixon—the Caliban or Mafia don of the Oval Office tapes. In the years after his resignation, Nixon at last fought his way to the creation of the last New Nixon—globe-trotting elder statesman, back-channel adviser to presidents Republican and Democrat alike.

So, over the years, the good new Nixons competed with the bad new Nixons. And the idea that there was such a thing as an implicitly unchanging, deep-down Real Nixon competed with the idea that he periodically became something entirely new. No paradox, really. The 1948 Ford and the 1968 Ford are both Fords. Still, John Ehrlichman had a good cautionary line for those pursuing the Real Nixon: "When I left, in May of 1973, Nixon was a different person than he'd been in 1969. That is not an extraordinary fact, given the circumstances of those four and a half years. Yet the bookshelves are jammed with writings that picture Nixon and his administration with an unrelieved and unchanging sameness, cutting a cross-section at a moment in time and extrapolating both forward and back."

The journalist Earl Mazo began his 1959 biography of Nixon with an extravagant statement: "Nixon is singularly complex, a paradoxical combination of qualities that bring to mind Lincoln, Theodore Roosevelt, Harry Truman, and Joe McCarthy." From Abe Lincoln to Joe McCarthy covers quite a range of American moral and political possibility. It took imagination, in the late fifties, for Mazo to think that Vice President Richard Nixon's character might possibly be an amalgam of such highs and lows.

Henry Kissinger believed that there was "no true Nixon," but rather that "several warring personalities struggled for prominence in the same individual." Kissinger said, "None of us really knew the inner man. . . . Each member of his entourage was acquainted with a slightly different Nixon."

Kissinger's verdict on the Nixon of the second presidential term might be thought to have an element of the self-serving because Kissinger worked in partnership with Nixon and shared his great accomplishments—notably the opening to China—and his (as their enemies saw them) crimes—in Chile and Cambodia, for example. Kissinger saw a Nixon who was alternately paranoid and visionary, disciplined and slovenly, courageous and craven, capable of high inspiration and of low cunning. He had an ugly, slurring streak of anti-Semitism, and yet, thought Kissinger, "he saw before him a vista of promise to which few statesmen have even been blessed to aspire. He could envisage a new international order that would reduce lingering enmities, strengthen friendships, and give hope to emerging nations. It was a worthy goal for America and mankind."

But that lay in the future.

The epigraph to David Greenberg's 2003 study, called *Nixon's Shadow,* an examination of the history of Nixon's image in the American mind over the years, is taken from T.S. Eliot's poem "The Hollow Men": "Between the idea / And the reality . . . Falls the shadow."

Instead of Kennedy's brilliant snow-dazzled inaugural "Ask not . . . !" or Reagan's crinkling movie-cowboy smile, Nixon left behind images of his signature five o'clock shadow and of the sweaty furtiveness of a man surprised in a criminal act. It must be remembered though that John Kennedy and Ronald Reagan were splendid actors with a genius for public self-presentation; Kennedy concealed much of himself (notably his physical pain

and debility) in the very act of presenting his magnificent performance self. Ronald Reagan, who could be stunningly vacuous
off-stage, had a nearly flawless sense of presidential occasion.
Nixon, on the other hand, did not develop his acting skills much
beyond the level of the Community Players in Whittier, or of the
lawyer's formal courtroom earnestness. He constantly needed to
have in his mind a sense of the role he was playing, but his resources as an actor were limited. It was when he sensed himself
losing his grasp on a particular role, a particular script and moral
context, that he fell into the manner that became famous; he had
lost the cover and authority and camouflage of his stated role. He
was like a student actor on stage who has forgotten his lines and
stands there exposed, naked, and waiting for humiliation.

Greenberg has a shrewd assessment: "'Any letting my hair
down, I find that embarrassing,' Nixon said in 1958, when he
was vice president. 'If you let your hair down, you feel too naked
. . . I can't really let my hair down with anyone . . . not even with
my family.' Not wanting to feel naked, Nixon covered up his
feelings, his illicit activities, his secret diplomacy. He hid behind
his pubic personae." In 1956, the columnist Murray Kempton
wrote, "Great care has gone into the construction of the shadow
which declares itself to be Richard Nixon." For Paul Johnson,
the conservative British historian and controversialist, "Nixon
remains the most enigmatic of American presidents. His character is elusive; the inner man is almost totally inaccessible." H. R.
Haldeman, Nixon's White House chief of staff, wrote that he
was "a multifaceted quartz crystal. Some facets bright and shining, others dark and mysterious. And all of them constantly
changing as the external light rays strike the crystal." Haldeman
thought Nixon "a man obsessed with maintaining what he perceived to be a correct public image. . . . [He] took pains with his
public image; he dressed neatly and conservatively, handled himself calmly in public . . . and yet, no matter what he did he
seemed to come across as flat, unattractive, unappealing."

Even the candid, uninhibited moment carried a suspicion of cynical premeditation. There was the night during the 1968 campaign, as Greenberg recalls, when Walter Cronkite was summoned to Nixon's hotel room where he found the candidate stretched out on the couch, shoes off, feet up. Over drinks, Nixon talked seemingly without restraint, using profanities: "The Nixon that Cronkite saw was so unlike the prim and awkward cardboard man he knew that he concluded not that he was seeing the 'real Nixon' but that the event was staged to make Nixon seem like one of the boys." (Years later, after he heard the growling scurrilities of the White House tapes, Cronkite concluded that the man he had talked to that night in 1968 was the real Nixon after all.)

The singer Country Joe McDonald produced this lyric in 1971, at the dead end of Vietnam, as hatred of Nixon was distilled into a countercultural art form and a virtual political program:

> Late last night I was watchin' the tube
> When I saw the most incredible thing
> They built a new mechanical man
> Looked just like a human being.
> I started to become terrified,
> Good God it was makin' me sick
> And then I began to realize
> It was no one but Tricky Dick.

A mechanical man. A sphinx without a secret, perhaps; or was it that, as the historian William Appleman Williams said, the search for the real Nixon was "a shell game without a pea?"

Greenberg summarized the various Nixons thus:

In his early career, Nixon's conservative supporters saw him as a populist everyman—a navy veteran, family man, and fighter for the American Dream. By the 1950s, liberal intellectuals challenged that image and proffered another interpretation: that of Tricky Dick, unprincipled opportunist. In the 1960s, more New Nixons emerged. Young radicals reinterpreted him as a dark conspirator. White House reporters who covered his administration saw an enemy of the First Amendment. Loyal aides and supporters considered him a victim of liberal enemies. And to psychoanalytic historians, Nixon was a case study in paranoia. After Watergate, foreign policy hands (along with Nixon himself) promoted the image of the former president as an elder statesman. And later still, revisionist historians argued that Nixon was, improbably, a liberal steward of the Great Society.

These were all facets of Haldeman's crystal. There were glints of truth—or more than glints—in every angle. But there are also many facets missing from the inventory.

Haldeman saw a crystal. John Ehrlichman described Nixon with a different and hauntingly metaphysical metaphor.

President Nixon was at Camp David one weekend when Wilkes-Barre, Pennsylvania, was devastated by a flood of the Susquehanna River. On an impulse, Nixon ordered up a helicopter and flew to the scene, taking with him only Ehrlichman, another aide, and a Secret Service detail. On this visit, Nixon was in high good spirits and made several movingly human gestures; seeing a bride and groom emerge from a suburban church after their wedding, for example, Nixon jumped out of his car, visited with the wedding party on the steps of the church for fifteen minutes, posed with the bride and groom.

Ehrlichman wrote:

Richard Nixon genuinely enjoyed the spontaneous. But . . . with sixty or seventy reporters in train, almost anything a president does is devoid of spontaneity. Thus the dilemma: When the press was around him, Nixon was stiff and stagy. So reporters filed stories about the wooden, insensitive man who looked at his watch as he shook hands with well-wishers. In Wilkes-Barre, he was sensitive, genuine and inspired as he moved among the flood victims, unreported.

This was Ehrlichman's metaphor: "So Nixon's propagandists were dealing with a paradox. They were not unlike florists who were trying to sell a flower that would bloom only in absolute darkness." Was the secret flower of Wilkes-Barre the "real Nixon?" It was one of them. Was it the Rosebud?

John Ehrlichman wrote his memoir in the early eighties, after he had served time in a federal prison camp for obstruction of justice in the Watergate case. The dark-blooming flower aside, Ehrlichman's Nixon—observed up close and in private by his consigliere—comes off most of the time either as a somewhat disorganized schemer, scattering black possibilities, or as a ranting, interminable monologist who thought through problems by pouring out a sometimes hilarious, sometimes shrewd, sometimes alarming stream of consciousness. Ehrlichman was always aware of that inveterate side of Nixon—in many ways the key to his political success—that worked the spin, the attitude, the public plausibility of an issue: Nixon's genius as a politician (and perhaps his greatest fault) lay in his manipulation of chimeras, his debater's sense of how the audience's moral view of a particular issue might be artfully colored by the use of certain rhetorical effects.

For example, when President Nixon formulated his administration's policy on court-ordered school desegregation in Texas in 1970 ("We carry out the law, and no more. We cooperate with local officials; we don't coerce them") he issued this profoundly Nixonian talking point: "Southerners will not be treated as second-class citizens."

That was a Nixonian twist: There is an old joke about a young man who murders his parents and then begs the court's mercy because he is, after all, an orphan. Nixon, from somewhere deep in his background, had a manipulative instinct for the theme of victims. He recognized almost throughout his life the tactical advantages of being able to portray oneself as a victim, and in an unexpected way, he was a forerunner of those people whom conservatives condemn for filing irresponsible lawsuits.

In his policy memo on school desegregation—and elsewhere in his famous Southern Strategy—Nixon presented the argument that white Southerners, the class that had dominated and suppressed blacks from slavery through Jim Crow, were not to be viewed any longer as oppressors but rather as . . . victims.

After Nixon defeated Helen Gahagan Douglas in the California race for the U.S. Senate 1950, the columnist Joseph Alsop invited Pat and Dick Nixon to his Georgetown house for a Sunday night supper—alien territory for the Nixons: Another guest, Averell Harriman, who was then a White House assistant to Harry Truman, arrived after the Nixons. He spotted Nixon. Harriman, who was slightly deaf, said loudly: "I will not break bread with that man!" He then turned off his hearing aid and stalked out of Alsop's house.

Nixon always hated the Washington social scene anyway. John Ehrlichman wrote: "He was particularly harsh in his criticism of the 'Georgetown crowd'; he would purse his lips and mince the words when he talked about their 'boring and time-wasting tea parties.' As a Congressman and Senator he had been uncomfortable at small Washington dinners he'd attended in the forties and fifties, and as Vice President refused most social invitations. As President he refused all of them."

Not entirely all. In September 1969, J. Edgar Hoover invited Nixon to dinner at his house on a quiet street in Northwest Washington. It was a strange evening. The walls of Hoover's dingy living room were covered by framed photographs and mementos—mounted Texas longhorns and plaques from civic groups, photos of Hoover with such celebrities as Tom Mix, or with Presidents Roosevelt, Truman, Hoover.

By way of small talk, the FBI director told Nixon he had his chili flown in regularly from Chasen's in Hollywood. Nixon responded that he had his cottage cheese flown in from Knudsen's Dairy in Southern California. Hoover discussed his efforts to infiltrate FBI agents among the workers building the new Soviet Embassy in Washington, the idea being that the agents could plant bugs in the walls as the building went up. He told stories about late-night entries and FBI bag jobs at other embassies. Hoover's friend and housemate, Clyde Tolson, came downstairs for a few moments, looking pale and pasty, and then vanished. Hoover described, in great detail, the woeful state of Tolson's failing health.

Ehrlichman, who was there at the stag dinner that evening, along with Attorney General John Mitchell, described how Hoover had decorated his dining room with custom-made lava lamps. In the spaces between the windows were

> . . . groups of tall Plexiglass tubes about three and four inches in diameter, lighted from their bases with different colors. They were filled with a watery fluid and with blobs of a plastic material that apparently became warm at the lighted base, then rose through the fluid, contracting as they cooled, finally achieving a mass that caused them to drift back down to the base to begin their rise one again. There were six or seven of these tubes, with red, purple, yellow and green dough bobbing slowly up and down, as the Director went on and on recounting the Bureau's triumphs over Weathermen and the NKVD.

After dinner, the men went down narrow basement stairs to "the recreation room" for a drink. "Near the door was a small bar. All the walls over and near this counter were decorated with girlie pinups of the old Esquire vintage. Even the lampshade of a small lamp on the bar had naked women pasted on it. The effect of this display was to engender disbelief—it seemed totally contrived."

It was a peculiarity of Nixon's character that he hated confrontation and, as a rule, found it difficult to fire anyone. In 1971, Nixon decided that Hoover, who had been FBI director since 1924, had to go. Hoover, among other things, had been strangely reluctant to pursue Daniel Ellsberg after his theft of the Pentagon Papers. (John Ehrlichman had the shrewd idea, ultimately rejected by Nixon, that the White House should simply declare that an investigation found that it had not, in fact, been Ellsberg who purloined the Pentagon Papers, but someone else, thereby instantly depriving Ellsberg of his hero-martyr's celebrity on the Left.)

But when Nixon brought Hoover to breakfast at the White House in order to drop the axe, the president flinched and, instead of sending Hoover at last out to pasture, wound up keeping him on and authorizing him to post even more FBI agents at U.S. embassies abroad. Hoover's immense accumulation over the years of personal and political secrets made him dangerous to presidents, and almost impossible to fire. His private dossiers were a toxic waste dump, hazardous to disturb, unpredictable. The Kennedys had treated Hoover with deferential anxiety; so had Lyndon Johnson.

At breakfast with the president, Hoover made it clear, as Nixon recalled in his memoirs, that he would "submit his resignation only if I specifically requested it. I decided not to do so."

But six months later, Hoover himself at last solved this intractable personnel problem. He died. Nixon laid him to rest with fulsome praise and ordered that the grandiose, unfinished FBI building be named after him. Nixon also immediately ordered the attorney general's office to seize Hoover's secret personal files and deliver them to the White House. But Hoover's secretary had already made off with them.

Anyone who has studied liars is aware that the first rule of lying is to look your interlocutor in the eye while telling him falsehoods. That is elementary mendacity. To communicate the sincerity that is indispensable to the success of lies, you must fix the other person with your gaze and direct your falsehood along the liquid beam of your sincerity, that open channel of candor and good will. So if his schoolmate was correct in saying that Dick Nixon did not look people in the eye when he talked, one wonders: Was Nixon such an incompetent liar that he could not master even the first lesson: —Look 'em in the eye!

Or did he suffer a discomfort with others, and with himself, that had its origins somewhere else—not exactly in the impulse to lie, but at least, in part, in his unique and lonely emotional agitations, or in the baffling mental interplay, characteristic of Nixon all his life, between transparency and front—indeed, between generosity and calculation, between selflessness and selfishness?

Nixon did have many spontaneously generous impulses. When he was in his first year of law school at Duke, he would carry a crippled classmate, Fred Cady, up the steep steps of the school. Cady had suffered infantile paralysis (like the man who then occupied the White House, although Franklin Roosevelt was careful not to allow himself to be seen when he was carried upstairs). There was of course no wheelchair access to the law school. Writes biographer Roger Morris: "Men who watched them would remember vividly how Dick Nixon grunted and staggered as he worked his way with Cady and crutches and books up the slate stairway, how gently he set him down on the landing, and then slowly walked along with the crippled young man as he dragged himself into the classroom."

In that instance, Nixon was perhaps remembering his mother's selfless ministrations to his tubercular brother, Harold, when she took him to Prescott, Arizona, and kept a boarding house for other TB patients.

Once when Nixon and another law school student were driving on a lonely stretch of road, they came upon a woman hitchhiker by the road. The other student started to pass her by, but

Nixon made him stop. "Richard was really pushing to help her," the other student said. "He said, 'Here she is out there, and what's going to happen?'"

A few years earlier, a customer—a Quaker mother of two boys, and a member of the community whom the Nixons knew—had been detected shoplifting at the family grocery store. Frank, Hannah, and Nixon's brother Don all wanted to call the police and report the woman. Richard said no. "You can't let them arrest her," he insisted. "You know what it will do to those boys to hear that their mother is a thief. Work it out some other way." So Hannah Nixon had a quiet word with the woman, who, mortified, confessed and agreed to make restitution. Hannah Nixon remembered: "My husband thought the woman would never pay us back. But Richard was sure I had done the right thing. It took months and months, but eventually she paid us every cent. Richard was right."

There was in Nixon a real gift of empathy and tenderness—an impulse mingling an inheritance of sweet formal charity from his mother's pious Milhous side and, from his father, an occasional flash of spontaneous human warmth.

Something else: Nixon's face betrayed an incessant struggle between the raw exposure of his true mind and thoughts and an almost panicky impulse to conceal what was going on in his mind and present instead a more earnest, manly, and mature façade. Of course he looked devious and discomfited. Nixon never quite learned what almost all other politicians learn—the necessity to immerse oneself in the part and decisively to conceal doubts and incriminating complexities.

Richard Nixon was a man unusually accustomed to solitary contemplation. The intellectual in Nixon—the monk, or, if you hated him, the schemer—was often disconcerted and surprised by the obligations of the political, public-performance side of his nature. The presence of others—the pressure of their thoughts, the pressure of his obligation to guess at their thoughts, the pressure of his obligation to decide whether he must satisfy their expectations of him or whether he should meet them more aggressively, the sheer pressure, among other things, of reading their eyes (for if he must read their eyes while he talked, how could he simultaneously think?)—all these made him appear to squirm. Tricky Dick's signature deviousness arose from the struggle of his mental solitude against his anxious sense of the dangers and obligations that other people brought upon him when they came close. His discomfort arose, one may at least surmise, from the zone of discrepancy between his anxious, imperfect mind and his saintly mother's judgmental telepathies.

That is my theory, with apologies: Nixon as an adult—as politician, campaigner, public official—may have become, in some respects, a bad man. But he remained—to an astonishing degree that people who hate such psychological analyses (Nixon himself loathed any effort to put him on the couch) cannot admit—a rather anxious good little boy interrogating his mother's gaze for approval or disapproval. Hannah Nixon was a mother of the quietly judging kind. She remained with Nixon, in his mind and heart, and not always entirely welcome, all his life. She remained as a powerful presence and it may be as a sort of never quite appeasable conscience embedded in that Nixonian core that had hardened around his Yorba Linda and Whittier childhood.

The elusive Nixonian core has been much explored—the atmosphere of hardscrabble and of near failure in the dust-bitten non-Eden of Southern California, the family lemon grove that succumbed to the non-paradisal California elements (Santa Ana winds, frosts, bad soil), the land that Frank Nixon did not buy (the family myth of the near-miss) where he might have struck oil and become as rich as Kennedy; the atmosphere of Hannah Nixon's hard-pressed long-suffering piety and of Frank Nixon's hard, root-hog-or-die household anger. If Frank Nixon had bought land with oil on it, then Richard Nixon might have gone

East to college; if his father had been wealthy when Dick went to Whittier College, he would have been a Franklin, not an Orthogonian, and, who knows, that hard energy of resentment that was, it seemed, at the heart of Nixon's personality and career might never have formed at all. He might have been a different man, and a different president, entirely.

Anyone studying the personality of Richard Nixon is struck, after a time, by the lack of humor in the man, and the absence of fun in his life—the absence of playfulness. One looks in vain across the stretches of his life for some shimmer or scintillation—some lightness of touch.

There are hilarious, humiliating stories about Nixon attempting such scintillations. Once in 1967 the almost rehabilitated presidential candidate Nixon was invited to a dinner at the home of Norman and Buffy Chandler, owners of the *Los Angeles Times.* As the guests stood drinking cocktails before dinner, Nixon announced to the company: "I probably shouldn't tell this. . . . But . . . Why did the farmer keep a bucket of shit in his living room?"

A stunned silence fell on the room.

Nixon, smiling one of his discomfited smiles, but looking increasingly panicked in his eyes, plunged on: "Because he wanted to keep the flies out of the kitchen!"

Longer stunned silence.

Mrs. Chandler spoke up: "You're right, Dick, you shouldn't have told that."

Nixon seemed to be missing some crucial inner circuitry—the wiring for humor, for example, even for the basics of social ease. He was an acutely uncomfortable man.

But now and then during adolescence and beyond, somewhat unpredictably, flashes of humor would break through. Assigned to write his high school class history in 1926, he parodied the famous "Psalm" by Henry Wadsworth Longfellow that his pious Quaker grandmother Almira had earlier sent to him:

Now the lives of great men all remind us
We can make our lives that sort
And departing, leave behind us
Footprints on the tennis court.

Not uproarious, but modestly irreverent. In February 1933 when Whittier was debating Southern California before a home crowd, Nixon, a star of the Whittier team, was said to have "brought down the house with humorous asides." A girl who attended the debate said the audience was amused when Nixon said, "The world is going to the bow-wows." Whittier seemed to be winning the debate easily. But then USC began scoring points and catching up, and Whittier needed to gain ground for a strong finish. An editor of the Whittier school paper, Lois Elliot, was sitting in the balcony just above the debaters. "I remember it clearly," she reported much later. "I sat in the gallery, and I saw when Nixon spoke in his rebuttal that he quoted from a blank paper. I told it later to my roommate; it was against all regulations, and very cunning. I remember it well." The implication was that Nixon, to support his case, simply conjured up facts or statistics out of thin air and pretended to getting them from a source cited on what was in fact a blank piece of paper.

That instance of Nixonian cunning offends the buried premise of an American sense of fair play: The Nixon of the Un-American Activities Committee would be for his entire career judged to be un-American in that sense—devious and inclined to make up his own rules. Homer's wily Odysseus prospered by such tricks and earned the poet's praise for them; Tricky Dick, however, would not be judged by the same yardstick—in part because the American rules and regulations were different from those of the ancient Greeks. Then, too, the people most inclined to use the term "Tricky Dick" were, in one way or another, his victims.

Pat Nixon recalled that in the early days of their marriage, Dick could be the life of the party. They socialized often with

Pat's friends from college. Nixon was an inept dancer and skater, but gamely went along with the others. They did living room skits. "I will never forget one night when we did *Beauty and the Beast*," Pat Nixon said. "Dick was the Beast . . . we had loads of laughs."

Now and then Nixon would be unintentionally and even endearingly hilarious. Once, when he contemplated an evening of music at the White House, he instructed his staff to invite all the best jazz musicians—"like Mantovani."

More often though, it may have been that Nixon's humor, if it could be called that, occurred on a different plane and worked the resentful man's dimension of the ironic and the saturnine. It may have been that Nixon conceived of revenge, artfully and unexpectedly achieved, as the funniest, most satisfying form of humor. When he became president, he appointed the Jewish publisher Walter Annenberg, son of Moe Annenberg (who had run an empire of race-wire parlors and had all kinds of unsavory underworld connections) as ambassador to the Court of St. James. He thus had the satisfaction of impassively sticking a finger in the eye of the Kennedys (as old anti-Semitic bootlegger Joe had held the job and thought of it as the ultimate sign of his own arrival in the aristocracy) and in the eye of the Eastern establishment blue-bloods whom Nixon despised: Annenberg, after all, replaced the highly aristocratic John Kennedy appointment, David K. Bruce. The darkly glinting and multifaceted humor in Nixon's choice of Annenberg was fully appreciated only, at last, by Nixon himself. But that was all right. Nixon was a man who did not mind savoring these pleasures alone. During his White House years, he would order cheap wine for his guests and have an expensive bottle of Lafite Rothschild set aside on the table for himself, wrapped in a discreet white linen cloth.

He did not seem to seek the company of other human beings for the pleasure and comfort and diversion of their company, but rather to display himself before them—to play a role of leadership, to argue his case, to struggle and so battle, as he constantly said. He thought of himself as a man "in the arena," which meant the cynosure of struggle, and if he was not in the arena, then he tended to melt into shadows or into the company of Bebe Rebozo, which amounted to being alone, Nixon's equivalent of a Zen experience. Rebozo was a sauna and massage—a visit to the club. Nixon offstage gravitated to the sanctuary of absolute noncontroversy—a natural reflex in a man who spent so much of his professional life as a controversialist. What suffused the private atmosphere of Nixon was the sense of loneliness— what might even be interpreted as a need for loneliness.

Rebozo had once been a mechanic who ran a small garage and then some coin laundries in Miami at the beginning of his career; he prospered in his investments; he eventually became a real estate speculator and the owner of a state bank. He began one of those odd American careers as discreet friend and companion of the powerful. How he managed it is difficult to say. He combined the qualities of Bernard Baruch with those of the Filipino houseboy.

John Ehrlichman hit on the secret of the Nixon attraction to him: "To be with Bebe Rebozo is to be with a genial, discreet sponge. He has cheerfully tolerated endless Nixon monologues with patience and equanimity." Especially as he grew older, Nixon developed the habit of thinking out loud, in rambling soliloquies. Bebe Rebozo became a listening equivalent of Nixon's yellow legal pad—an instrument for thinking through ideas, venting grievances, trying out poses and self-presentations. Rebozo impassively absorbed the Nixonian stream of consciousness.

In Florida, Ehrlichman recalled, "Nixon and Rebozo would go cruising on Bebe's boat or simply sit by the water, drinks in hand, Nixon talking and Rebozo impassively listening." If Nixon was, as commentators said, uncomfortable in his own skin, he felt better in that skin when he was around Bebe. He was reassured by Rebozo's unquestioned and unquestioning loyalty. Bebe did not gossip. The two men had a friendship that had advantages over marriage: It seemed to involve a freer, less complicated exchange that was unshadowed by the past and by a history of resentment. If Pat Nixon, a strong-minded, independent woman, found herself constrained and silenced over the years by her husband's career and by the difficult, covert side of his character, Bebe was, it seems, absolutely undemanding, worshipful without grievance, Sancho Panza without sarcasm: sounding board and acolyte and, by the way, an excellent bartender. He was, for Nixon's purposes, the perfect parallel spouse—a Stepford wife.

Rebozo was a friend of Florida's Senator George Smathers, who was also a friend and companion in womanizing of John Kennedy's. In his successful and scurrilous primary campaign against Senator Claude Pepper in 1950, Smathers regaled backwoods Floridians with accusations that Pepper's sister was a "thespian" and Pepper himself an "extrovert" who had "practiced nepotism" with his sister-in-law. (Such tactics—polysyllabic malapropism as character assassination and creative rube-scamming, the Mel Brooks school—had been perfected in the 1930s by Senator Robert Rice Reynolds of North Carolina—"Buncombe Bob"—who used to describe a Harvard-trained opponent as a man whose favorite dish was "cav-eee-awww—that's right, cav-eee-awwwww! You know what cav-eee-awww is? It's fish eggs! Fish eggs from Red Russia!")

Some thought that Smathers's campaign of deft insinuation against Claude Pepper ("Red Pepper," as the Smathers's forces' nickname had it) served as a model for Nixon's strategy against Helen Gahagan Douglas.

When Nixon became president, Smathers had already left the Senate. He worked as a lawyer-lobbyist in Washington and leased an oceanfront villa at the Key Biscayne Hotel. Ehrlichman remembered that in the late sixties and early seventies, when Nixon, through Rebozo, had bought a house in Key Biscayne, "I would sometimes see Smathers emerge [from his villa], blinking at the afternoon sun, always with a different young lady of great beauty as his swimming companion. He was a great example to those of us beginning to enter middle age."

Fastidiousness, a motif of cleanliness and uncleanliness, played through Nixon's character all his life. It was perhaps not surprising that a boy with a tubercular older brother would become fastidious. A fatal uncleanness had made its way into poor Harold's body. He and the other TB patients carried "sputum cups" in which they expectorated the unclean discharge of their lungs.

The metaphor of uncleanness and germs comes to convey moral and political messages. This of course has always been a reliable chord and trigger of paranoia and race hate: the danger of the invisible, the menace undetectable by the human eye. Goebbels made a Nazi genre of the Jew as insidious germ, burrowing into German society, corrupting it, destroying it. Much of the postwar American anti-Communist fear drew its energy from the idea of unseen malignant forces at work on the wholesome body of America. When Whittaker Chambers came before the Un-American Activities Committee, Alger Hiss made a point of remembering that the characteristic by which he remembered Chambers (or "George Crosley," as Hiss insisted on calling him) was his conspicuously rotted teeth. The unsmiling Chambers was seen to conceal a secret rot, and if he only opened his mouth it would be visible.

The word "American" in those years acquired a moral-political shadow, an evil twin: un-American. When the flier for the Sales Executives Club said that Richard Nixon was "American," it did not, of course, mean that he was American as opposed to French or Italian; the term had become powerful and, as it developed, a somewhat dangerous value judgment. To be American was, precisely, not to be Un-American—not to be . . . foreign, infected by foreign ideas, unclean. To speak of "the American people" is to apply a morally inert descriptive label. But to speak of "Amer-

icanism," and of its shadow, its nemesis, "Un-American activities," was to plunge into a realm of conflict, controversy, anger,
danger: and the political manipulation of fear.

In 1947, Nixon stayed out of the committee's notorious and
circus-like hearings on communism in Hollywood. His moment
would come some months later. Even as a young congressman,
Nixon had a fine sense of timing and opportunity.

By November 1947, the American atmosphere had become so
inflamed on the Communist issue that Eric Johnston, president
of the Motion Picture Association of America, found himself delivering an aggressively defensive speech at the Plaza Hotel in
New York, threading his way between the Hollywood Ten and
their HUAC accusers:

> A terrific fury against communism has whipped itself together in
> this country, and the wrath of the American people cannot be
> taken lightly. That wrath is going to increase should our rela-
> tions with Russia grow from bad to worse. . . .
>
> But there's a danger in the wrath we've kindled. There's a dan-
> ger of being swept away by hysteria; a danger of our anger get-
> ting out of hand until every American who stands for progress is
> damned as a red and a communist. We can't let that occur. It
> mustn't be a crime in this country to criticize. We know the real
> answer to communism is to make democracy here in America—
> work so well that no man would want to be a communist.

A letter to Nixon from a Baltimore man named G. C. Hart in
January 1948, inquired: "Did it ever occur to you that a good
way to stop communism would be to make capitalism somewhat
decent? I think it is just as easy."

Un-American, in the postwar context of the committee,
meant, first of all, in one way or another, sympathetic to communism. It is true that at the time of Harry Truman's Loyalty Order
of 1947, the Loyalty Review Board of the U.S. Civil Service

Commission listed many organizations deemed to be subversive to American interests, including the Ku Klux Klan and various paramilitary neofascist groups (American Patriots Inc., the Dante Alighieri Society, Friends of the New Germany, the Italian Black Shirts, the Silver Shirt Legion of America, among others). But after Winston Churchill's Fulton, Missouri, speech about the "Iron Curtain," in the atmosphere of (often justified) anxiety about atomic secrets and about the expansionist ambitions of communism, Un-American meant mostly an "activity" or state of mind aligned with communism against "the Free World" in the new bipolar struggle for the hearts and minds and political control of the world.

Un-American also carried an old freight of American xenophobia. The Un-American was something or someone foreign, wearing a beard, carrying a bomb, speaking with a foreign accent, preaching subversion at basement meetings. To be American was to be clean. To be un-American was to be unclean. As the Nixon flier said, an American "pulls no punches." Presumably an un-American does pull punches, meaning, one supposes, that he is weak, devious. (Thus the flier in 1947 described Nixon, destined to be regarded as one of the more memorably devious characters in American political life, as "straight-from-the-shoulder non-devious.") To be an American, in the patriotic sense, implied a certain manliness. If someone needs to be punched, he will be punched.

What Congressman Nixon brought to Washington was a consummately lawyerly soul. His entire political approach was based on a lawyerly model—adversarial, "in the arena" meant essentially "in the courtroom," and his sense of struggle was a sense of "trial," of testing, of wits and guile. He spoke constantly of combat and struggle and crisis. His first book was called *Six Crises.* His favorite quotation—one he used as the title for another book—was Teddy Roosevelt's passage about life and politics as heroic struggle "in the arena." But such struggles were always circumscribed. Politics to him was analogous to a trial—a campaign was a trial. Different points of view were brought into collision and "tried." Tough but fair. He felt that you could play rough because the battle occurred within the bounds of the democratic system, as a trial occurs within the bounds of a courtroom. Intense argument and partisanship become possible because of the overall legitimacy of the arena.

His was a very American frame of mind. Nixon's philosophy of politics and law and Americanism depended on the idea of a stable arena in which to compete—depended upon the solidity of the American legal and political (ultimately constitutional) system. Anything that smacked of revolution was un-American in the profoundest sense; later, it was the revolutionary energies of the late sixties and early seventies that shook the institutional solidity of Nixon's political framework and led him to condone or encourage the ruthless countermeasures (as he conceived them) involved in what became known as Watergate. Nixon was destroyed—or destroyed himself—when the moral architecture of his America was so shaken by the times that he could no longer fight, he thought, as lawyers fight, in the arena of a fair trial. Now there was breakdown and *sauve qui peut,* and screw them before they screw you.

It was intergenerational warfare, to some extent: The terms of political battle that Nixon knew changed in the sixties; America turned upside down, and what Nixon had assumed to be good and reliable and virtuous and unquestionable—the virtue of America in making war, for example—was now described as wrong, or even as evil. American values underwent abrupt realignment; and it was that shift in values that caused the turbulence in which the great degringolade of Watergate occurred. Nixon was accustomed to seizing his opportunities in the stable universe he had mastered as lawyer and politician in the postwar years. When that universe began to shake in the divisions of the Vietnam era, Nixon, now the most powerful man in the world, made mistakes encouraged by his cruder instincts. He was the chief executive now. "When the president does it, that means that it is not illegal," he astonishingly thought. The result was violence in political judgment, extremism in the defense of the presidency, stupidity arising from disrupted conscience and aroused machismo, default to ruthlessness as a necessity of war.

The Orthogonian idea presupposed an Orthogonian (square) normality as the dependable foundation: The sixties represented the crisis of the Orthogonian, the shaking of the foundation— and indeed, the revolt of the Franklins. And when the very foundation was attacked, Nixon instinctively came to think he himself was the foundation. He had come to think of himself as guardian and embodiment of American normality. Against such widespread un-Americanism, he felt empowered to take all measures, even those that might be illegal under the rules of the normality, rules now superseded or suspended, as habeas corpus was suspended under Lincoln because Lincoln, like Nixon, faced civil war and an insurrection against normality so profound and dangerous that any step at all was justified to preserve it.

It has always been misconceived in Nixon's critics to claim that the abuses of the law in Watergate resulted from a sinister hunger for power. No. Watergate represented a desperate nostalgia for, quest for, the restoration of prelapsarian American normality. Watergate was very much like the anti-Communist work of HUAC at the beginning of the Cold War: That, too, was an effort to restore American normality, to protect it against the deforming abnormality of foreign (Communist) ideas.

Both HUAC and Watergate were reflexes of Nixon's moral and political immune system, seeking to expel foreign intruders and protect the wholesome American organism. Of course, those who do not share Nixon's sense of Orthogonian normality as a foundation of American life (Norman Mailer viewed it as a malignant world cancer) are bound to see Nixon himself as dictatorial, criminal, dangerous. They do not accept the Nixonian view that certain hard countermeasures were necessary to save the country. Tyrants have always put forth such a rationale. But whether you accept the Nixon view or the other depends on your Orthogonian orthodoxy.

The Franklin-Orthogonian distinction began as a class distinction, an income distinction. The Orthogonians did not have the money that the Franklins had. Today, is it still so?

The Franklins tend to be either moneyed information class people, with admixtures of what might be called the ideological poor. The Orthogonians still draw their basic strength from the square-rigged middle classes—the "faith-based," as Bush-era vocabulary has it, with their "values issues" and their embattled nostalgia. The Franklin mind, which was oriented in Nixon's youth to a country-club Republicanism, has now gone over into the secular elitism of the urban information classes—Democrats mostly.

JACK AND KICK: MAY 1948

IN MAY 1948, Kathleen Kennedy, Marchioness of Devonshire, the sibling to whom John Kennedy was closest—the third of the Kennedys' golden trio (Joe, Jack, Kick)—died in a plane crash in a thunderstorm in the Rhone Valley of France. She was flying to the Riviera in a chartered plane with her married lover, Peter Fitzwilliam, a wealthy English peer whom Kathleen intended to marry, even against the vehement wishes of her deeply Catholic mother: Rose Kennedy had threatened to cut Kathleen off, to disown her. As far as Rose was concerned, if Kathleen married Fitzwilliam, it would be as if she were dead. For her sin, Rose Kennedy decided, Kathleen would be excommunicated from the Kennedy tribe as she would be from the Catholic Church. With the plane crash in the Rhone Valley, someone brutally remarked, Rose thought that "God pointed his finger and said, 'No!'"

John Kennedy heard the news of Kathleen's death when a reporter for the *Boston Globe* telephoned Kennedy's house in Georgetown and talked to Kennedy's aide and court jester Billy Sutton. Kennedy was listening to a phonograph record of the musical *Finian's Rainbow.* Ella Login was singing "How Are Things in Glocca Morra?" Kennedy said to Billy Sutton, "That girl has a sweet voice." Then he began to cry.

For months after this, Kennedy, normally lively and buoyant, fell into a deep and distracting depression. He thought of Kathleen often. He would suddenly ask friends what they considered to be the best way to die. (His answer: To die in battle.)

At the time of the plane crash, Joseph P. Kennedy was in Paris. The Ambassador, more tolerant than his puritanical Catholic wife of Kathleen's love affair, had agreed to have lunch at the Paris Ritz with Kathleen and Fitzwilliam and discuss their plans for eventual marriage. The lunch never occurred.

When Ambassador Kennedy received word of the crash, he responded, even in his shock and grief, by lying. The mythmaking, myth-preserving public relations lie was an inveterate reflex and family technique, one that he passed on to his son.

Ambassador Kennedy told reporters that Kathleen had only by chance accepted a ride in the chartered plane with Fitzwilliam. She barely knew the man. The truth—that the married man with whom she died, known among the British upper class as a rich and somewhat unreliable rogue, was her lover, whom she hoped to marry (despite the strictures of her church) after Fitzwilliam had obtained a divorce from his sometime alcoholic wife, Olive—would do violence to images and myths (about Kathleen's widowhood, about her piety, about the family's bright, energetic wholesomeness and virtue) that might compromise Jack's political career; in any case, the insouciant upper-class squalor of the business (the married lover, the lover's betrayed wife, the widow Kathleen's inferentially betrayed dead hero-husband, the private plane winging off for an adulterous weekend on the Riviera) did not square with the shining family image that the Ambassador had carefully put together over several decades.

And so Ambassador Kennedy without hesitation lied, as the family lied about Jack's Addison's disease, as Joseph Kennedy had concealed (even from his wife) the botched prefrontal lobotomy he had had performed on their daughter Rosemary in 1941. Rosemary, born mentally retarded, had become difficult; after the operation, she was put away in a religious house in Wisconsin for the rest of her life. Rosemary's condition did not square with the family image, either. Reality would be trimmed and colored to confirm and elaborate the image; the truth must not be allowed to emerge, candid and unadorned—not if the truth played for the wrong team. That was elementary political public relations, of course—spin, damage control—but the Kennedys, starting with the ambassador, possessed a precocious and far-sighted gift for their tribal image making. They knew how to present themselves in a golden light. They had an instinct for camera angles. And the mythmaking worked.

Georgetown was a village of red-brick row houses a mile west of the White House. It had been in business as a river port, trading in tobacco, for a half century before L'Enfant designed the capital. Georgetown was densely but pleasantly distributed on a hill descending from north to south, from R Street and Oak Park Cemetery and Montrose Park, to the hillbilly bars and liquor stores along M Street, and below them to wharves and sheds and small factories beside the Potomac. On the rise at the western edge of the village was Georgetown University, and on the eastern edge, Rock Creek. The walks of the side streets were brick, and the streets themselves often paved with cobblestones. Wisconsin Avenue formed a T-square with M Street and bisected Georgetown north-south. The trolley line up Wisconsin climbed to the National Cathedral at the highest point of the city, just before Cleveland Park and the run out to Friendship Heights.

In 1948, Georgetown's residents comprised working-class whites and blacks living beside the mansions of the wealthy and the rickety wooden houses of the poor. Housing was still affordable. Roosevelt's New Dealers—including William O. Douglas, Ben Cohen, Harry Hopkins, Tommy Corcoran—had moved there. One author wrote that "the [Roosevelt] Brain Trust represented the first wave to arrive in Georgetown during its gentrification process, its transformation from a 'black ghetto,' as Washington society referred to it, into the city's most historic district." Diplomats, journalists, intelligence people came to form the core of a socially interwoven Georgetown set. Philip and Katherine Graham, owners of the *Washington Post,* lived in a mansion on R Street.

In November 1946, after his election to the House, John Kennedy signed a rental agreement to pay $300 a month for the three-story row house at 1528 31st Street. The house had a small garden and patio in the rear, and enough room to accommodate Kennedy and his twenty-six-year-old sister Eunice, along with a black valet-butler named George Thompson and a Kennedy family cook named Margaret Ambrose.

Eunice, who had taken a job in Washington on the Justice Department's Committee on Juvenile Delinquency, would act, more or less, as hostess. Kennedy invited his congressional aide, Billy Sutton, a factotum of the kind that the Kennedys liked to employ as part of their court, to live at the house. Sutton paid $2 a month in rent.

Life in the house on 31st Street was active, informal, and hectic, and had the unsupervised air of a sort of aristocratic commune. Joe Alsop is said to have looked behind some books on the mantlepiece and found the remains of a half-eaten hamburger. Kennedy was cheerfully slovenly about money, clothing, appointments, and women. He had the lingering habits of a kid, and often looked like one: Early on he would wear khakis and sneakers to the Capitol. George Smathers remembered that when Kennedy was campaigning, he would stick out his hand and say, "I'm a candidate for Congress," and they would look at him and think, "Why, you're not old enough to be the baby-sitter."

Margaret Ambrose fed Kennedy a diet of cream of tomato soup, lamb chops, creamed chicken, and other bland foods to soothe his chronically sensitive stomach. To rest his bad back, Kennedy often ate his dinner from a tray in his bedroom, sometimes joined (innocently) by a woman he had invited for a date.

Kennedy was in love, during the war, with the beautiful, slightly older Danish-born Inga Arvad—"Inga-Binga," he called her—whom he had met in Washington when he worked there as a naval intelligence officer. Their affair continued when the navy

stationed him in South Carolina. But it was a dangerous attachment. Inga, as a very young woman, had worked as a Danish reporter in Germany, had covered Hermann Goering's wedding
and there met Adolph Hitler, who, much taken with her Nordic
beauty, had invited her to sit with him as his guest at the 1936
Olympics. The FBI had learned all this, and kept its eye on her
as a possible Nazi spy when she was working as a reporter for the
Washington Times Herald. The FBI even bugged her apartment
and listened when she made love to Ensign Kennedy, the ex-
ambassador's son.

After Joe Kennedy broke up the affair, Jack was transferred to
PT boats, to the Pacific. Inga ended up married to the cowboy
movie star Tim Conway.

Jack Kennedy remained wistful and tender about Inga-Binga.
In 1947 and 1948, his approach to other women, and to sex, was
considerably more casual. He had many women, often secretaries
and stewardesses whose names he hardly bothered to learn, calling them "sweetie" and "kiddo" and dispatching Billy Sutton in
the morning to drive them to their offices or to the airport.

There were different readings of his sexual/social life—the innocent version, which presented Jack as essentially boyish, and
the racier version, slightly more corrupt, which cast him as a
fully grown, amiable rake.

According to his secretary, Mary Davis:

I don't know where the rumors got started that he was such a
dater—a swinger. He couldn't have been less interested in girls,
really. He dated very infrequently. He wasn't that interested in
exerting himself. His idea of a big date was to call up one of the
airline stewardesses and go to a movie! Margaret Ambrose would
fix dinner for them, they'd go to the movie, then back to the
house again where Margaret would have a little snack for them.
That was his idea of a big date! There were plenty of girls who

were serious about Jack. But he wasn't serious about them. He'd hit it off beautifully with girls, enjoy their company, but he wasn't ready—he'd not go beyond that.

But Kennedy's friend from Choate, Rip Horton, remembered the 31st Street house as something of a French bedroom farce:

> I went to his house in Georgetown for dinner. A lovely-looking blonde from West Palm Beach joined us to go to a movie. After the movie, we went back to the house and I remember Jack saying something like, 'Well, I want to shake this one. She has ideas.' Shortly thereafter, another girl walked in. [Kennedy's aide] Ted Reardon was there, so he went home and I went to bed figuring this was the girl for the night. The next morning, a completely different girl came wandering down for breakfast. They were a dime a dozen.

Kennedy was recreationally involved with a number of women, none of whom he wanted to marry. There was the model Florence Pritchett, the British tennis star Kay Stammers. The reporter Nancy Dickerson, whom he also dated, said, "He was young, rich, handsome, sexy, and that's plenty for starters. But the big thing about him was that he was overpowering. You couldn't help but be swept over by him." Kennedy told Clare Boothe Luce: "Dad told all the boys to get laid as often as possible. I can't get to sleep unless I've had a lay."

He had an affair with the actress Gene Tierney, who was then separated from her husband, Oleg Cassini (who would later become Jacqueline Kennedy's dress designer). Remembering Kennedy, Tierney said, "He had the most beautiful eyes. And he knew the strength of the phrase, 'What do you think?' He made you feel very secure."

In sexual behavior, as in much else, including, for a time, politics, Jack followed his father's example—not always a good one.

A friend of his, the Washington socialite Kay Halle, told a strange, mildly disturbing story: "I was at some posh restaurant in Washington, and the waiter brought me a note inviting me to join friends at another table. It was Joe and his two sons Jack and Bobby. Jack was a congressman then. When I joined them, the gist of the conversation from the boys was that their father was going to be in Washington for a few days and needed female companionship. They wondered whom I would suggest, and they were absolutely serious!"

There was always with the Kennedys a peculiar vibration of predatory clannishness that might now and then strike that note halfway between competition and incest. It was thought that Inga Arvad had gone to bed with the father as well as the son. Bobby and Jack shared Marilyn Monroe. The Kennedys swarmed densely, and sometimes it was hard to tell where one left off and another began.

If Jack Kennedy was in no rush to marry, it had much to do with the confusing and sometimes uninviting story of his own parents' marriage. The union of Joe and Rose Kennedy had, of course, produced the vigorous, numerous, numinous tribe. But the patriarch's energetic infidelities over many years, continuing now, in his fifties, dramatized a great Kennedy theme of moral dissonance between public life (including the bright façade of wholesome family) and private life that included Gloria Swanson and countless other mistresses, to say nothing of the mostly hidden financial piracies that paid for everything.

Kennedy biographers Peter Collier and David Horowitz quote a classic study of Irish rural life written by Conrad Arensburg:

> The father and husband is normally owner and director of the enterprise. The farm and its income are vested in him. . . . The sons, even though fully adult, work under their father's eye, and refer necessary decisions to him. . . . The subordination of the sons does not gradually come to an end. It is a constant. . . . For

"boyhood" in this instance is a social status rather than a physiological state. . . . "You can be a boy forever," one Irishman said, "as long as the old fellow is alive."

It was one thing for the old man to be the domineering, omnipresent proprietor-progenitor, moneybags and autocrat. It was a still more complicated transaction—an embarrassment, a source of pride, of envy, of intimidation—for the old man to be a sexual competitor: "The primal father of Freudian myth," as Collier and Horowitz observed, "blocking his children's entry into adulthood by the sheer force of his own appetite."

QUESTIONS OF CHARACTER

THE SINKING OF *PT-109*

PT-109 WOULD MAKE John Kennedy a hero, with an asterisk. History—and Kennedy himself, in rueful moods—would remark that although it is valiant for the officer to rescue and protect what was left of his crew after the boat was destroyed and two of his men were killed, there was nonetheless not much distinction in so inattentively allowing a PT boat to be rammed by a destroyer; it was the only such instance during the entire war.

The incident would become a conspicuously attractive item in Kennedy's political resume. Hollywood would make a heroic movie about it in 1963 in which Cliff Robertson played Kennedy. The film was released six months before the assassination. *PT-109* would enter into Kennedy lore and myth, remembered in its religious relics—the *PT-109* tie-clips worn by favored courtiers, the carved coconut shell on his desk in the Oval Office. On inauguration day in 1961, a large *PT-109* float came down Pennsylvania Avenue, the surviving crewmen waving from the plywood decks at their skipper, the new president, as if it were the Rose Bowl Parade. John Hersey, an old friend of Jack's who had gone to work for Henry Luce and become a fair-haired boy at *Time,* wrote a heroic account of the episode, published in the *New Yorker* in mid-1944; it was reprinted later in *Reader's Digest.* Joe Kennedy would see to it that hundreds of thousands of copies of the *Digest* article would be distributed during Jack's 1946 congressional campaign, and during the 1952 Senate campaign against Henry Cabot Lodge. The writer Robert J. Donovan declared in 1961 that "it is even possible that he might never have reached the White House if it had not been for *PT-109.*"

Douglas MacArthur, who was unenthusiastic about Lyndon Johnson's one combat mission, was said to have been even less impressed by John Kennedy's misadventures. MacArthur is supposed to have remarked that Kennedy should have been court-martialed for allowing his boat to be cut in two by a destroyer.

A squadron skipper later observed: "This was not a little stream. It was a big strait. Kennedy had the most maneuverable vessel in the world. All that power and yet this knight in white armor managed to have his PT boat rammed by a destroyer. Everybody in the fleet laughed about that." But Kennedy received the U.S. Navy and Marine Corps medal for *PT-109*. His commanding officer put him in for the Silver Star. Joe Kennedy went to his friend James Forrestal for help after the ambassador's initial bid for a Congressional Medal of Honor failed.

The *PT-109* episode would become an ink-blot test of people's judgment of Kennedy's character. The argument over *PT-109* anticipated other either/or perceptions of him—as either the graceful prose stylist who wrote the Pulitzer Prize–winning *Profiles in Courage,* or the political hack who had Ted Sorensen write it and then cynically accepted the prize in the same spirit in which he collected his navy medal. *PT-109* in fact anticipated the larger historical debate over whether Kennedy was the prince of Camelot and martyred hero of a generation, or a relatively inconsequential president who was also a reckless sex addict.

PT-109 asked whether Kennedy was a war hero who saved his men or a slovenly skipper whose inattention got his boat sunk and two men killed.

The answer on *PT-109* is—a little of both.

Kennedy's commanding officer, Albin Payton Cluster, put him in for the Silver Star, as he put it, "for the survival phase, not for the preceding battle."

At the time the Amagiri hit Kennedy's boat, he had only one of his three engines in gear.

It may be that Kennedy deserved the Silver Star for the courageous way he handled the situation in the days after the disaster, but deserved a court-martial for allowing the boat to be sunk in the first place.

Kennedy seems to have agreed with that reading. Inga Arvad's son said that Jack joked about it with her when he got back to the States: "He told her it was a question of whether they were going to give him a medal or throw him out."

Writes Thomas Reeves: "In the White House, shortly after the Bay of Pigs disaster, Donovan tried to get Jack to talk about the night PT 109 was hit. The president paused a few seconds, shook his head, and said, 'That whole story was more fucked up than Cuba.'"

THE RETURN FROM WAR inevitably involved a psychological deflation, a descent from adrenal highs—and, as it would seem later, a descent from participating in a myth to reentering merely domestic quotidian time and returning to marrying and breeding and working and drudgery and aging. War had been the worst and the dullest drudgery of all, most of the time, but the veterans had a tendency to forget that.

Some veterans of war also absorb a sly understanding that a certain amount of the mythic heroics represent sham—and for those who enter politics after wars, a certain amount of exploitable sham. Kennedy was acutely aware of the less-than-heroic aspects of *PT-109*. The episode would have been funny slapstick—if the two had not died. But Kennedy exploited *PT-109* for all it was worth politically: He encouraged the transmogrification of the (in some respects squalid) story into bright myth—though not quite as disgracefully as Wisconsin's "Tailgunner" Joe McCarthy fluffed up his own service in the Pacific for political effect.

THE CARACAS THESIS

IN MAY 1958—midway between his opening battle against Alger Hiss in 1948 and his triumph in the presidential election in 1968—Pat and Dick Nixon went to South America on a goodwill tour. A crisis occurred there that would reverberate years later, in Watergate.

Riots erupted, Communist-inspired. The worst trouble came in Caracas. The local police and the army looked the other way, or vanished entirely, while mobs menaced the Nixons—surrounded their cars, shattered the windows, covered the Nixons with spit, rocked the vehicles and threatened to set them on fire and to tear the occupants apart in the street.

Pat and Dick endured the assaults with admirable bravery and grace and presence of mind. Later, naturally enough, Nixon was enraged.

As Nixon told his early biographer, the journalist Earl Mazo:

When we left the airport [after "welcoming" demonstrations there], I had a chat with the foreign minister of Venezuela. He wiped the spit off me with his handkerchief and said he was sorry but the people are very expressive because they have not had any freedom for so many years and the new government did not want to suppress freedom. I told him that if his government did not learn how to control the type of people that I saw there at the airport and control the excesses in which they were indulging, there wouldn't be any government and there wouldn't be any freedom either.

Nixon instinctively hewed to models of the orderly and the seemly; when he was young, the homeless migrant Okies who showed up in Whittier brought with them a suggestion of the alien and even the unclean. Their desperation had in it possibilities of anarchy (Communist organizers were working among the migrant pickers) that would be alarming to someone whose own situation was hardbitten and only precariously respectable and who was, as it were, clawing toward the country club. Nixon carried very early impressions of humiliation along those lines; nothing is more intolerable to a child than shame, especially if it is a family shame.

All his life, Nixon praised—embodied—a bourgeois seemliness and order in public, even while, in private, in masculine company (as the White House transcripts show), he would swear and slur darkly.

In Caracas, Nixon saw anarchy armed and dangerous. The Venezuelan government initially did nothing to stop it or to protect the Nixons. Mazo, who was in the press party accompanying the vice president, remembered that "half the Venezuelan police escort vanished when the attack began." Nixon's life was truly in danger.

"Masses of men and women, young and old, poured from a dingy alley a hundred feet away shouting and waving banners, placards, pipes, clubs, and bare fists, like a scene from the French Revolution. At least five hundred swarmed around the Nixon car, the excess overflowing to envelop the other cars. Practically all the remaining Venezuelan police quickly disappeared."

A handful of Secret Service agents did what they could, pushing and shouldering aside the mob. They did not draw their guns lest that inflame the crowd further; when finally one of them drew his gun inside the Nixon car, the vice president warned him sharply to put it away.

"The car doors," Mazo wrote, "were the principal objective of the gang bent on dragging the Vice President from his limousine to tear him apart—the most degrading death possible, by Venezuelan standards."

Nixon remembered, "When the first window broke, I realized we were in very serious trouble. . . . It looked as though their tactics were to turn the car over and burn it." He described looking into the faces of the mob: "What went through my mind was the complete unreasoning hate in their faces—hate, just hate. I'd never seen anything like that before. Never. This mob was a killer mob. They were completely out of hand, and I imagine some of them were doped up to a certain extent."

Nixon said that he had never seen it before, but then he would see it again, in the late sixties, in the streets of America, where, right there at home in the nation of which he had become president, mobs and dope and violent anarchy would be loose and, as he told the foreign minister in Caracas that day, there was a danger, as he thought, that if the mobs were not brought under control, then "there wouldn't be any government and there wouldn't be any freedom either."

And so it was out of the violent memory of Caracas that Watergate, Nixon's presidential undoing, began.

Nixon, well before his experiences in South America in the late fifties, had sometimes practiced a politics of dirty tricks. In Watergate, he brought the techniques of such extra-legal espionage and subversion (practiced by a collection of operatives scarcely more competent than the Three Stooges) to bear upon the antiwar movement and upon his political enemies (the two had become the same) in order, as he saw it, to put a lid upon the American outbreak of the Caracas danger.

Henry Kissinger and others have theorized that Nixon might have been a different man and come to a different political destiny "if only he had been loved when he was a child." There is perhaps some truth in the thought. But an explanation of Nixon also lies in his anger and heartbreak over the disparity between what he thought America ought to be and what he saw it had become in the sixties—the Caracas-come-to-America effect. He came to feel as if he were as walled up in the White House during the ferocious antiwar demonstrations sweeping the country as he had been in Caracas when he finally made it to the U.S. embassy and holed up there until the army regained control of the streets. The rioting American elites of the late sixties and early seventies (the college-educated, the children of the professional-class Franklins) all represented to him an Orthogonian heartbreak and an Orthogonian outrage.

In the House HUAC days of 1948, Hiss was the snake in the American Eden. In the late sixties, subversion had become so general that it threatened to take over the very future of the country; it was the young of the leadership classes who had turned against the government, against Nixon, and against his idea of America; and it was out of his sense of anger and beleaguerment that the mentality of Watergate emerged.

Against anarchists and mobs, you had to play rough. Nixon, a man happiest when working alone, in the isolation of his own intellect, liked to play the tough guy. The vocabularies of Caracas and of the Watergate-era Oval Office were remarkably the same and derived in some distant way from thirties gangster movies, from Humphrey Bogart and Edward G. Robinson: a language of saturnine knowing self-sufficiency and masculine competence that gives off certain warning signals. Men who were young in the 1930s sometimes liked to affect a snarling gangster savvy and toughness.

And so when Nixon compared notes with Mazo about the scene in Caracas, he said: "They had allowed the airport to be completely dominated by the Commies and their stooges. The minute I stepped off the airplane, while getting the salute, I cased the place."

You had to be as tough as a gangster to defeat gangsters. You had to be as ruthless as they (the Communists, the Franklins, the enemies) were, because they did not play by the rules and they did not give an inch, and only a sucker goes all Marquis of Queensberry when the going gets ugly.

Besides, it wasn't just Nixon (Nixon would think to himself, again and again). The Kennedys played dirty all the time. American history was full of a ruthlessness not taught in civics books. When the Civil War started, Abraham Lincoln suspended habeas corpus, and a lot of suspected Southern sympathizers went to jail, without due process, and stayed there for a good long time, in specific contravention of the civil liberties guaranteed by the Constitution. But Lincoln argued that if he did not do such things, the government would fall, and, if that happened, the Bill of Rights and the rest of the Constitution would be lost.

There was in this something of the Vietnam logic of "We had to destroy the village in order to save it." But it did have a pedigree in American experience.

JOHN EHRLICHMAN SAID that Nixon's favorite movie was not, as had been reported, *Patton,* but rather Mike Todd's endless and bouncily anodyne travel epic, *Around the World in Eighty Days,* the Jules Verne story starring David Niven as Phileas Fogg and Cantinflas as his Sancho Panza/valet, Passepartout. Ehrlichman said that Nixon watched the movie repeatedly during the White House years and, at moments when he was excited, would bounce up and down in his chair: "Watch! Here comes the elephant!"

If Nixon could see himself as Patton—slashingly bold in conception (*"L'audace, toujours l'audace,"* as Patton said, quoting Frederick the Great) and uncompromisingly tough—it might also be easy to understand something of his identification with the Phileas Fogg character. Nixon had been around the world many times. He was a seasoned traveler, knowledgeable and proud of his sophistication about the customs of other countries and about their leaders. His subtle and thorough and sometimes visionary knowledge of foreign affairs had been ripened in wide travels in and out of public office. His memorable encounter with violent mobs in Venezuela had given him a sense of his own skills at improvising in difficult situations in foreign lands. He would have made, he must have thought, a perfectly serviceable Phileas Fogg himself.

John Kennedy's Anglophilia—his admiration for Melbourne and for the spirit and style of John Buchan—had detailed literary and historical origins. Nixon arrived at something of the same admiration by way of Mike Todd. Kennedy had Melbourne and John Hannay and Ian Fleming's 007. Nixon had Phileas Fogg.

All these characters—the fictional James Bond and Hannay and Fogg, the historical Melbourne—had in common their gift of urbane, unflappable improvisation under pressure. Good men in a tight spot. It was an American idea of manhood dressed up in formal clothes and civilized by America's idea of British veneer: manhood with manners and the witty riposte, manhood that knew which fork to use, which wine to order. Lyndon Johnson's idea of manhood was drawn from the opposite model—John Wayne, Texas, nature's noblemen rather than Debrett's. Johnson, like other Texans, savored the humor of playing against other people's expectations of Texan behavior, and so would sometimes exaggerate the note of rural crudity and unsophistication—the oldest American social game, in which would be revealed the true virtue and intelligence and courage and worth of the simple, the unsophisticated, when the fancypants gentlemen are exposed as frauds or cowards.

More recently, George W. Bush played such a game. Once, when feeling in some parts of America was running high against the French, Bush said with a straight face: "The trouble with the French is that they have no word for entrepreneur." The French and many Americans cited this as yet more evidence of the hopeless stupidity of the American president. They were unfamiliar with such Texas tropes in which the Texan, Bush, says something hilarious—"the trouble with the French is that they have no word for entrepreneur"—in the sly knowledge that his critics will reveal their own obtuseness by not getting the inner Texas joke, which is that the Texan knows full well what they will think, and trusts, with half a smile, that it will dawn on them, in a moment, that it is they who have been had, and look stupid, because the Texan has given their smugness a little thumb in the eye.

No one ever accused Richard Nixon of sexual impropriety. Indeed, Nixon's persona had about it a curious asexuality. Kissinger's maxim—that power is the most powerful aphrodisiac—has become a banality; modern politics is filled with case studies affirming the point—such public figures as Clinton and Kennedy and Nelson Rockefeller, even those who, like Kissinger, are unprepossessing in a physical sense, have emitted a sexual energy, as if it were a part of their life force and their will to power, or, more simply, an expression of their political gregariousness. Lady Bird Johnson, stoically and heroically mum for decades about her husband's exuberant and (to her) heartless infidelities, finally gave an interview after his death in which she absolved him in public. Lyndon had affairs, she said, because he loved all people, and it would have been unnatural for him to exclude women, half of the human race, from expressions of his love.

But Nixon manifestly did not love all people; he did not even seem to like very many people. There would never be need for Pat Nixon, who endured much, to endure or excuse Nixon's sexual conduct. Nixon's apparent asexuality is part of the mystery of the man. And yet is it fair to judge him in such terms? He obviously loved his wife, and he was faithful to her. Does such conduct make a man mysterious?

Why should the amorality of Kennedy or Johnson imply the asexuality of Nixon?

Do Kennedy and Johnson earn demerits for their marital infidelities? If so, does Nixon receive extra credit for his fidelities?

Lyndon Johnson had an active extramarital sex life—with, among others, Alice Glass, a beautiful Texas woman who was the mistress of one of LBJ's benefactors, Charles Marsh. In that affair, Johnson betrayed not only his wife but his friend and benefactor. He bedded many other women besides. Yet there has never been the fuss over Johnson's sex life that there has over Kennedy's, or Clinton's. Johnson's sexual escapades have almost never been mentioned in the bill of particulars against him. Perhaps that is because there was so much else on the list.

Johnson has mostly been arraigned for his lying, for an inveterate habit of untruth that culminated, his critics said, in his deceits regarding the Vietnam War. It was Johnson's famous Credibility Gap that began the unraveling of his administration and his Great Society, and drove him from office.

Johnson was president during 1) an American sexual revolution, and 2) a war in Southeast Asia. Both events were of intimate concern to the young. The first promised sex, and second threatened death. The immense baby boom generation that had been born around 1948 and now came of age in the Johnson-Nixon years was not likely to criticize a president for sexual activity. It was the war that menaced their lives.

But Johnson would have seemed to them too old and too gross a figure to imagine in a sexual context. The same was true of Nixon. Kennedy had been young and beautiful and sexual—and he was dead.

JOHNSON'S INFANTILE DISPLAY of the normally private functions of defecation and urination—he liked to discomfit "the
Harvards," aides such as McGeorge Bundy, by forcing them to
confer with him while he sat on the toilet, and he was a lifelong
exhibitionist who in college had dubbed his penis "Jumbo"—
tended to divert attention from his sexual behavior. Maybe his
toilet displays were a form of what magicians call misdirection,
conferring upon his private parts a disgusting sort of innocence
and suggesting, subliminally, the candor of a child pointing to
his own mess with the delight of achievement. Johnson's toilet
behavior was obscurely prelapsarian: It spoke of functions previous to sex, and therefore, it may be, provided moral camouflage
behind which the more exuberant and pleasurable barnyard activity of sex might more safely be conducted.

It is impossible to imagine Nixon's behaving as either Johnson
or Kennedy did in private quarters. Johnson frequently referred
to his sex life with Lady Bird: He pointed to her bed in the family quarters of the White House and remarked that she was "still
the best lay in the United States." Kennedy notoriously brought
women into the White House for sex whenever his wife was out
of town. One night, during a private dinner in the family quarters, Kennedy even pursued Toni Bradlee, wife of his friend Ben
Bradlee, when she went to the bathroom, and tried to seduce her
there.

Nixon's improprieties were driven by different impulses.

Kennedy had a casually foul mouth. He would ask people
(men and women both), "You getting any?" And sometimes add
the rather sweet afterthought, "Not as much as you deserve." All
three men, Kennedy, Nixon, and Johnson, employed elaborately

crude, profane vocabularies that would have surprised and offended a lot of Americans and that were not any particular evidence of classiness.

Kennedy accepted a Pulitzer Prize (for *Profiles in Courage*) that he perhaps should have shared with his assistant and speechwriter Ted Sorensen. (In fairness, the controversy over the authorship of *Profiles* has never been resolved; Sorensen has always insisted that Kennedy did indeed write it.) Kennedy lied to his wife about his women and to his country about his health. He used drugs (Dr. Max Jacobson's amphetamine cocktails) recklessly. He had an affair with a Mafia boss's girlfriend, Judith Campbell Exner. He got mixed up with Marilyn Monroe. None of that was terribly classy.

Ben Bradlee also reported that in the fall of 1962, after Nixon's loss in the California gubernatorial race and his notorious "last press conference," Kennedy remarked that Nixon was "beyond saving." He was "sick."

The casual sneer in Kennedy's use of the word "sick" was much like that in his phrase "no class." Kennedy meant "sick" in an informal, slangy sense, signaling aesthetic distaste rather than a medical diagnosis. But "sick" was a word that, like the phrase "no class," had interesting layers of meaning.

In fact, on the morning when he held his last press conference, Nixon was indeed sick—physically sick. He had a terrible hangover. His hands were trembling. Never able to hold his liquor, Nixon had gotten stinking drunk the night before as he watched the election returns and contemplated what he considered the final ruin of his political career in the coup de grace humiliation of a loss to Pat Brown in his home state after he had lost the presidency to Kennedy two years earlier. Fate, and the press, were rubbing it in.

It was a foolish display—not because he lost his temper, but because, hung over, he allowed something raw, something authentic and pained, to emerge for a moment from his inner fortress and to shake its fist at his tormentors. He gave those tormentors what they thought was the evidence they needed to confirm what they had been saying all along.

No politician has ever picked a fight with the press and won in the long run. Nixon never learned that; he paid a politician's ultimate price in 1974 when he had to resign the presidency. It was not the press that destroyed Nixon's presidency; he and his men did that by committing illegal acts and then trying to conceal them and to obstruct investigations into their misconduct. But the political climate of 1974 would have been far different, more favorable to Nixon, and possibly to his survival, if he and Vice President Spiro Agnew and the Nixon hatchetmen, H. R. Haldeman, John Erhlichman, Charles Colson, and others, had not declared war upon the media. All presidents despise the media as a matter of course. But most have the wit to manipulate the relationship, to humor reporters, to flatter them, to work around them, to manage them in such a way that they do not actively damage the president's public image.

Franklin Roosevelt was contemptuous of the press, and especially of publishers, who in his era were mostly conservative—men such as William Randolph Hearst and the *Chicago Tribune*'s Colonel Robert McCormick and *Time*'s Henry Luce. But FDR understood the press and handled reporters with a master's touch, cultivating them in his jaunty, paternal way, granting them access to his presence, inviting them into his office for frequent "press conferences" that resembled nothing so much as a cheerful zookeeper tossing fish to the grateful, barking seals.

Harry Truman hated the press with an unsuspected depth of feeling. Dwight Eisenhower held the press in that remote disdain that generals accustomed to order and discipline and being obeyed and exercising great power have for disorderly rabble.

John Kennedy possessed a genius for public relations. He had learned from his father's lessons. Joe Kennedy taught him to cultivate reporters, to send them notes whenever they wrote anything about him, to be friendly, interested, accessible—comradely with them. He also learned from his father's mistakes—notably from the catastrophically bad press his father earned during his last days as ambassador to England and in a surreal interview he gave in the fall of 1940, in the midst of Roosevelt's third-term presidential campaign, to the *Boston Globe,* in which he said he thought democracy was finished in England, and possibly in the United States as well.

But Kennedy, in the colder premeditations of his political nature, detested the press. As much as Nixon, he thought the media were unfair to him. Kennedy, unlike Nixon, understood how important the media were to him, and he knew how to manage them.

ALL THREE PRESIDENTS EXHIBITED, at one time or another, behavior that was "sick"—that might be called pathological.

Nixon and Johnson, especially toward the end of their terms, showed signs of clinical paranoia. Richard Goodwin, a Kennedy aide who stayed on and worked for Lyndon Johnson, believed that, in 1967 and 1968, Johnson was paranoid—mentally ill. Many who worked in the White House toward the end of Watergate—including Chief of Staff Alexander Haig—believed that Nixon had become mentally unstable.

Kennedy, who had been physically sick for many years with Addison's and his catalog of other ailments, also indulged himself in sexual conduct so reckless and dangerous to his presidency and to the country that it might reasonably be called pathological. A man whose sexual needs or drives have become so urgent is willing to risk too much.

There is the matter of Johnson's Silver Star—a decoration that he boasted of repeatedly at political rallies during the 1948 campaign against Coke Stevenson. Johnson had a bardic gift of self-glorification.

In 1943, Congressman Johnson decided that he would have to do something to get into uniform and then be sent overseas to compile some sort of war record, because he knew that after the war a politician without a war record would be a dead duck. The war had been going badly for the Allies, with disastrous news from Wake Island and Guam and Bataan and Corregidor, and it had begun to be conspicuous that Congressman Johnson, who had made brave statements about what he would do to join the boys in "the front lines, in the mud," was still wearing civilian clothes. Some newspapers in Texas published editorials that came close to questioning his courage. The *San Antonio Light* had asked Johnson to enlist "some time ago." The *Fredericksburg Standard,* largest newspaper in the Texas Hill Country, published a sarcastic editorial: "We believe the Congressman will live up to his often repeated promises. But of course we may be wrong and the Congressman's disparagers may be right."

He was a member of the House Naval Affairs Committee and held a lieutenant commander's commission in the U.S. Navy Reserve. Johnson asked Admiral Chester Nimitz to sign the forms putting him on active duty. Then he went to his friend James Forrestal, secretary of the navy (who was also a friend of the Kennedys and would take Jack Kennedy along on his plane to the conference at Potsdam at the end of the war) and sought an assignment. Forrestal wrote a note back to him: "Lyndon, how do you want these orders to read?"

Johnson had entertained grandiose hopes for an admiral's rank and a job as head of all wartime production for the navy. Getting nowhere with that idea, he had Forrestal send him, not to a war zone, but to Texas and the West Coast, for an inspection tour of shipyard training programs. He arranged for his aide John Connally to accompany him. It became an odd and feckless interlude. In the early days of a terrible world war, Johnson put on his uniform, and then, in effect, immediately went AWOL.

Johnson managed to leave the impression that he was embarking on secret and possibly dangerous work, and that he would surely soon be in combat. He stood in the House and dramatically told his patron, Sam Rayburn, "Mr. Speaker, I ask unanimous consent for an indefinite leave of absence." Rayburn saw Johnson and Connally off at Union Station—"standing silently amid the tumult of the giant concourse jammed with men in uniform going off to war, their women kissing them goodbye."

Johnson and Connally did not go into combat but, rather, at the worst moment of the war for the United States, when almost all the news was bad, they spent the next ten weeks visiting shipyards in San Diego, Burbank, Los Angeles, San Francisco, Portland and Seattle. They also, as Connally said later, "had a lot of fun." Connally was to Lyndon Johnson what George Smathers was to John Kennedy, and a little bit of what Bebe Rebozo was to Nixon (although, for Nixon and Rebozo, without the women). As Caro wrote: "They traveled by train, two tall, black-haired young Texans, dramatically handsome in their Navy blue and gold uniforms, having the good times of young sailors at war, but not at sea. . . . There was a lot of partying." They went to parties with movie stars, met Veronica Lake and Alan Ladd and Bonita Granville.

Johnson worked with a Hollywood photographer and had campaign pictures taken that were better than the ones he was sending to his constituents. He worked with a Hollywood voice coach to improve his delivery.

As the weeks passed, it became difficult to sustain the charade that Johnson was engaged in heroic war work that must remain veiled in secrecy. One of his advisers and backers, the newspaper publisher Charles Marsh, wrote to him with brusque advice: "Get your ass out of this country at once to where there is danger, and then get back as soon as you can to real work."

That is what Johnson did.

In later years, especially in the 1948 campaign, he shamelessly embellished the story of how he "won" the Silver Star—he rode along as an observer on a B-26 bombing raid against the Japanese air base at Lae on the coast of New Guinea—until his incredibly brief wartime service became an epic war story of heroism and shared danger.

In rural Texas, there was no manlier virtue than bravery in battle. Johnson saw to it that, as often as possible during the 1948 campaign, the person introducing him at political rallies would be a veteran, preferably one who had lost a limb in battle. "So successful was the Johnson campaign in locating pro-Johnson amputees for this task," wrote Robert Caro, "that the percentage of men introducing Johnson who still possessed all their limbs was surprisingly small. And the introductions stressed the war service: 'Congressman Johnson was fighting in the Pacific until he was recalled to his congressional duties.'"

Johnson, a man who might have been invented by Mark Twain, would warm to the rural crowd and the gaudy emotion of his theme, and he would tell them that he knew what it was to see boys die, because he had had a friend who died. "He was the boy I roomed with, he was a country boy, too. He was a pilot, and he flew a B-17 . . . his name was Francis Stevens, but we all called him Steve." They had been on a mission together, but Steve had been shot down. And Lyndon had had to collect his personal effects and mail them to his mother. "I sat in that little room we had shared together, and got all the letters his mama had written him, and I tied them up to send back to her. And I packed up his clothes. I remember I rolled up his socks. They smelled bad, but they were his, so I sent them to his mama, too."

That line about the socks smelling bad had just the touch of Johnson authenticity; he was a man who knew how to cross the sentimental with the crude to achieve some deeper, weird believability: It must be true, Lyndon didn't pretty it up. All his political life, Johnson would enlist his grossness, in an original way, to vouch for his honesty—or, more than that, to vouch for some raw truth he wished to present. Johnson's famous bathroom displays and performances, like the one in which he pulled up his pajamas to show the scar from his gall bladder operation, cunningly forced others off their native accustomed turf (where people did not do such things). He surprised them, a little, into a different terrain, one that belonged to him, where he made the rules. His grossness was an exercise and tactic of power. The stink of the dead man's socks, mailed home to mother, had the touch of the political artist.

In 1948, Johnson would wave his lapel at the crowds and show them his Silver Star ribbon and say, "That's the Silver Star. General MacArthur gave it to me." Later, he would even start complaining that the Silver Star was insufficient recognition for his sacrifices and bravery—an astonishing embroidery of the original self-delusion of his combat experience. It can be explained only, as Caro says, by understanding that in time Johnson himself had come to believe the fantasies that blossomed in his imagination as he told and retold his one experience of war (as a passive observer) until it became an Iliad.

In this capacity for self-myth, Lyndon Johnson bore a striking resemblance to Ernest Hemingway and to the poet James Dickey. Hemingway, an ambulance driver wounded in World War I, over the years—under the influence of alcohol and possessing an ego that liked to give itself a parade—concocted the myth of himself as a bandit warrior and slaughterer of men, a regular Achilles. James Dickey embellished his war record flying combat missions in the Pacific, and turned it to his literary uses. Senator Joseph R. McCarthy—"Tailgunner Joe"—claimed heroics after the war that had no basis in actuality.

The truth is that Lyndon Johnson, once aboard the bomber and under attack from Japanese Zeros, displayed a coolness and presence of mind that could be interpreted as bravery; but it was, so to speak, a passive bravery. Johnson was not called on to do anything—fly a plane, or man a gun. He watched: He stood on a stool with his head in the navigator's bubble on top of the fuselage and, without flinching, the others said, stared at a Japanese Zero coming in with its guns blazing. But Johnson did nothing other than watch. None of the men on the bomber crew who did fire the guns and bring down the Zero, and who then took the plane safely back to its base in Australia, received medals.

MacArthur seemed irritated that Johnson had risked his life merely to ride along on the mission—a needless risk, one that accomplished nothing, at least from a military point of view. MacArthur said almost offhandedly that he would be giving Johnson a Silver Star, but there did not seem much enthusiasm in the gesture, which was surely touched by the contempt that a professional soldier would feel for a politician who had contrived to come all the way to the war zone just to have his combat ticket punched, and then was about to return to domestic politics wearing the army's third highest decoration for gallantry; hundreds of thousands of men would remain stuck in the trenches where Johnson, in brave campaign speeches, would claim to have been. MacArthur told Johnson that he had no actual medals on hand, but there were some ribbons in the outer office and Johnson could pick one up on his way out.

Johnson's moment in combat was worthless militarily. But from a political point of view, that is, from Johnson's point of view, it accomplished everything. He turned it into a politically useful myth.

In Johnson's Texas past, his biographer Robert Caro picked up stories that as a young man he had been a physical coward—that he had

> displayed a conspicuous hesitancy and timidity at participating in [wrestling and fist fighting], or at riding an unruly horse or diving from a not very high bank into the Pedernales River—at any of the routine rough-housing of youth. And at college, if a fellow student, antagonized by him, approached him to fight, Johnson would immediately, without a gesture of resistance, fall

back on a bed and kick his feet in the air with a frantic wind-milling motion to keep his foe away, while yelling, "If you hit me, I'll kick you! If you hit me, I'll kick you!"—a scene which astonished other students, one of whom said, "Every kid in the State of Texas had fights then, but he wouldn't fight. He was an absolute physical coward."

But if he did not do any fighting in the bomber over Lae, he was certainly admirably cool under fire. Perhaps Lyndon Johnson refused to fight, and kicked his feet on the bed in college, for the same reason that in Washington during the forties he was known, quite often, to doze off during dinner parties when the conversation did not focus on him—when he was not the center of attention. Johnson was a brilliant and scintillating talker when he was the hero of the dinner table. In an analogous way, he would be cool under fire in the bombing raid because he understood, instinctively and perfectly, that what he was doing at that moment amounted to a magnificently efficient political move: Johnson was such a political animal that a display of physical courage would be worthwhile only if it yielded political result. Johnson brought home a politically priceless Silver Star from his dangerous ride over New Guinea. It would occur to him only later, as his imagination reworked the experience to flashier effect, that he should have brought home something even grander. Such were Johnson's powers of self-aggrandizement that, if he had fabulated on it long enough, he might have decided he deserved the Congressional Medal of Honor.

SUPREME COURT JUSTICE Oliver Wendell Holmes summarized an honest soldier's contempt for the exploitation of war by manipulative egos playing to a home audience. Holmes was a young man of twenty when he went off with the twentieth Massachusetts Infantry Regiment to fight in the Civil War. Severely wounded at Antietam (a bullet in the throat), Captain Holmes lay recovering in Maryland when his concerned but self-important father, having heard the news, bustled down from Boston by train to search for his son. Dr. Holmes, the father, who wrote a well-known column for the *Atlantic Monthly* as the "Autocrat of the Breakfast Table," finally located his wounded son, and put him onto a train to return to Boston. On their way home, as Holmes the younger noted with a certain buried sardonic scorn, the father busied himself in writing a florid and egotistical article for the *Atlantic* titled "My Hunt After the Captain." The son had taken the bullets. The father would contrive to put himself at the center of the drama. After the war, Captain Holmes refused to discuss his experiences in the war with any except those who had actually been in the combat. But politicians, like the Autocrat of the Breakfast Table, instinctively understood the self-dramatizing uses of wartime service, and exploited it. Career military men, too, have always understood, as instinctively as politicians, the necessity to get one's ticket punched through wartime service. MacArthur's award of the Silver Star to Johnson amounted to mutually comprehending professional courtesy extended from a supremely political career military man to a briefly visiting career politician in need of a touch of combat ormolu to parade at home. Nixon himself exaggerated his wartime service to some extent—usually in a complicated Nixonian now-you-see-it-now-you-don't in which he first deprecated his service by saying he had not done anything special during the war but had "only been there when the bombs fell," and then talked, in hyperbole that obscurely falsified the overall experience, about "sharing the foxholes with the troops." The audience was left with the impression that Nixon was 1) a modest young man who, unfairly to himself, deprecated his contribution to the war effort, and 2) maybe more of an everyman hero than he was letting on. Nixon had a genius for playing with the lighting effects. He knew how to retouch the photos of himself. The slightly doctored campaign memories of his wartime service sometimes bore a resemblance to that press release from young Congressman Nixon's office talking about him as "a husky ex-footballer." He did play football at Whittier, of course—doggedly, badly, unsuccessfully. And he did jump into bomb shelters on Bougainville on the occasions when Japanese bombers came around. But his claims as both a husky footballer and as a combat veteran left an impression not quite warranted by the facts.

But then the war records of John Kennedy and Lyndon Johnson also left impressions (Kennedy as the hero of *PT-109*, Johnson as the Congressman worthy of MacArthur's Silver Star) that did not quite square with the facts.

All wars leave both an idealizing battlefield nostalgia and, in the other direction, a certain bitterness in the young who did the dying at the orders of the old men who made the decisions. Johnson, Kennedy, and Nixon were the young men of the Good War (again, Johnson far less than the others, for his war was brief and symbolic—he had already in spirit joined the old men); the three men would also become the presidents who made the decisions that took America into its Bad War, Vietnam. America got into the Bad War because of the Good War. It was precisely the apparent moral and strategic lessons of the Good War—such lessons as Munich that guided Kennedy, Johnson, and Nixon in their response to what they perceived to be the Communist threat in Southeast Asia. John Kennedy's 1961 inaugural address bristled with a hard-edged Wilsonianism informed by Munich and organized around almost unquestioning confidence in the American Century. Kennedy's famous rhetoric made a dangerously open-ended promise: "Let every nation know, whether it wishes us well or ill, that we shall pay any price, bear any burden, meet any hardship, support any friend, oppose any foe, in order to assure the survival and the success of liberty."

CHAPTER FOUR

LATE
SUMMER

THE HISS CASE

THE HISS CASE WAS Richard Nixon's political origin myth.

He often referred to the case in later years—to the lessons it had taught—as if it had been the formative struggle, the primary text of his political education. It was the chief of his *Six Crises,* a *fons et origo* of his political technique and moral attitude. Nixon's conversation on the White House tapes contains numerous references to the Hiss case, as if for him it had served as a model and a warning and, in its triumphant outcome years before, a promise of future vindication. The Hiss case had worked. Hiss went to jail. Nixon went to the White House. The story showed that Nixon was right, and that if he persisted, and played the cards adroitly, he would be vindicated again and again, no matter how beset he might be, or how unpromising the cards might seem at the moment.

There was in Nixon an alert, improvising intelligence, present in the present, and always learning; it was the part of his mind that, for example, formulated the opening to China.

There was another part of his mind that was frozen in patterns of the past and referred backward to the imprint of the first political steps, the first lessons—and, in some more primitive and almost preconscious way, that referred back to earlier traumas.

The Hiss case represented some early truth to Nixon, about the division of forces in America, about the role of the treacherous, wrong-headed press. Above all, it taught a lesson about the great rewards available to the man who did battle with the soft-headed, overprivileged, elitist Franklins (the Hiss supporters) who were dupes of darker forces—the "useful idiots," as Lenin said—of dangerous foreign ideologies and agents. The question always was this: Did Nixon deeply believe that domestic communism was a real threat to American life and institutions, or did he think that an artful exploitation of the idea of such a Communist threat could be the making of his political career?

The answer lies in an indeterminate zone; Nixon was a lawyer. A lawyer advances the interests of a client. Lawyer Nixon's client was Politician Nixon. Lawyer Nixon seized an opportunity when he saw the path (Hiss-Chambers) by which Politician Nixon could most successfully advance his ambitions. *L'audace! Toujours l'audace!*

At the same time, Nixon undoubtedly believed, quite rightly, that there had been, and was in 1948, a great deal of subversive Communist activity in the United States. In the closing years of the century, the Venona decryptions of radio traffic between Communist agents in America and their bosses in Moscow— along with Soviet secret documents made public after the collapse of the USSR—showed unmistakeably that Communist agents were busy in America, in the federal government, in the labor movement, in Hollywood, and elsewhere. The Communist threat was not the hallucination of cynics or of right-wing fanatics. The question, which remains unresolved, is how great a threat the Communist influence represented. Did generous, good-hearted leftists merely wish to see America move more humanely toward socialized medicine, toward a more equitable distribution of wealth, and toward better relations with the Soviet Union? Or did such leftists, as witting or unwitting representatives of Soviet interests, wish to see private property and free enterprise undermined in America, and America coaxed toward centralized government and, ultimately, toward a totalitarian model? Some leftists have argued that it was the right wing's efforts to ferret out Communists that made America totalitarian. Plenty of Democrats were fiercely anti-Communist. It was Harry Truman who established the Loyalty Boards. It was also Harry Truman who acquiesced to a reporter's description of the Hiss case as "a red herring."

The Voorhis campaign was the success of Nixon's political novitiate. Hiss was the triumph of his juniorate.

One day in November 1943, the conductor of the New York Philharmonic, Bruno Walter, became ill, and his understudy, a twenty-five-year-old named Leonard Bernstein, took over for him, going on stage at Carnegie Hall with virtually no advance notice, and magnificently conducting a program of Schuman, Rózsa and Strauss. A star was born. (Something of the same story as Lana Turner's discovery at the Top Hat Café.)

The Hiss case had for Richard Nixon a touch of that satisfyingly American quality of young talent's seizing a Big Chance and striking it rich.

Would the Hiss case have made as much of a splash if it had not happened in early August 1948 in a comparatively dead news time—a moment when it did not have to share the front pages without urgent other stories? Perhaps not.

In one sense, the Hiss case was not news at all—not news, at least, to the FBI, which kept files on Hiss, and not news to the White House, either. In 1939, Whittaker Chambers had gone to a high State Department official, Adolph Berle, to report on the Communist cell in Washington of which Hiss had been a member. Berle duly reported the information to the Roosevelt White House, but a world war was starting, the Soviet Union was an ally, and neither the president nor anyone else in the White House showed any interest. But Nixon and Chambers and HUAC formalized and dramatized the charge (the fact) of Alger Hiss's identity as a former Communist agent, and in the public spectacle of the hearings, composed the story into theater, into American folklore. It entered history as intensely interesting drama, with an indelible cast of characters—Chambers and Hiss, and Nixon as one of those Tom Dewey/Dana Andrews straight-arrow prosecutorial good guys, dark-browed and serious and lawyerly and businesslike, with a brisk let's-get-to-the-bottom-of-this air: faithful husband and scoutmaster, the best of America back from the war, alert, reliable, responsible. Our kind of guy. Neither Chambers nor Hiss was "our kind of guy."

Each was a kind of foreigner.

Chambers—dank, disheveled, obscurely unwholesome, vexed by un-American thoughts and readings in dangerous foreign texts (Dostoevski, Kropotkin, Bakunin: neurotics and bomb-throwers)—represented no America that postwar Americans cared to embrace. Chambers and his foreign influences merely confirmed the American instinct to recoil from a world that had drawn the nation into catastrophic world war (twice) and that now menaced America in a new way with a new enemy: expansionist, subversive, conspiratorial communism.

Chambers had repudiated the Communist plague, but nonetheless bore its traces still—the impression of its danger, its damage, its uncleanness. Americans could not feel at home with such a character as Chambers. He was too strange and deep, deflected, shadowed: Uncomfortable. Un-American. His was not an American experience (so it seemed), but a European drama, a Russian story. He seemed not to be formed by American influences.

There was the further discomfort of his apostasy. A turncoat stirs uneasiness, not so much gratitude for the bounty he has brought with him as dowry and earnest money filched from his former master, but, rather, a perfectly natural mistrust. If he could betray the cause to which he was once so loyal, then— whatever the eloquence of his explanations, however fierce and anguished the avowals of his repentance—still, here, sitting before us in all his squirming, sweating unease, is the evidence that he is a man who betrays. How is it possible to trust a traitor, even when his latest betrayal seems to be one committed in your favor?

The American instinct especially hates traitors. The darkest negative cautionary story of American folklore concerns Benedict Arnold, whose name became the generic term for treason and denoted an unforgivable sin. The frozen floor of Dante's Hell, the ninth circle, was reserved for those who had committed treason against relatives, party, or homeland, against guests and rightful lords. Disobedience to God was the original sin. Disloyalty was the primal sin against the state. Harry Truman had codified the offense and brought it up-to-date a year before the Hiss case when he instituted the government's Loyalty Board and required each federal employee to take a loyalty oath.

Chambers had a citizen's loyalty to United States; did he betray that loyalty by working to ferry American secrets to the Soviet Communists in the thirties? Turn it around: Chambers had given his loyalty to the Communist Party and then turned against it. Hiss held fast to his loyalty to the Communist Party, but betrayed his duty and oath as an American government official.

All this residual meaning and passion flowed beneath the surface in 1948—never quite articulated. The seeming consequences of disloyalty had, after Hiroshima, become apocalyptic. The Rosenbergs would die for their sins of disloyalty. In film noir—in *Double Indemnity,* for example, and in *The Postman Always Rings Twice*—a wife and her new lover (a virtual stranger to her) would conspire to kill her husband in cold blood for the insurance. Sexual treason blurred into homicide all is permitted—as Count Ugolino della Gherardesca's treason in 1280 led on, via Dante, into cannibalism (eating, it was said, his two sons and two grandchildren while imprisoned so that he could stay alive himself) and Dante's memorably macabre image of Ugolino's wiping his lips on the hair of the skull he was consuming: If there is a more savage or ruthlessly accurate metaphor for conscienceless political survival, it is difficult to think of it. In the last months and weeks of Watergate, the president's men— Ehrlichman, Haldeman, Mitchell, Colson and the rest—were fed into the maw. It did no good. The presidency perished anyway.

It helped that Richard Nixon vouched for Chambers.

As for Hiss, he seemed all right at first, though in the manner of a fancy New Deal public man, all Harvard Law and elegant tweeds. He was not authentic, either, not in the real American way, and became radically less so as the case went on. To some extent, the Hiss case was a subliminal referendum on the matter of who was a real American.

Richard Nixon first heard about Alger Hiss in February 1947, just after he came to Washington as a freshman congressman. Someone introduced Nixon to Father John F. Cronin, who was a professor of philosophy and economics at St. Mary's Seminary in Baltimore. Cronin had been working to organize labor unions. But the more he saw, the more he became worried by the way that Communists were infiltrating American war plants. He took a leave from his teaching to make an extensive study of Communist Party activities, an investigation that brought him to Washington. As Earl Mazo wrote, "He ran across all the names and episodes that subsequently became familiar to the public through Congressional hearings—Alger Hiss, Elizabeth Bentley, and the whole litany. The information was not hard to come by, and Father Cronin was startled by the apparent indifference of responsible officials."

And so Father Cronin told Nixon about it. Nixon was interested. But Nixon was a busy man in his first year in the House, and he had other projects in the works. He served on the Herter Committee, whose reports led to the Marshall Plan. He worked on a small subcommittee of the House Labor Committee that drafted the Taft-Hartley Labor Law. It was on that subcommittee that he worked closely with John Kennedy—the two taking opposing sides, and, on one occasion in the spring of 1947, traveling to McKeesport, Pennsylvania, where they debated Taft-Hartley before a local civic group.

In *Kennedy and Nixon,* Chris Matthews offered a snapshot of the two men in McKeesport, a sort of preview, thirteen years before the fact, of their individual styles and their impact on the audience in the 1960 presidential debates.

"There, in a chandeliered ballroom," wrote Matthews, "they offered a stark contrast in style. Nixon, a prize-winning debater at Whittier, drove a wedge through the audience. Ignoring cat-calls from the blue-collar crowd, he warned that big labor's power was growing 'by leaps and bounds.'"

Nixon bore down aggressively: "We have had unprecedented labor strife—the automobile strike, the steel strike, the coal strike, and even the railroad strike, in which the president was forced to intervene." The labor people jeered loudly. A local business leader wrote to Nixon to apologize for the reception.

Nixon, always combative, nerved himself up for struggle. He did not seek conciliation so much as vindication. Each debate was a trial. Years later, when he accepted the presidential nomination in the tumultuous year of 1968, he read the American mood correctly—people were sick of all the conflict—and spoke at length about conciliation. He mentioned a little girl's sign that he claimed he had seen on a roadside while campaigning: "BRING US TOGETHER."

But most of the time his combative instincts had the upper hand. In McKeesport he attacked the labor position frontally.

But Kennedy, who opposed the Taft-Hartley Act in a nuanced and provisional kind of way (he thought there were good things in the bill, such as the prohibition on wildcat strikes), was far more conciliatory and ingratiating. Wrote Matthews: "More telling than their argument. . . was the difference in manner. The Californian maintained a fighter's edge, challenging his more genteel seeming opponent on every point. The slender law-maker with the slight limp focused on the audience, seducing the steel-town folk with his smooth delivery and youthful charm. While Nixon debated, Kennedy simply ignored his opponent, carefully making sure that the businessmen in the room understood his justified concern that the Republican's get-tough approach to labor might create more trouble, not less."

The audience was impressed, in different ways, by both men. A stockbroker who moderated the debate told his wife afterward that Nixon was "going to go places." Everyone seemed to agree about that. The man said, "It was hard to tell who had come from the wealthy family and which had worked his way up. Neither could be called a stuffed shirt."

But, remarked Matthews, "it was Kennedy who won the media battle." The next morning's editions of the McKeesport Daily News had a photograph of Kennedy, tanned and smiling and engaging. Nixon's eyes were darting sideways in that characteristic hunted look—his jowls darkened by five o'clock shadow. "Even in the black-and-white photo, the charisma gap was stark."

But Kennedy and Nixon seemed to hit it off together. At the Star Diner afterward, they had a lively talk about the new baseball season. A local Democratic organizer said they were "young fellows whom you could like." They showed "genuine friendliness." They rode back to Washington together on the Capital Limited, leaving McKeesport at midnight. They drew straws for the lower berth, and Nixon won. "Then, as the train rolled on toward Washington, the two spent the early morning hours talking about their true interest, foreign policy, especially the rising standoff with the Soviets in Europe, which Bernard Baruch had just christened the 'cold war.'"

As a freshman, Nixon was a humorless, calculating, utterly focused workaholic. In a memoir, his office manager, Bill Arnold, gave this picture of Nixon:

Mr. Nixon was always a restless soul carrying out his duties. He pushed himself hard, as all who worked for him were supposed to do. He never left his office to get to the airport or railroad station until the last possible minute, for fear of having to sit around and wait at a terminal. It was often my responsibility to drive him to such places and I always cautioned that we were going to miss a plane or train some time. One day this happened as we were attempting to cross the Potomac on the 14th Street drawbridge, which opened while we were en route to the airport to permit a boat to pass beneath. Sure enough, we missed the plane. But did we sit around and wait for the next one? We did not; instead we went back to the office to put in another hour's work.

George Smathers said that Nixon was "the most calculating man I ever knew." Everything he did, it seemed, smacked of focused premeditation. Once he gave a small cocktail party in his attic office for reporters covering HUAC. He memorized the name of each journalist and even his favorite drink. George Reedy, a UPI reporter who in the sixties would be President Lyndon Johnson's press secretary, remembered that Congressman Nixon gave him a big "Hi, George!" when he entered the suite, even though the two had never met. Most politicians make it their business to know names, and to practice such bonhomie, but in Nixon, throughout his career, the exercise would have an artificial quality. The politician's trick is sincerity, and as said, once you have learned to fake sincerity, you have it made. Nixon was either 1) a hopelessly insincere man whose social instincts were made of naugahyde, or 2) simply a politician who did a bad job of faking sincerity, and therefore looked insincere to those who did not know him (and who really knew him?). The second possibility would be a verdict in his favor   somewhat.

The truth may be that Nixon's insincerity was perfectly genuine (sincere, if you like) but also, in a sense, irrelevant, because sincerity is, after all, merely one of the decorative hypocrisies of an inherently insincere profession; sincerity lacks substance, and may be neither here nor there, and Richard Nixon on the whole was inwardly impatient with the conventional pageant and therefore did it badly.

Or perhaps it is more accurate to say that sincerity was something he simply did not understand. He aped it badly when he felt it necessary to trot out something like sincerity, in something of the way that he made wistful stabs at other forms of, shall we say, unnecessary human contact—manly locker room talk, for example, and cocktail party chitchat, or discussions of whether a constituent's son got into Dartmouth.

He was a mental man, his mind a highly active and sophisticated calculator, a political gamesman. He appeared to be an incredibly banal man in part because he had no gift for banalities and was ill at ease with them. So when he recognized the need to dispense a banality of some kind, he would give it a try, but the result was quite often painful, like those early attempts at ice-skating when he was courting Pat in California. He had no natural grace at such things. His social instincts were retarded, or, at least, they were not wired up for everyday use; that "Hi, George!" to Reedy—indeed, the entire impulse to have a small cocktail party for reporters—had a complex savor a) of the lonely geek that Nixon surely was; b) of the press-baiter momentarily suppressing his contempt for reporters and their dishonest, indeed whorish, profession; and c) of a young congressman-on-the-make engaged in the perfectly conventional politician's business of plying the jackals with whisky.

Nixon's earnestly focused work had begun to pay off before the Hiss case began. In March 1948, the House Un-American Activities Committee (HUAC) took up a bill to outlaw the Communist Party. Nixon judged that a bad idea. Why not draw Communists into the light rather than force them farther into the shadows? Nixon and his colleague, Karl Mundt of South Dakota, proposed a substitute bill that would require all members of the Communist Party to register with the federal government. Ironically, this was a measure that Jerry Voorhis, whom Nixon had described as something of a Communist stooge, had introduced eight years earlier but had failed to pass.

Nixon expertly floor-managed the Mundt-Nixon Bill on the floor of the House, where it was debated for three days. Leading the opposition was New York's Vito Marcantonio, the leftist Democrat whom Nixon had made the gold standard of Communist dupes in running against Voorhis, and whose record he would cite again and again when he ran against Helen Douglas for the senate in 1950.

The full Nixon was on display in those three days—thoroughly prepared (he was the most careful and intelligent member of HUAC, and no one knew the bill better than he), formal, courteous to Marcantonio, businesslike. Throughout his career, Nixon profited by the comparison between himself and others who shared his opinions; he presented the opinions in a way that seemed reasonable, civilized. Serious and thoughtful were adjectives that people used about the young congressman.

He told the House: "Member after member has expressed the fear that this bill strikes at all progressive organizations. That is exactly the trouble in the country today. There is too much loose talk and confusion on the Communist issue. By passing this bill the Congress will go on record as to just what is subversive about communism in the United States." His colleagues would overwhelmingly vote for the bill, he predicted, "not because the bill happens to be against communism and this is a political year—I am not asking any Member of the House to vote for the bill on that basis."

The biographer Stephen Ambrose remarked: "This was a Nixon technique that already was beginning to drive his opponents to distraction—denying that he had said what he had just said." Nixon was a sort of rhetorical fan-dancer. Like Gypsy Rose Lee, he knew how to display, and then with coquettish prudery to rescind, the most titillating ideas: He would flash one and then cover it up with ostrich feathers. But the audience had seen what it had seen, or, rather, had heard what it had heard, and remembered that. But the covering up, the ostrich feathers, had also left an impression of modesty—judiciousness, probity, fairness.

Nixon was learning how to have it both ways (anti-Communist but not McCarthyite, a conservative in touch with the party's far right wing, but also an internationalist/moderate who would talk to the Eastern establishment) a skill that would propel him onto the national ticket with Eisenhower in 1952, and then take him to the top of American politics sixteen years later.

But he could have it both ways only up to a point. Nixon insisted: "This bill, far from being a police-state bill, is a bill which will prevent the creation of a police state." But not only did the American left oppose the bill; so did the liberal Republicans from the Northeast, led by Governor Thomas E. Dewey of New York.

Dewey fulminated against the bill: "I am unalterably, wholeheartedly, and unswervingly against any scheme to write laws outlawing people because of their . . . ideas. . . . I am against it because it is immoral and nothing but totalitarianism itself. . . . Stripped to its naked essentials, this is nothing but the method of Hitler and Stalin. It is thought control. . . . It is an attempt to beat down ideas with a club."

The bill died in committee in the Senate.

But the bill had made Nixon a national figure, in a minor way. In June 1948, he swept both the Democratic and the Republican primaries in the Twelfth District, and thus was assured of reelection. His home base was solid.

His second daughter, Julie, was born on July 5. He wrote to a supporter in Alhambra: "As you have probably read in your paper by now, July 5 was a big day for the Nixon family. Our little girl, Patricia, now has a baby sister, Julie, to hand her clothes down to! Pat and I are, of course, really thrilled about the event."

Nixon's biographer Stephen Ambrose quoted that letter and then added censoriously: "Not a word about how the delivery went for Pat, or how she was recovering. With Nixon, it was first things first; when he wrote his old college professor, Paul Smith, also the day after the birth, he did not even mention Julie. He went into analysis of how the campaign would go ('Although Dewey is an excellent administrator and fine speaker, he lacks the warmth that is essential to a really effective national campaigner')."

Ambrose displays an odd obtuseness about the man and the era. It would have been wholly out of character for a husband in 1948, especially one as private and reticent as Nixon, to discuss the details of his wife's delivery with anyone outside the family, let alone a comparative stranger, a political associate. It must also be said, however, that one reads Nixon's remark about Dewey's lack of warmth with a wondering smile: It was shrewd of Nixon to see that one of the things that would defeat Dewey in the famous 1948 presidential election was his cold-fish problem; not only did Dewey, as Alice Longworth cracked, look like the groom on a wedding cake, but it was impossible to imagine that the groom could summon the heat to make it successfully through the wedding night.

Nixon was his own kind of cold fish, of course; he, too, "lacked warmth." But it was a different problem from Dewey's. The governor of New York, at least in the 1948 campaign, had a mind that seemed to have gone smug and inactive. He said such things as "The future lies before us!" The congressmen from the Twelfth District of California, however, had a mind that was almost too active; it gave off not precisely heat, but a dark intensity.

In January 1948, investigators from the House Un-American Activities Committee approached Chambers and asked him to repeat the story he had told to Adolph Berle nine years earlier about his work in the Communist Party during the thirties, and about the Hiss brothers and the others who had been Communists while they held high positions in the New Deal. Chambers demurred.

But now, at the end of the July, Elizabeth Bentley's testimony reopened the can of worms.

In *A Streetcar Named Desire,* Tennessee Williams struck, with eerie fidelity, characteristic notes of 1948 secrecy (Blanche's past, her family's financial ruin) and brutal power, unrefined by manners or tradition or intellect—or by a past now impotent or dead.

Marlon Brando was so smolderingly beautiful as Stanley Kowalski that his performance managed to make moronic rapacity (which was getting to be the way of much of the world, in a political sense) seem titillating and, well, almost worth it: In Broadway audiences' excitement over *Streetcar,* one could make out an unwholesome strand of covert sadomasochistic acquiescence to the rape at the end that drives Blanche mad and leaves her simpering about "the kindness of strangers."

If—instead of Brando—the director had cast an ugly brute in the role of Stanley (imagine Ernest Borgnine in the part, for example), then the true implications of the role would have been clear.

The casting of Marlon Brando as Stanley Kowalski—again, with an eerie precision—replicated a pattern in the civilized liberal Western imagination that could surrender, with perverse romantic satisfaction, to the idea of brute, savage regimes and ideologies. It was a variation on what came to be known in later years as the Stockholm Syndrome—people who are held hostage going over emotionally to the hostage-taker's point of view; the heiress Patty Hearst, who, in the 1970s, joined up with the radical gang that had kidnapped her and participated in their depredations, is an example.

All through the thirties some overbred liberal impulse had flirted, in a nearly overt sexual way (in a mode that might be called sexual/intellectual) with the idea of brute force that would sweep aside—or had already swept aside—the effete, bloodless, sexless old civilization: Kowalski, the rough beast slouching toward Blanche as Yeats's "rough beast" had slouched toward Bethlehem. All power comes from the barrel of a gun. The world had fallen apart. Maybe we needed strong brainless gangsters to put it back together.

Many liberals embraced the gangster communism with a frisson of orgasmic self-annihilation. Communism became the liberals' fascism—as brutal and overpowering as fascism, but with a more respectable intellectual rationale that was based on universal humanitarian claims rather than on nationalistic or even tribal furies. Communism sounded like a humane and progressive agenda, and the Lenin ruthlessness was just the antidote to what George Steiner called "the Sundays and suet of the bourgeois life form," the bad conscience, the unearned privilege, the sheer disgusting blubber of the inane middle-class capitalism.

In the Western romance with totalitarian communism, there was that strange quality of almost erotic self-surrender, the St. Sebastian note. Brute power had a seductive sexual vibration.

The impulse lingered through the era of Kennedy, Johnson, and Nixon. Twenty years after *Streetcar*, the French playwright and soi-disant pervert Jean Genet would cover the 1968 Democratic convention, and would write rhapsodically about the massive thighs and the billy clubs of the police beating up the antiwar demonstrators on Michigan Avenue; the Chicago police were all Stanley Kowalski. Genet loved them.

In *Streetcar*, Blanche's sexual past—what in those days was called nymphomania, a lonely tendency to seduce the newspaper boy, the rot behind the genteel façade—was a secret that chased her from place to place, as Chambers's Communist past pursued him in the period after he quit the Party and went into hiding, a hunted man, or at least a man who fancied he was hunted, who carried a pistol and, in restaurants, sat facing the door, his back to the wall. Chambers thought of himself as Hugo's Jean Valjean, driven endlessly by his secret past; Chambers saw himself as the Bishop of Digne, too. Nixon was a relentless Javert.

The past would pursue the present—catch up with it, confront it. Secrets would emerge, and justice would be exacted—justice in Tennessee Williams's heartless fantasy, taking the form of a brutal rape that drove Blanche off the deep end, irretrievably. For Chambers, the great public exposure of the Hiss case amounted simultaneously (in Chambers's reading) to his own crucifixion and to his ultimate vindication: the triumphant suffering of his *Witness;* truth at last retrieved from history's wreckage. Hiss's friends, meanwhile, thought that he was the one crucified; it is an unusual drama that features two competing Christs.

All these historical or cinematic dramas revolved around issues that were essentially religious, even when the conflicts were staged in the arena of politics. America began by declaring itself (through Thomas Jefferson) to be entitled to "life, liberty, and the pursuit of happiness." But the deepest Christian premise assumed that man was not entitled to happiness in this world, that he would attain it in only in the next through redemption purchased by the sacrifice of Jesus Christ upon the cross.

The FBI had come to interview Chambers five times in 1946 and 1947. Chambers was known to have been a Communist in the thirties, and to have turned against the Party in 1938, but he had always been a guarded and cagey and deeply reluctant informant. He did not wish to betray people who had been his accomplices and even his friends; he did not want to expose himself to prosecution and punishment. He had a family and a farm in Maryland to take care of. In fact, he lied to the FBI. He told the FBI that he had never "participated in [a] Soviet espionage ring or any branch of Soviet intelligence." He said he had no "documentary or other proof" of espionage by Communist agents in Washington. The lies would haunt him later.

There was in Chambers an understandable let-this-cup-pass-from-me reluctance to get involved. He was a handsomely paid ($25,000 a year—big money in the journalism of those days) senior editor at *Time,* a happy family man, and, in his time off from New York, a hard working Maryland farmer who, with only his wife and one hired man, kept fifty head of dairy cows and tended crops. He had, he hoped, left behind a dank and anguished past that included not only the fugitive work in the Communist underground but also the secret life of his intermittent homosexual episodes. Now that he had two children, a devoted wife, and a life that made him happy—the physical labor of farming balancing the intellectual stimulation of his writing and editing. Chambers can hardly have wished to jeopardize his own peace of mind, and his family's, by descending again into the foetid basement of the past and sort through such complex old business—to compound old guilts with new betrayals and to hurt others as well, whose lives, like his own, had moved on.

The postwar red hunts had the urgency of the incipient cold war and the sinister expansionism of communism, which had laid Stalin's hand upon Eastern Europe and had ambitions farther west, in Italy and France and Great Britain, and was on the verge of taking over all of China.

But the red hunts also, relevantly and irrelevantly, tapped the poisons of the past; no matter how the FBI investigations and HUAC hearings and Loyalty Board proceedings might address present dangers, they sometimes merely prosecuted the naïvetes and stupidities of long-ago youth, Communist dreams since abandoned, and regretted. Once politics became involved in red hunting, it was almost impossible to distinguish the truly dangerous espionage going on in the postwar period from the often blameless idealisms of the thirties, or, for Alger Hiss and Whittaker Chambers, to sort out even more complicated histories that were a combination on the one hand of otherwise harmless leftist thirties zeitgeist of the Steinbeck kind and, on the other hand, of active espionage and treason. What would be the statute of limitations on youthful folly? Or, so to speak, on peacetime treason?

And so for a long time before the subpoena compelled Chambers to come before HUAC and Richard Nixon, he was guided by an instinct to evade and conceal. From childhood, he had harbored a tendency toward the covert. About his parents' unorthodox lives (including his father's homosexuality) and the savage inner life of the house in Lynbrook, Long Island (mad grandmother Whittaker wandering the house at midnight, armed with butcher knives) Whittaker had felt a sense of shame and humiliation. At the same time, it was the deep sense of privacy and concealment that nurtured Chambers's melodramatic ego: Who is there to contradict fantasies that are conceived in the dimly lighted privacy of one's secret mind. Chambers had a high sense of theater. So did Richard Nixon. Both men possessed sharp interior intelligence; from the backstage workshops of their minds would emerge sensational dramatic productions. Each had a sense of occasion.

But for the moment, in the comparative contentment and normality of his immediate postwar years, Chambers put all his sense of drama into the eccentric doomy fables he wrote for the Luce publications. The world had just been through titanic traumas—the Great Depression, a world war, Auschwitz, Hiroshima—and what was needed was not more shock and dislocation but an assimilation of what had happened. Chambers had hoped to write about history now instead of trying to live it.

ELIZABETH BENTLEY, a thirty-seven-year-old former schoolteacher who held a degree in languages from Vassar, was "a troubled, unhappy woman who had joined the Communist Party in 1935 and gone underground in 1938." She became the agent who took over Chambers's job as courier to the Washington spy apparatus when he left the party.

The House Un-American Activities Committee had been founded in 1938. Its first chairman, Martin Dies of Texas, was a flag-waver and publicity hound who would rouse himself periodically during hearings to denounce the New Deal's "sinister cadre" of "idealists, dreamers, politicians, professional do-gooders and just plain job-hunters." HUAC acquired a reputation as the megaphone of blowhard Southern reactionaries and anti–New Deal Republicans. It is one of the ironies of Nixon's progress that Jerry Voorhis himself served on HUAC for a time as a kind of liberal anti-Communist outrigger—one of the House leadership's periodic attempts to give HUAC credibility and a veneer of intelligence. House Republican Leader Joe Martin asked freshman Nixon to serve on the committee for just that reason—to raise its collective IQ and give it a touch of polish.

But it was hard work. The committee's idea of "Un-Americans" tended to be people who were eastern-educated liberals from the big cities, and especially Jews. Its current chairman, J. Parnell Thomas, a New Jersey Republican, was hardly an improvement over Martin Dies. Thomas, if anything, solidified HUAC's image as being reckless in its work, ineffectual, primitive, and dangerous to the civil liberties of American citizens—as being, in effect, un-American itself, a cartoon of not-very-bright Neanderthals, armed with clubs, wandering up and down the landscape.

In 1946, the Republicans gained control of Congress for the first time since Herbert Hoover. Their nemesis Roosevelt was gone; the wartime Soviet ally had turned into a potentially menacing enemy in a world that had seen what an atom bomb could do. Anti-communism became an instrument of domestic politics in America. It took on a life of its own. A flow of dangerously high political voltage pulsed through the Communist question. The Roosevelt administration at its highest levels had been slovenly about the real problem of Soviet espionage; it had indeed harbored many Communists in government, some of them active agents of the Stalin regime. After Elizabeth Bentley defected from the Party in 1944, she told the FBI what she knew about Soviet spying and implicated more than eighty agents.

The hearings the committee had conducted the year before into Communist influence in Hollywood had been, on the whole, embarrassing. The "Hollywood Ten" became martyrs to the cause of free speech. It was an amateur's mistake to enter into a posturing contest with glamorous professionals.

The hearings brought to Washington a parade of stars, including some vociferous anti-Communists such as Adolph Menjou and Robert Taylor, but also, on the other side, Humphrey Bogart and Lauren Bacall, among others. The hearings represented one of the first displays of the American merger of politics and the California entertainment industry—a fusion that would bring forth Senator George Murphy, Governor Ronald Reagan, and Governor Arnold Schwarzenegger, as well as initiate the tradition of Hollywood political activism practiced by Barbra Streisand, Jessica Lange, and Sean Penn.

Politics and movies were fraternal twins—not only the dominant modes of American entertainment, but even along with the churches, and the mobile society's unraveling ties of community—the dominant modes of American moral thought. Politics and movies increasingly replaced the churches as the theaters of the moral imagination. Politics and movies told stories filled with meaning and choice. They engaged the constituent audience's faculties of moral speculation and judgment. Movies and politics explored possibility, guided behavior, colored and interpreted experience. HUAC was not wrong in its instinct to look at the movies because, in their dim, vociferous way, the members understood that what would matter in the struggle for the control of the American mind would be the version of the story that sold, that drew the public into its narrative—the moral coloration, the interpretation. John Steinbeck's *Grapes of Wrath* told the stories of Oklahoma farmers, driven off their farms by the Dust Bowl, who headed west with dreams of paradise. They became fruit pickers, and were, in Steinbeck's telling and in the 1940 movie, victimized and brutalized and even communized (in a wholesome, fraternal, thirties common-man kind of way—Henry Fonda in overalls groping fervently toward the truth that all mankind is just "one big soul": "It looks thataway to me . . . ")

But the Okies arrived in Richard Nixon's California back yard. People like the Nixons were inclined to tell a different version of the story, from the fruit-farmers' point of view (Frank Nixon had, of course, failed at his lemon farm). Hannah Nixon received some of the strangers with charity and with handouts. But her Quaker's generosity and Christian charity was often overwhelmed in the family by a harder tribal defensiveness that saw the Okies as illegal aliens, invaders—rascals and pie-stealers at best, Commies at worst.

It was the same story, told from different sides of a struggle. America has always been a drama of interpretation—and, in some ways, amounts only to its interpretation of itself. America, with a kind of neurotic ideological need to think well of itself and its place in the world, sifts its stories of itself to see what it amounts to in the sight of God and the sight of others. Who are the heroes, what are their stories?

Nixon's Whittier boyhood had been somewhat straitened, but insular; if he had had enough hard-bitten experience—illness, death, hard 4:00 A.M. labor—in his childhood (Frank Nixon's "Root, hog, or die!"), his instinctive loyalties in the larger American dramas of the time tended to lie not so much with the hardbitten laborers, not with the migrant workers and the poor and rootless, not with the Joads, but rather with the Chamber of Commerce, with the California small businessmen, the farmers, employers and professionals whose work implied a settled community—the moral foundation on which Nixon's America rested. It was from that solidity that he came; and threats to that solidity—revolution, anarchy, rioting, the dissolution of middle-class moral norms—mobilized his deepest energies of resistance. Such threats reverberated so deeply in him that he would be willing later on to override his usual lawyerly, constitutional responses in an effort to suppress the danger. When he perceived that the courtroom itself was in flames, his instinct told him it was useless to go on with a legal argument. He even proceeded to the fatal idea that it was useless in such circumstances, or irrelevant, for a president of the United States to obey the law.

The years after World War II represented a moment when American stories and heroes were changing. *The Grapes of Wrath* was the thirties sentimentalized; it ended in a kind of flirtatious dream of mystical communism to come. But what came instead was World War II, the Bomb, a massive disillusionment and de-mystification as far as the monster Stalin's communism was concerned. What came was the postwar rise of suburbs and Rotary Club and technology and family—more a Nixon kind of world than a Steinbeck kind of world. And those who had been Communists back in the Depression, no matter how good-hearted and generous and even mystical they might have been, would become targets in the new version of the story.

WHITTAKER CHAMBERS began the great case by being deeply evasive.

In June, 1947, a grand jury in New York started hearing evidence on whether the Communist Party in the United States was a conspiratorial organization whose purpose was the overthrow of the American government. The Justice Department suggested calling Chambers to testify. But the prosecutors decided against it: Chambers was considered a cagey, difficult, unproductive witness. He spoke in generalizations, rarely offered names and dates and other hard information. Don Levine, editor of the anti-Communist weekly *Plain Talk* was later indignant when Chambers got credit for being an anti-Communist crusader. Levine insisted that Chambers had gone out of his way not to pursue Communists. At just the moment when the country at large was awakening to the "Red menace," "Chambers had lost his zeal for Red hunting," Sam Tanenhaus noted. "He was willing to state his case in *Time,* keeping the argument on the plane of ideas." He had resigned, too, from the informing business. He had always found it repellent.

But in late 1947 and early 1948, items in the *Washington Times-Herald* and the *New York Sun* referred, though not by name, to Chambers and his Communist background and defection, and the information that he might have to offer about the coming scandal. In March, 1948, an ex-Communist named Ben Mandel, who was tracking down witnesses for HUAC, visited Chambers at the Time-Life Building in New York and asked whether he would testify in upcoming hearings. Chambers declined to appear voluntarily, and he begged to be spared a subpoena.

Chambers had been happy at *Time* magazine. His eight years there had been productive and satisfying, though he was controversial among the staff, especially writers and correspondents contributing to Foreign News when he edited that section and argued a hard, uncompromising anti-Communist line. Chambers by this time had already stepped down from Foreign News and become an occasional special projects essayist. Now he advised the managing editor, Tom Matthews, that he intended to resign from the staff and become a contract writer, doing occasional pieces for *Time* and *Life* from his Maryland farm. His heart was fragile. A new generation of writers and editors, young men back from the war, was taking over the magazine; they were animated less by the old ideological struggles so central to Chambers than by a certain bright-eyed postwar briskness (somewhat like Nixon's) that was attuned to the commercial energies of an economy expanding and exploring new technological possibilities.

On the morning of Monday, August 2, 1948, Whittaker Chambers had a cup of coffee with Henry Luce in the Time-Life Building in New York. Chambers disconsolately advised his editor in chief that he thought a subpoena from HUAC was imminent. He offered to resign, in order to spare the Luce publications any embarrassment.

Luce replied, "Nonsense. Testifying is a simple patriotic duty."

Chambers went back to his office. At noon, the subpoena arrived. The committee was in a hurry. Chambers was directed to appear at a public hearing the next morning, August 3, at 11:00.

That night after the magazine had locked up that week's edition, Chambers boarded his train at Penn Station, but instead of getting off at Baltimore to go to his farm, he continued on to Washington and spent the night at the home of *Time* correspondent Frank McNaughton in suburban Takoma Park. It was near midnight when Chambers arrived in a taxi from Union Station. He seemed agitated. He asked McNaughton to close the curtains to cover a picture window overlooking the street and to lower the blinds on the other windows. Chambers paced the living room floor, sucking on an underslung pipe.

Chambers slept for barely three hours. As he and McNaughton walked toward the hearing room, Chambers saw a familiar face in the crowd. He recognized a Communist he had known in the thirties. Chambers asked McNaughton to sit between him and that person in the hearing room.

If Chambers had been reluctant to come before the committee, he brought to Washington that day his sense of occasion and high history. In a melodramatic opening statement to the committee—a soliloquy, an apologia—Chambers said that as a young man he had "become convinced that the society in which we live, Western civilization, had reached a crisis, of which the First World War was the military expression, and that it was doomed to collapse or revert to barbarism." Marx and Lenin seemed to his young mind to answer the question, "What to do?" But thirteen years in the Party showed him that the Communist dream was in reality "a form of totalitarianism" whose "triumph means slavery to men wherever they fall under its sway, and spiritual night to the human mind and soul." And so he quit the Party. But at the time, he told "someone" [in fact, his wife, Esther] that "I know I am leaving the winning side for the losing side." But he judged that it was "better to die on the losing side than to live under communism." He reported that, for a year, he had lived "in hiding, sleeping by day and watching through the night with gun or revolver within easy reach."

The Communists might kill the apostate. "That was what underground communism could do to one man in the peaceful United States in the year 1938."

In an executive session of the committee earlier in the morning, HUAC's chief investigator Robert Stripling had asked him whether he had been "aware at any time while you were a member of the Communist Party of a so-called espionage ring that was being set up or functioning in Washington." Chambers lied. He said, "No, I was not." In the successive stages of the Hiss case, Chambers would show the authorities only one or two cards at a time, only as many as he had to. If the committee had been more alert that morning, it might have wondered why, if Chambers had merely been a member of the Party and not an agent, his apostasy would lead him to fear that the Party would try to kill him. In 1938, after Stalin's Moscow show trials, thousands of disillusioned American Communists had quit the Party; it would have been ridiculous to think that the Party would try to kill people simply because they turned away from the faith. Killing such a man could only mean that the Party feared he knew too much about its espionage operations and must be silenced. That gaudy touch about watching through the night with a revolver suggested that he might be guarding even more dangerous information than he now disclosed.

On the other hand, Chambers did hint that his knowledge of the Party was unusual. He told the committee that the Communist underground group in Washington with which he was familiar had been engaged in "infiltration" of the American government, although "espionage was certainly one of its eventual objectives."

His prepared statement reached a symphonic crescendo:

The publicity inseparable from such testimony has darkened, and will no doubt continue to darken, my effort to integrate myself into the community of free men. But that is a small price to pay if my testimony helps to make Americans recognize at last that they are at grips with a secret, sinister, and enormously powerful force whose tireless purpose is their enslavement.

At the same time, I should like, thus publicly, to call upon all ex-Communists, who have not yet declared themselves, and all men within the Communist Party whose better instincts have not yet been corrupted and crushed by it, to aid in this struggle while there is still time to do so.

He named the Washington group, called the Ware Group: Nathan Witt, John Abt, Lee Pressman, Henry Collins, Charles Kramer, Victor Perlo, and two brothers, Donald Hiss . . . and Alger Hiss.

There it was.

Richard Nixon watched Chambers carefully and tried to make out what kind of man he was. In a memorandum he wrote after the session, Nixon remarked: "He impressed me as being extremely shy and reticent, and also as if what he was doing was being done because he thought he should, rather than because he wanted to. . . . He was not a crackpot." Nixon was especially attentive toward the end of Chambers's prepared statement, when he said he knew the consequences of what he was doing but felt that duty to his country compelled him to do it. "His voice broke," Nixon remembered, "and there was a pause of at least fifteen to twenty seconds during which he attempted to gain control of his emotions before he could proceed. This one incident was to have considerable bearing upon my own attitude toward him because I did not feel it was an act."

On the morning of August 5, a Herblock cartoon in the *Washington Post* depicted an innocent man cornered by a tiger that was labeled "Smear Statements." That day, two days after Chambers made his charges, Alger Hiss, at his own request, appeared before the committee and, with an easy, self-confident grace, denied that he had ever been a Communist, or worked for the Communist cause, and denied as well that he had ever known anyone by the name of Whittaker Chambers. He was applauded by the crowd in the hearing room.

Nixon remembered later: "As Alger Hiss stood to be sworn in on the morning of August 5, the difference between him and Chambers could not have been more striking. Hiss was tall, elegant, handsome, and perfectly poised as he categorically denied Chambers' charge. In a firm voice, he said, 'I am here at my own request to deny unqualifiedly various statements about me which were made before this committee by one Whittaker Chambers the day before yesterday.'" That "one" before the Chambers name was a good touch. Hiss lowered his voice (for dramatic emphasis, said Nixon), and stated: "I am not and have never been a member of any communist front organization. I have never followed the Communist Party line, directly or indirectly."

Chief Investigator Stripling asked Hiss to review his impressive professional history. Hiss listed his clerkship for Justice Oliver Wendell Holmes and his rapid rise in the State Department to a senior position one rank below assistant secretary—and his performance as secretary-general of the UN conference in San Francisco and his appointment to head the Carnegie Foundation: a record of rock-solid achievement in the highest circles of the American establishment. The men who had sponsored and endorsed him over the years included Justice Holmes, Justice Stanley Reed, the distinguished diplomat Francis Sayre (Woodrow Wilson's son-in-law), and Edward R. Stettinius, the last secretary of state appointed by Franklin Roosevelt.

Among his sponsors was John Foster Dulles, board chairman of the Carnegie Foundation and the man everyone presumed would be the next Secretary of State, after Thomas E. Dewey had defeated Truman in November: a foregone conclusion. When

HUAC's F. Edward Hebert asked Hiss whether Dulles had had anything to do with his appointment to head the Carnegie endowment, Hiss replied: "He urged me to take my present position."

Karl Mundt, the acting chairman of the committee, pointed out that Chambers had testified under oath when he said that he knew Hiss, and Hiss replied: "I do know that he said that. I also know that I am testifying under those same laws to the contrary."

Nixon described the scene: "When Hiss finished his testimony, people surged around him, to shake his hand and congratulate him on his performance, and to commiserate with him on the damage the committee had done him." That morning, Nixon remembered, Truman had held an informal press conference in the Oval Office, and when a reporter asked him, "Mr. President, do you think that the Capitol Hill spy scare is a 'red herring' to divert public attention from inflation?" the president agreed, and then read a prepared statement that said the hearings were "doing irreparable harm to certain people, seriously impairing the morale of federal employees, and undermining public confidence in government."

All this caused consternation in the committee. Some members with an air of sheepish ingratiation congratulated Hiss after his appearance. Democrat John Rankin stepped down from the podium and led a procession over to the witness table to shake Hiss's hand. The committee began to panic. In executive session that afternoon, Mundt said, "We've been had. We're ruined." They had made a terrible mistake, they decided, one that might threaten the continued existence of the committee. HUAC had backed a crackpot. The press seemed mostly convinced by Hiss. A *Washington Post* editorial compared Hiss to "an innocent pedestrian, spattered with mud by a passing vehicle."

Only freshman Congressman Richard Nixon held out for pursuing the Chambers-Hiss connection. He volunteered to take over the investigation himself.

The chief investigator, Stripling, supported Nixon. As Sam Tanenhaus pointed out, "In pushing for the extended inquiry, Nixon and Stripling had withheld something from their colleagues. Both men were confident Hiss, not Chambers, had lied. While many in Washington had professed astonishment at Chambers' charges, those plugged into the busy anti-Communist circuit knew of rumors about Hiss dating back to the early 1930s."

Hiss made the error that Nixon might have warned him of. Hiss did not foresee the danger in his denying that he knew "one Whittaker Chambers."

Nixon had been tipped off earlier by Father Cronin about Hiss, of course, and Hiss's name had floated around in Berle's report and in FBI files. Hiss to the end of his life in 1996 would maintain that the only source for the story that Alger Hiss was a Communist was, all along, Whittaker Chambers—that the nightmare calumny had begun on the occasion, just after the Hitler-Stalin nonaggression pact in August 1939, when Chambers visited Assistant Secretary of State Berle and described Hiss as part of a Communist apparatus in Washington.

Hiss had set off a fatal chain of events for himself when he fired off the telegram to Chairman Parnell Thomas of HUAC in response to Chambers's charge. Hiss began:

My attention has been called by representatives of the press to statements made about me before your committee this morning by one Whittaker Chambers. I do not know Mr. Chambers and insofar as I am aware have never laid eyes on him. There is no basis for the statements made about me to your committee. I would appreciate it if you would make this telegram part of the record, and I would further appreciate the opportunity to appear before your committee to make these statements formally and under oath. I shall be in Washington on Thursday and hope that that will be a convenient time from the committee's point of view for me to appear.

Hiss should never have sent the telegram. Lots of charges of Communist affiliations in the thirties were flying around in the postwar period. So many people had been denounced to HUAC that the charges had relatively little meaning—unless the one accused chose to respond, to play the game, to accept a villain's part in HUAC's morality play. Furthermore, HUAC had a yahoo reputation for indulging reckless charges, for trampling constitutional rights, and for being plain stupid. The press tended to sneer at HUAC, to view its work with contempt. When reporters asked Hiss about what Chambers had said about his having been a Communist, before the war, Hiss might have smiled and scoffed and replied, "Well, that's nonsense. Charges of this kind do not even deserve a reply."

When Hiss heard about Chambers's accusatory, on Tuesday, August 3, he went to lunch with friends in New York. They, like his colleagues at the Carnegie Endowment, advised him not to respond—to let the moment pass—and, above all, not to yield to the temptation to enter into an arena where the committeemen, yahoos or not, used live ammunition and had legal powers, and where a witness might become entangled in dramas of perjury and contempt and Fifth Amendment. The president of the Carnegie Corporation of New York, Charles Dollard, wrote to Hiss on August 4: "For heaven's sake, don't lose your sense of proportion. Your peers have a confidence in you which is not to be undermined by the reckless charges of a hysterical renegade. . . . I think you now have the Endowment on the high road and I should hate to see your attention distracted by a campaign against termites." Letters poured in from powerful friends. One came from Mrs. Vincent Astor, who had been a friend of Hiss's in his days at Harvard Law School. The *Washington Post, Baltimore Sun, Boston Herald,* and other papers wrote withering editorials about the recklessness and stupidity of the House Un-American Activities Committee.

If Hiss had not risen to the bait, impatient HUAC would eventually have cranked up its engine and roared off to fish in some other part of the lake. The likelihood is that interest in Hiss would have died down. He probably would have survived as head of the Carnegie Endowment, and even if Hiss's sponsor, John Foster Dulles, the Endowment's board chairman, had judged that a discreet resignation might be a good idea, Hiss could have returned happily to the practice of law. There were hundreds of thousands of honorable people in all kinds of professions in America who had, during their idealistic youth in the economic turmoil of the Depression, believed that communism was the way to a better world.

Besides, Whittaker Chambers, for all the melodrama of his appearance, had come only reluctantly before the committee. Whatever his thoughts about the cosmic historical struggle between communism and the West, he was not eager to destroy his former associates and to place himself at risk of prosecution. It was only reluctantly, and under extreme pressure, that he later produced the documentary evidence, the Pumpkin Papers, and the other items that brought down the roof around Hiss.

Whether Hiss had actually been a Communist during the thirties—and if so, what kind of Communist he had been (a Washington cocktail party idealist, or an agent working for the government in Moscow), and with what consequences (the USSR had been recognized by the United States, was not an enemy, and indeed would become America's wartime ally) would have been tedious questions to pursue, especially for an embattled, vaguely discredited HUAC with a short attention span.

So there were two issues, two sets of doors that Hiss would have to pass through before he came into the presence of trouble: Hiss should have declined to walk through either. First, there was the question of whether he had been a Communist. Second, there was the question of whether Alger Hiss knew Whittaker

Chambers. The first was problematic. The second was an immense banana peel. Alger Hiss marched arrogantly and heedlessly down the stone corridors of the Old House Office Building and slipped on the banana peel.

Now, on the afternoon of August 5, 1948, Nixon saw the opening—the play of possibilities that might wait on the other side of that simple question: Did Hiss know Chambers? Nixon's alert, predatory instinct sensed the improbable Franklin-slaying Orthogonian vindication somewhere out there, and he ran through the opening, to the Senate, to the vice presidency, and to the presidency of the United States.

"In most cases," Nixon wrote, "we were in an almost impossible position of having to prove whether or not an individual had actually been a Communist. This time, however, because of Hiss's categorical denials, we did not have to establish anything more complicated than whether the two men had known each other."

Why did Hiss make such a mistake so early in the case? Partly because it *was* so early in the case, and Hiss could not foresee what was to come. He faced a dilemma. He judged, wrongly, that it was necessary for him to reply categorically to Chambers's charge that he had been a Communist. Of course, he might have done so without specifically saying in his statement that he did not know "one Whittaker Chambers." He might have left that question alone. But a member of the committee would surely have asked him whether he had ever met Chambers, and then he would have had to answer. If he had admitted that he had known Chambers in the thirties, then the admission would have been an invitation to the committee to ask under what circumstances they had known one another . . . and a grilling on such circumstances would have been awkward. Hiss had not yet thought out that story—though later, when the case heated up and Hiss saw he could not simply walk haughtily away, he would claim that he had known this man Chambers by a different name, as one George Crosley, a down-at-the-heels freelance journalist.

But for the moment, at the opening of play, Hiss bluffed.

His judgment may have been dulled by complacency. He had friends at the highest levels of American life.

Hiss's judgment may also have been impaired by his contempt for the House Un-American Activities Committee. There was a telling moment later in August when Nixon, heading a small HUAC subcommittee to pursue the matter in New York, summoned Hiss to appear. It was inconvenient, it was irritating, and Hiss had begun to see the danger; in a remarkably clumsy display, he impatiently told Nixon and the others that he had an appointment at the Harvard Club, and if the [uncouth] subcommittee insisted on detaining him, would they at least have the decency to have someone phone the Harvard Club to explain that Mr. Hiss had been held up. Hiss would sound this note throughout his trials, and on into his later life, after he had served eighteen months in a federal prison for perjury, after he had returned to New York and found a job as a salesman for a stationery manufacturer and settled into a modest life conducted well below the radar of celebrity media. In the 1970s, after the disgraced Richard Nixon had resigned from office, Hiss gave his version of the old case to a journalist named John Chabot Smith, who wrote a virtually hagiographic book called *Alger Hiss: The True Story.*

The note was caught perfectly in something that Hiss's wife, Priscilla, said to a friend on Tuesday of that week, up in Peacham, Vermont, where the Hisses had a summer cottage. Mrs. Hiss had allegedly been trying to recall whom the newspaper photographs of Whittaker Chambers reminded her of; he seemed vaguely familiar. She told a friend, "I remember a dreadful man named Crosley." A dreadful man. The phrase shivers with a certain genteel horror—a well-bred horripilation—at the memory of Whittaker Chambers and his bad teeth and his foetid air of the lower depths. Thirties radicals could be terrible snobs, and the Hisses if anything overplayed the snob card. Chabot Smith almost hilariously fell in with this tone.

Writing of Alger's idealistic arrival in Washington in 1933, the depth of the Depression, to begin work at the Agriculture Department in the exciting turmoil of the New Deal's Hundred Days, Chabot Smith reported: "On a bright sunny afternoon in early April, Hiss stepped off the train at Washington's Union Station, and walked through the huge vaulted lobby and triumphal arches that formed in those days a gateway to the nation's capital. It was the beginning of Washington's spring, when the blossoms were opening on the magnolias around the Capitol and the Japanese cherry trees beside the Tidal Basin."

Thus exhilarated, "Hiss checked in at the Racquet Club," where he would be playing the bachelor for a while. Chabot Smith reported on Hiss's friendship with the Labor lawyer and New Dealer Lee Pressman, whom Hiss remembers as "an extremely attractive young man, tall, handsome, well built and well spoken." Chabot Smith commented: "He wasn't one of Hiss's social crowd; he didn't ride horseback or play tennis, and he didn't enjoy music and the theater as Hiss did."

Hiss came from an old Baltimore family (of German immigrants, original name, Hesse) that went back to the mid-eighteenth-century. Alger's mother, Mary Lavinia (Minnie) Hughes, claimed descent from the Earl of Leicester and, on her mother's side, from a leading Baltimore family, the Grundys. Alger's family was not rich. Chabot Smith wrote, "The Hisses were not wealthy by any means, but they were prominent, respected people. They kept their own horse and carriage, and on occasion Charles [Alger's father] would hire a private railroad car for a family outing. They were seen at concerts and art galleries, they cultivated a life of good taste and literary interests, they knew everyone they wanted to know in Baltimore, they belonged to the best clubs, and they were recognized wherever they went." In such descriptions, which Chabot Smith got from Alger Hiss, one picks up a Dreiserian vibration of beleaguered American gentility, of a respectability (like that of Blanche Dubois, for that matter) that dangles over an abyss.

Alger was the youngest of five children, and, in addition, his parents had undertaken to help raise the six children of his father's brother John, who had died of a heart attack when he was thirty-three. When Alger was two and a half, the country suffered the panic of 1907, the worst financial crash in America before the Great Depression. Alger's father Charles—an erstwhile salesman for a Baltimore dry goods store—could not get a job. His health was poor. His elder brother, George, brought him down to North Carolina to work as partner in running a successful cotton mill, but "the simple life of a North Carolina mill town was not what Charles was accustomed to or what Minnie had been brought up to believe in."

So they returned to Baltimore, and Charles's depression deepened; only seven days later, he sent Minnie out to fetch a doctor, and while she was gone, he lay down on his bed and cut his throat with a razor. Minnie found him when she returned. Alger did not learn the truth about how his father had died until years later, when he was a teen-ager.

Minnie managed the disaster energetically and admirably, and raised the children on what was left from insurance and investments, about $100,000. She gave up the horse and carriage. All the children took music lessons. Alger made spending money as a boy by collecting cold spring water from a public spigot in Druid Hill Park and trundling it around on a wagon to neighborhood customers, to whom he sold it for fifteen cents a quart. Hiss went to Johns Hopkins, where he earned a distinguished record, and, like Richard Nixon at Whittier, enjoyed performing in college theatricals. (During the Hiss case hearings, Congressman F. Edward Hebert, perplexed at the absolute contradictions between Hiss's version of the facts and Chambers's, would throw up his hands and declare: "Whichever one of you is lying is the greatest actor America has ever produced." In fact, all three men—Hiss, Chambers, and Nixon—were actors.)

Hiss went on to Harvard Law. Later, when he was practicing law in Boston, he revived a childhood interest in bird-watching. In the days of August 1948, when Whittaker Chambers was persuading Nixon and others on the committee that he had indeed known Hiss and his wife, and had known them well in the thirties when Chambers claimed they were Communist agents together, there would pop into the narrative, unbidden, a gorgeous, apricot-colored bird called the prothonotary warbler. Chambers told the committee he remembered that Hiss was very excited one day at home in Georgetown (the house where Chambers and his wife were staying as guests of the Hisses) because he had spotted a prothonotary warbler. And later, when Nixon cross-examined Hiss, Nixon mentioned, off-handedly, in a lawyer's sly courtroom way, the prothonotary warbler, and Hiss unthinkingly, innocently, lit up and said, "Yes! Gorgeous bird! Have you seen it?"

It was after Harvard Law, at the recommendation of his professor, Felix Frankfurter, that Hiss received his appointment as law secretary (now called clerk) to Justice Oliver Wendell Holmes, then in his late eighties. Among Hiss's duties was reading aloud to the justice, whose eyesight was failing. At the urging of Holmes's friend Harold Laski, the British Socialist intellectual (who later would tutor young Joe Kennedy, to no avail, ideologically) one of the books selected for Holmes's reading was Trotsky's autobiography. Holmes detested it. Hiss told Chabot Smith that the book "made no impression [on Hiss] of any kind."

In a letter to Laski in 1930, Holmes commented on the Sacco-Vanzetti case, a trial that was to the 1920s what the Hiss case became in the 1940s—a bitter American cultural divide. Hiss sought to bestow upon himself some of the martyrs' charisma that emanated posthumously from Sacco and Vanzetti. He would quote Holmes's letter about that case as if it were a gloss on

Hiss-Chambers and on Alger's own fate (which, of course, was somewhat less fatal than that of the Italian immigrants): "I doubt if those two suffered anything more from the conduct of the judge than would be a matter of course in England. It was their misfortune to be tried in a community that was stirred up, if not frightened by manifestations the import of which was exaggerated, and, without knowing anything about it, I presume that the jury felt like the community."

In the twenties, Hiss's future wife Priscilla had an ill-fated four-year marriage to a man named Thayer Hobson, who was a friend of young Henry Luce, a Yale man who, with his classmate Britton Hadden, had founded *Time* in 1923, the great middle-class editorial phenomenon that would later give a home to Whittaker Chambers, after he broke with the Communist Party. Luce gave Priscilla a job as his office manager.

In 1926, there fell across Alger Hiss's life one of those odd co-incidental shadows.

His much-admired older brother, Bosley—lively, gregarious, feckless, a drinker, a sometime journalist for the *Baltimore Sun*—died of Bright's disease (an acute inflammation of the kidneys).

Two and a half years later, after a midnight quarrel with her husband, Alger's older sister, Mary Ann, depressed by money worries and marital trouble, swallowed a bottle of caustic household cleanser and killed herself.

Hiss lost his father and sister to suicide, and a beloved brother to a disease evidently brought on by dissipation.

Whittaker Chambers had lost his beloved, despairing, feckless, drunken brother Richard to suicide—and in a different way, had lost his father as well, first by the father's abandonment (when he vanished into a parallel life in New York City) and then, after the prodigal father had returned, by a grisly death in Whittaker's presence.

Richard Nixon lost two siblings—Harold to tuberculosis and Arthur to tubercular encephalitis.

John Kennedy lost his older brother, Joe, and his sister Kathleen.

Deaths happen, and large families inevitably witness more deaths among their own. Still. The shock of the loss of a sibling dead before his time—a death that is therefore, by the reckoning of human nature, unnatural—may cause hidden cracks deep in the foundations of personality. There is first of all the business of survivor guilt. Nixon's mother would say: "I think it was Arthur's passing that first stirred within Richard a determination to help make up for our loss by making us very proud of him. Now his need to succeed became even stronger."

Richard Chambers had sometimes tried to persuade his brother Whittaker to commit suicide along with him—on the argument that the rottenness of the world was overwhelming and the Chambers character was too weak and sweet to withstand it. Chambers was deeply stricken when Richard finally succeeded in suicide; but, he said, one night after visiting his brother's grave, "I went to look inside the little house, where I had once narrowly saved my brother [from death in an earlier suicide attempt]. There I made my decision: 'No. I will live. There is something in me, there is some purpose in my life which I feel but do not understand. I must go on living until it is fulfilled.' I added to myself: 'I shall be sorry that I did not go with my brother.'"

It is difficult to doubt that Chambers's later strange career in the Communist underground and in the (as he saw it) Golgotha of the Hiss case had something to do with the shock of the losses he had suffered. Chambers made it easier to speculate about such matters because his mode was grandiloquent confession, and he confided even his own temptations to suicide during the Hiss case in excruciating detail, as if, in the immense Manichaean dynamics of his mind, all his meaning had become a struggle between the will to survive and the temptation to die—a struggle that he saw projected upon the clouds above and upon history itself, in the titanic conflict of communism ("the winning side") and the West ("the losing side"). In an essentially Christian metaphysical criss-cross, to die meant to live and to live meant to die. One who vanishes into other lives and other selves (the Communist underground, various aliases and disguises) plays games of death and rebirth, of self and not-self, and may indeed alternate between, on the one hand, an abnegation of self so total as to amount to symbolic suicide, and, on the other, a fierce and even triumphant reassertion of self that may be like nothing so much as the gasping, surfacing burst of a swimmer who has held his breath underwater to the limit and now breaches wildly into the upper air. And, in effect, into another life.

Who can know whether, in Alger Hiss, the terrible losses of his father and sister and brother touched off some analogous dynamic? If Chambers was given to melodramatic self-disclosure (or, as Hiss claimed, to malicious fictions masking as confession), Hiss himself throughout his life was given to keeping himself somewhat concealed behind a veil of what seemed to be either genteel reticence or else, more simply, a guilty man's desire to hide what he did.

Hiss would later say that the man he knew as George Crosley (that is, Whittaker Chambers) reminded him in some respects of his dead brother, Bosley, who would have been about the same age as Chambers if he had lived and who had talked in the same romantic way when he worked for the *Baltimore Sun*.

So in the violent collision of Chambers and Hiss in 1948, there was a faint peculiar echo of the lost-brother-reborn. Or, in a dynamic in which something like love had turned to something like its opposite, each had turned into the other's evil twin. And physical opposite as well: Chambers short and fat and dumpy, Hiss tall and elegant; Chambers a blinkingly, squirmingly private man, Hiss a masterpiece of public veneer.

Tabloid psychological speculations have little standing in the face of hard facts, and it is frivolous to try to explain any of these men by counting the untimely deaths in their families, or to try to confirm Alger Hiss's guilt or Whittaker Chambers's mendacity by persuading oneself that one or the other arose from the trauma of a sibling's death. Or to attempt to explain Richard Nixon's character and career by positing a brother's death as the key to the mystery.

But character, which is irrational, may sometimes be inaccessible by rational routes or by logic and rules of evidence. Sometimes, such mysteries of personality—and Hiss, Chambers, and Nixon were all three mysterious men—may be glimpsed only by the grace of coincidence, or a kind of biographical body language, certain evident inclinations of mind, the spirit's reflexes.

In any case, it is striking that around the three principals in the Hiss case there should accumulate such dramatic family coincidences.

It is also a strange circumstance that all three men, Chambers, Hiss, and Nixon, were Quakers. One of the details of home life with the Hisses that Chambers mentioned to Nixon was the revealing fact that, between themselves, *en famille*, the Hisses used the Quaker plain speech, addressing one another as thee and thou. As a Quaker himself, Nixon understood that only someone close to the family would know that.

Chambers belonged to a Quaker meeting in Maryland, near his farm in Westminster. It was part of Chambers's vexed, forlorn history (so filled with betrayal and abandonment) that after he testified against Hiss before HUAC, some members of his Quaker meeting shunned him. Chambers angrily left the Quakers.

As for Nixon, his Quaker principles never seemed terribly deep, though they represented for him his mother's high-minded and intractable character. His father's bellicosity was a sort of counterweight. When Nixon decided to join the navy during World War II, instead of taking the conscientious objector status to which he was clearly entitled as a Quaker and to which his

Quakerism urged him, his mother, Hannah, fell into one of her awkward disappointed silences, as if Richard's manly impulse to go to war (approved and expected by his wife) were simultaneously censured by his mother, who always held claim to some deep and perhaps seldom visited region of her son's mind.

Alger Hiss presented himself in the HUAC drama as an accomplished and privileged Franklin—old-family Baltimore by way of Harvard Law and the Racquet Club and the State Department and Yalta; in Hiss' case, the callow Franklin snottiness had been redeemed by his leftish noblesse oblige New Deal liberalism, a well-tailored paternalism that had been learned, after all, at the feet of the supreme well-born paternalist, the Hudson River Valley squire Franklin Roosevelt.

The Hiss case shaped up as a variation on the American inside/outside game. Hiss was very much inside the American elite. Chambers was Outside in an almost mystical sense: Outside had, quite poignantly, been Chambers's life. He had felt it always—his isolation, his otherness. He had elevated his loneliness to a metaphysical status—the loneliness of the miserable child, of the Communist agent, and (though he did not say so), of the furtive homosexual. Even at *Time* magazine, where he rose to senior editor on his brainpower and ideological rhetoric, he was embattled and often despised.

So Chambers was distinctly outside Hiss's accustomed ambit of clubby power. Franklin Roosevelt starting in 1933 had much altered the intellectual tone of government, attracting armies of academics and idealists (Hiss among them) to Washington. Such a long tenure in the exercise of power, working among mostly like-minded people of leftist bent and, in any event, of little inclination (yet) to censure Communists, had surely given Hiss a sense that, despite postwar changes in the air, he remained on the Inside of power, insulated and fortified there by his government background and powerful friendships and a social unimpeachability—insulated as happily as a man sitting in his leather chair, in the great hall of the Harvard Club, under the head of the elephant that Teddy Roosevelt shot in East Africa on safari in 1908.

As for HUAC, its members were surely Outside—not technically, of course, not according to the Constitution, if it came to that, but Outside in a class sense: NOCD (Not Our Class, Dear). The committee savored of rural primitives, of a coarse, unthinking mentality easily ridiculed in the atmosphere of New York and Washington where civilized power met to exchange ideas and gossip.

In Nixon the reflex of self-pity and outsiderness was so strong that, years later, he wrote: "While there is no doubt that my reputation from the Hiss case launched me on the road to the vice presidency, it also turned me from a relatively popular young congressman, enjoying a good but limited press, into one of the most controversial figures in Washington, bitterly opposed by the most respected and influential opinion leaders of the time."

In this subtly tilted reading, it was Richard Nixon who was the victim—as if the Hiss case were something that had happened to him, as if his role in the matter had been almost passive, and as if, from his happy garden of youthful popularity, he had been cruelly expelled into a bitter world in which powerful ("the most respected and influential opinion leaders") enemies unfairly assaulted and pummeled him. In these periodic flickerings of self-revelation, Nixon offers himself as St. Sebastian, punctured by the arrows of tormenting injustice. Except, of course, that Nixon was a martyr who, unlike the saints, always lashed back; the attacks of his oppressors were a moral precondition—the rationale for what he saw as justified retaliations. His self-declared victimhood was a setup to position him morally for the attack.

Whittaker Chambers's psychology functioned along the lines of the same dynamic—more so, perhaps. Chambers, a gifted writer with a grandiose and even an apocalyptic imagination, had an infinitely larger sense than Nixon of being persecuted.

Nixon practiced a petty tactical martyrdom. Chambers's was operatic, cosmic, explicit.

In *Witness,* his autobiography published in 1952, Chambers wrote, "I did not wish to testify before the House Committee. I prayed that, if it were God's will, I might be spared that ordeal." His act of witness would be a crucifixion.

"I was doomed," he wrote. The morning of August 3, 1948, before he began his testimony, Chambers remembered,

> I did not sleep much. I felt something that was not only fear, though I felt fear, too. What I felt was what we see in the eye of a bird or an animal that we are about to kill, which knows that it is about to be killed, and whose torment is not the certainty of death or pain but the horror of the interval before death comes in which it knows that it has lost light and freedom forever. It is not yet dead. But it is no longer alive.

Chambers was a man fully as complex as Nixon. He gave a dimension odd and penetrating to the story of postwar, pre-McCarthy anti-communisma narrative depth more peculiar and interesting than Nixonian opportunism, or the shallow partisan controversy of HUAC. Chambers's book, *Witness,* is a forgotten classic of American autobiography.

Like Kennedy, Nixon, and Johnson, Whittaker Chambers remains a mystery.

He was a man with a large historical conception of himself, and a romantic, religious sense of history and the motion of Big Ideas at a time when the skeptical, deflating American imagination increasingly committed itself to the domestic, the banal, the secular, the commercial, the material.

Chambers, like Nixon, came from a hard American childhood that had been shadowed by poverty and family illness. Chambers, like Nixon, had been solitary and lonely and even friendless—although in Chambers the story took on a lurid, melodramatic tone in which the note of self-pity became sonorous and metaphysical.

Chambers said that his family "could scarcely have been more foreign in China than in our alienation from the life around us. . . . My father was not a father. My mother was not a mother. . . . That left me absolutely alone."

In an unforgettable chapter of *Witness* called "The Story of a Middle-Class Family," Chambers gave the excruciating history of his childhood.

He began: "I was born in Philadelphia on April 1, 1901. When my father, Jay Chambers, who was then a young staff artist on the *New York World,* received the startling news, he crumpled the telegram and threw it into a waste basket. He did not believe it and he did not think April Fool jokes were in good taste."

Even as he began, Chambers raised shadow questions about his own credibility: Or about the lengths to which he might go to dramatize a cosmic wretchedness and sense of abandonment. How could his father have been startled by the news of Whittaker's birth? He had had nine months to get used to the idea. How did the newborn Whittaker acquire the details of a scene far away in which his father scathingly crumples the telegram? No doubt Chambers's mother, nicknamed Lala, told him about the scene later on. Over the years, she seems to have told Whittaker altogether too much. She kept telling him about the ordeal of his own birth: "My terrible birth was fixed indelibly in her mind. Throughout my boyhood and youth, she repeated to me the circumstances of that ordeal until they were vivid to me. They made me acutely unhappy, and her repetition of them made me even unhappier."

Lala almost died. "Mine was a dry birth and I weighed twelve pounds and measured fourteen inches across the shoulders. I had to be taken with instruments."

A note of thin Dreiserian American bleakness (again, the Dreiser note) moans through the story. In his writing, Chambers displayed an acute, melodramatic sense of weather. The characteristic temperature of his life was cold, chill. The characteristic time of day was twilight. It rains often. Dark clouds drift across his prose. In the "Letter to My Children" that opens *Witness,* he wrote: "My children, as long as you live, the shadow of the Hiss case will brush you. In every pair of eyes that rests on you, you will see pass, like a cloud passing behind a woods in winter, the memory of your father."

The day of Whittaker Chambers's birth, "Snow was falling and soon turned into a blizzard. From her high bed, my mother could look into the whitening world outside the window and see the cemetery across the street. She wondered if, in a day or two, she would be lying under the snow." Doom. Doom. The secret of Chambers—his prose, his mind—was tragic premonition, and a metaphysical self-abnegation so cunningly uncompromising that it was transformed (as he intended) into colossal self-inflation. When a man describes his life as a passage through Gethsemane to crucifixion, he is, after all, claiming quite a bit for himself.

Emerson wrote, "I am a god in nature, I am a weed by the wall." Chambers told the world, in effect, "I am a worm. I am the Savior." Like Lana Turner and Richard Nixon, Chambers had his ups and downs. But he claimed to be working on a grander scale. A saint and a mountebank sometimes fought for prominence in Chambers's character.

Sometimes Chambers's writing achieved a splendid and sustained eloquence. Sometimes it became vulgar and tiresome, like, say the ham performances of Eugene O'Neill's father, James O'Neill, playing *The Count of Monte Cristo* for the umpteenth time, right around the time of Chambers's birth.

Chambers grew up in Lynbrook, Long Island, across Long Island Sound from the summer home in New London, Connecticut, of the O'Neill family, whose melodramatic troubles had an unhappy resonance with those of the Chambers family; O'Neill's brother, James Jr., for example, was an alcoholic and a suicide, as was Whittaker's brother Richard. When Tolstoy claimed that all happy families are the same and all unhappy families are unhappy in different ways, he had the formula backwards.

Whittaker was the son of a bisexual magazine illustrator who would vanish for long periods into another life in New York. Chambers himself would, like his father, marry and father two children, but he would also dodge in and out of homosexual episodes from time to time. The unpleasant father's appearances and disappearances seem to have impressed upon the son's character a pattern of evasiveness and legerdemain—and the habit of secrecy. Whittaker's embrace of communism, and then, after fourteen years, his renunciation of it, manifested, like the drama of his bisexuality, the struggle of an intense, unstable personality to find a satisfactory working identity—to find his true self.

But apart from the earnest and conventional idea of a search for identity, a somewhat more cynical dynamic of legerdemain, of sleight-of-hand, appealed to Chambers the magician. He was, in 1948, an ideological jack-in-the-box—popping out of nowhere to save the world. Now you don't see him, now you do. The old secret agent, denizen of the underworld, burst into the upper air to expose the secrets of the secret-stealers. He was a reluctant witness, at least at first; but as at Gethsemane, reluctance was an integral part of the drama.

"We were poor," Chambers remembered, "and there was something humiliating in knowing that the poverty was unnecessary—that my father was making a good salary, which he did not share with us." When he was off in New York, Jay Chambers sent his wife and children eight dollars a week for living expenses. Whittaker's mother baked cakes to sell and make extra money to live on, just as Richard Nixon's mother got up at four in the morning in Whittier to bake pies for sale. "I would go out and hustle orders [for cakes]. The next day I would deliver the cakes. In summers, I peddled vegetables."

It is a curiosity that Lala—like the three presidential mothers, Hannah Nixon, Rose Kennedy, and Rebekkah Johnson—thought that she had married somewhat beneath herself, beneath her social and intellectual station. Chambers wrote: "In her heart of hearts, my mother always felt, or at least she made me feel, that she had married the cook."

Jay Chambers was a small-bore bohemian who affected to disdain middle-class convention. The Lynbrook house was defiantly threadbare. When he was off leading an alternate life in New York, Jay refused to give Lala the money to replace the browned and bubbled wallpaper, or to fix the living room ceiling after a piece of it fell down, exposing the laths. Lala pawned her jewelry to re-paper the house. Neither parent bothered to send the boys to a dentist—a neglect that would manifest itself years later in the bad teeth by which Alger Hiss remembered "George Crosley."

Mrs. Chambers had been an actress (that theme again) before she was married. She sometimes dreamed of returning to her career on the stage. They would pack the trunks, and his mother would make the rounds of theatrical agents in the city, but nothing came of it. Whittaker Chambers remembered that "the saddest of such excitements, and the most persistent, was the one about buying a farm." The mother and her two boys would send for a farm catalog and dream about milking cows and slopping pigs on their own place. But they never did.

After he broke with the Communist Party and became an editor at *Time*, Chambers bought a farm in Westminster, Maryland, and happily worked the land as a real, practicing farmer. It was the farm with the pumpkin patch where Chambers hid three canisters of microfilm in the fall of 1948—the famous "Pumpkin Papers" with their evidence that Alger Hiss had been guilty of espionage. Chambers wrote that it was Hugo's *Les Miserables*—The Wretched of the Earth—that carried him into the Communist Party, and the same book, years later, that brought him out of it: "It taught me two seemingly irreconcilable things—Christianity and revolution. . . . It taught me that in a world of force, the least act of humility and compassion requires the utmost exertion of all the powers of mind and soul." The saintly Bishop of Digne became his hero. Hugo wrote: "He inclined toward the distressed and the repentant. The universe appeared to him like a vast disease; he perceived fever everywhere. And without trying to solve the enigma, he sought to staunch the wound. The formidable spectacle of created things developed a tenderness in him."

Chambers delivers a disquisition on what might be called the Holy Lie—a fascinating subject in the light of the role of lies in so much of his life: The struggle of the Hiss case was a drama of truth and lies—not only the crude, dogmatic collision of stark truths and stark lies, but also a far more complex human interplay of partial truths and modulated lies.

Victor Hugo's concept of the Holy Lie becomes a paradigm. That exemplary lie is the one that Hugo's character Sister Simplice—famous for her absolute integrity and inability to tell an untruth—told Inspector Javert toward the end of the story. Jean Valjean was hiding in Sister Simplice's room. Javert asked her, twice, whether she was alone in the room (the inspector had found her on her knees, praying). And twice, without hesitation, she had insisted that she was alone.

"Your pardon," said Javert, and withdrew.

Chambers quotes Hugo's words, which "became a part of my mind: 'Oh, holy maiden . . . may this falsehood be remembered to thee in Paradise.'"

The Holy Lie means an untruth presumably sanctified by the virtue of its intention. Sister Simplice lies to the System (Javert) in the overriding interest of common humanity. But when the System itself (Hitlerism, Stalinism, George Orwell's Big Brother) lies to the people in the name of its supposedly virtuous larger intention, it produces only monstrous inhumanity. The tragedy of such early Communists as Hiss and Chambers arose from the conflict between their original Sister Simplice impulses to encourage compassion and justice and the cannibalism of the system they naïvely endorsed.

Chambers understood this, and left the Party. Hiss, if he understood, suppressed it, and remained loyal to the Party and to his lies about it—either because he still believed in the higher truth of the Communist analysis of history or because, by 1948, he was so entangled in lies (and so entrenched in his other life as a respected member of the American foreign policy elite) that he could not see a way out. There is a sort of bracketing irony of history that Hiss's dilemma in 1948 was so much like Nixon's in 1972–1974. Hiss was immobilized by the discrepancy between his private secrets and his public façade. During Watergate, Nixon suffered similar paralysis. The photographic equivalent is a double exposure—truth and lies set down irreconcilably on the same frame. Hiss went to jail. Nixon lost the presidency.

Chambers added a certain depth to the Hiss case and the Nixon story through his ability to see clearly and presciently what Nixon could not see. Chambers reflected on Hugo's text. "We live in a sad society. Succeed—that is the advice that falls, drop by drop, from the overhanging corruption." In *Witness*, Chambers wrote: "I, for one, would not want to live a life in which money, comfort, appearances and pleasure mean success. There is something wrong with a people that measures its happiness and success in those terms. It has lost its mind. It has no mind; it has only activity."

Grandmother Whittaker, his mother's mother, came to live with the already disturbed Chambers family in Lynbrook. The old woman was insane. She had been staying at the YWCA, but she reported that at two in the morning, "they" ("There was always a 'they,'" commented Chambers) had driven a spike through the ceiling and pumped gas into her room. In her terror, Grandmother Whittaker ran downstairs into the street and tried to board a trolley.

When Grandmother Whittaker moved in, Lala Chambers gave her son an order: "You will have to stay up tonight. She may try to kill us all." Whittaker sat downstairs all night, reading. Grandmother began to throw open windows and doors. "They're pumping gas in here," she cried. "The house is full of gas." Finally, Chambers got her back to bed. "Ten minutes later, she was throwing open the doors and windows again. This kept up all night. For years, in addition to our old tensions, this dark, demoniac presence sat at the heart of our home."

She suffered spells. She muttered and growled, and late at night, she would "float downstairs, take a knife from the kitchen, and sit by the window in [Lala's] bedroom, where she knew she should not go . . . an ominous figure in her sealskin coat, she would rock back and forth, the knife clutched defiantly in front of her." His mother told Whittaker, "'You will have to take the knife away from her again." Chambers added: "My grandmother was quite powerful and there was usually a sharp scuffle before I got the knife. I suppose nobody ever sleeps quite peacefully in a house where a woman sometimes wanders around with a knife."

The teen-aged Whittaker Chambers ran away from home. He ended up working in Washington, D.C., as a laborer on the Capitol Transit System, laying or tearing up electric railway track. There he learned a job that he regarded as perfect training for his later life as a Communist agent. He was sent down into a shallow tunnel, four feet deep, where two naked and fully electrified third rails hung. The concrete in the tunnel had to be chipped out with a cold chisel. "I had to lie prone on a heap of rubble. The third rails, with the full power of the Capitol Transit System flowing through them, were about two inches above my sweat-soaked shoulders. In that cramping position, I had to break concrete. A sudden turn of my head, a slip of the hammer or chisel would have brought me in contact with the rail. It was an invaluable experience."

On August 17, Nixon and other members of the House Un-American Activities Committee gathered in a two-room suite that they had rented for the day in the Commodore Hotel in New York City. The living room, Nixon noted, was decorated with Audubon prints. Whittaker Chambers was asked to wait in the bedroom until Alger Hiss arrived to confront—at last—the accuser whom Hiss claimed he did not know.

Hiss was irritated when he arrived; his guests were waiting at the Harvard Club. As Nixon remembered the encounter, Hiss was asked to be seated, and then Chambers was invited to enter from the other room. Hiss was seated with his back to Chambers. Chambers walked behind him and sat on a sofa. For the first time Hiss would be able to look at the man whom he claimed he did not know—but may have known by another name, George Crosley—the man who had accused him of being a Communist and set in motion a sensational political controversy. Hiss had told the committee: "I will be very glad of the chance to confront Mr. Chambers. . . . My desire is to see him face to face."

Nixon watched Hiss intently at that moment in the hotel suite. Not once, Nixon claimed, "did Hiss turn around to get a good look at the man he claims he did not know. Instead he looked at all times stonily straight ahead at the members of the committee."

Nixon concluded that Hiss "acted the part of a liar who had been caught, rather than the part of the outraged innocent man, which he had so successfully portrayed before then." Chambers had earlier offered to take a lie detector test, and predicted that Hiss would refuse one. When Hiss was asked, he fudged and said he thought that lie detector tests were unreliable. During the HUAC investigation, Hiss (as Nixon noted later) always insisted on reviewing the transcripts of previous testimony and always had a lawyer with him when he testified. Chambers never asked for transcripts, and never brought a lawyer with him.

In the hotel room, Nixon finally said: "Mr. Hiss, the man standing here is Mr. Whittaker Chambers. I ask you now if you have ever known that man before."

Someone raised the window blind so that there would be more light.

Hiss and Chambers stood up to confront one another, standing four or five feet apart. Hiss inspected Chambers impassively.

Hiss, addressing Nixon, said, "May I ask him to speak? Will you ask him to say something?"

Chambers said, "My name is Whittaker Chambers."

Hiss stepped toward Chambers until he was a foot from his face. He asked Chambers to open his mouth so that he could see his teeth.

As Nixon recalled the scene, "[Hiss] actually reached up with his hand and made a gesture of opening the fingers to indicate what he wanted Chambers to do. I would say that his hand was not more than six inches from Chambers' teeth. I wondered why Chambers didn't reach out and bite his fingers."

Now it was Chambers who did not look at Hiss. He stared straight ahead of him and then up at the ceiling.

"The voice," Hiss commented, "sounds a little less resonant than the voice that I recall of the man I knew as George Crosley."

Hiss, who was six feet tall, lowered his head to peer into the mouth of Whittaker Chambers, who was some six inches shorter.

Hiss remarked: "The teeth look to me as though either they have been improved upon or that there has been considerable dental work done since I knew George Crosley."

Chambers said that four years earlier his Westminster dentist had extracted some teeth and installed "a plate in place of some of the upper dentures."

At that—in what Nixon described later as a "very loud, dramatic voice as if he were acting in a Shakespeare play"—Hiss "rose from his chair and pointed his finger" and declared to the committee that he was now prepared to identify this man as the one he had known, thirteen or fourteen years before, as "George Crosley."

Tiny violent fantasies: Nixon wondered why Chambers did not bite Hiss's finger. Now Hiss said he would know "Crosley" "if he had lost both eyes and taken his nose off."

But Alger Hiss seemed to be the only man in the world who had known a short, seedy freelance writer in the 1930s who went by the name of George Crosley.

In a sense, everyone was acting in a Shakespeare play. They repeated the confrontation performance a week later in a formal public hearing in Washington, in the midst of a late August heat wave. Twelve hundred spectators packed into the caucus room. Hundreds more were turned away.

For the first time in history, television cameras were set up, as big and cumbersome as steamer trunks perched on tripods, to witness a live congressional hearing—a civic art form that would ripen in later years through the U.S. Army–McCarthy hearings, Estes Kefauver's Senate rackets hearings, and, of course, the Watergate investigation, which would mark the end of Richard Nixon's political career just as the Hiss-Chambers hearings marked the beginning. There were only 325,000 television sets in America then, but it was just at that moment, in the summer of 1948, that television had begun to assert its presence as a new dimension in American life. Millions had watched the political conventions that nominated Harry S. Truman and Thomas E. Dewey for the presidency earlier in the summer.

So in a steaming, session that lasted nine and a half hours, the Un-American Activities Committee repeated, as public circus and TV pageant, the Hiss-Chambers confrontation scene they had rehearsed at the Commodore in New York. Hiss fingered "George Crosley."

Chambers's bad teeth came up again.

Nixon asked Hiss, "Did you ever see Mr. Crosley with his mouth closed?" The loud laughter that greeted Nixon's sarcasm indicated the degree to which public opinion had begun to turn against Hiss. His legalistic evasions had undermined the earlier story line of the unimpeachable public servant maligned by a passing mugger. John Foster Dulles had quietly asked Hiss to resign as head of the Carnegie Endowment. Hiss said he would prefer to wait until the congressional hearings were over, and Dulles agreed. If Dulles and his friends in the Northeastern Dewey establishment wing of the Republican Party had stood by Hiss, Nixon would have had to abandon the case.

F. Edward Hebert of Louisiana modified his earlier line about Chambers or Hiss as "the greatest actor." Now he told Hiss: "Either you or Mr. Chambers [is] the damndest liar that ever came on the American scene."

Against Hiss there had now accumulated a fascinating and damning tangle of specificities—not only the details of Chambers's knowledge of the Hisses' life (the prothonotary warbler, the Quaker plain speech, the houses where they had lived and the way they were furnished, and where their veterinarian was located) but also the Ford roadster Hiss had given to Chambers (or, as Chambers claimed, had donated to the Communist Party), the rent-free use of the Hiss apartment.

"Crosley" was of course Chambers, and under HUAC's big tent the melodramatic cast performed its lines. The crisply tailored Hiss—his indignation wearing a little threadbare now—tried to dismiss Chambers as "a self-confessed liar, spy, and traitor," "unbalanced or worse." "Is he a man of sanity? Getting the facts about Whittaker Chambers, if that is his name, will not be easy. My own counsel have made inquiries in the past few days and have learned that his career is not, like those of normal men, an open book. His operations have been furtive and concealed. Why? What does he have to hide?"

It was not, on reflection, Hiss's strongest line of attack, for it invited the question "What does Hiss have to hide?" It was Chambers who was exposing—indeed humiliating—himself in the process of accusing Hiss. But why?

Nixon asked: "Mr. Chambers, can you search your memory now to see what motive you can have for accusing Mr. Hiss of being a Communist at the present time?"

Chambers's spenglerian sonorities rose to the occasion. His voice was close to tears. He replied: "The story has spread that in testifying against Mr. Hiss I am working out some old grudge, or motives of revenge or hatred. I do not hate Mr. Hiss. We were close friends. But we were caught in a tragedy of history. Mr. Hiss represents the concealed enemy against which we are all fighting. I have testified against him with remorse and pity, but in a moment of historic jeopardy in which this nation now stands, so help me God, I could not do otherwise."

In the months that followed, Richard Nixon—working in consultation with Bert Andrews, of the *New York Herald Tribune*, and with HUAC's chief investigator, Stripling, presided over a deepening melodrama.

Chambers at first accused Hiss only of having been (and perhaps still being) a member of the Communist Party. He had not spoken of spying. He had not specified exactly what it was that he and Hiss had done on behalf of the Party or against the American government.

After much delay, Hiss sued Chambers for slander. Chambers, to defend himself in the suit and to make his statements about Hiss stick, gradually but theatrically unpeeled layers of new evidence. From its hiding place in a dumbwaiter in the Brooklyn apartment of his wife's nephew, Chambers extracted a sealed package of documents and microfilm that he had asked the nephew to hide there ten years earlier when he broke with the Party. At the time he anticipated that one day he might need "a life preserver." This was it.

Chambers turned over the package to the court. It contained transcripts of memos and reports and diplomatic cables, some marked "strictly confidential," sent to Secretary of State Cordell Hull from American ambassadors in Paris and Vienna and from the chargé d'affaires in London. Some of the documents were in Alger Hiss's handwriting.

It was espionage. Chambers acted as a courier, receiving documents from Hiss in Washington and delivering them to a Soviet agent, Boris Bykov, in New York. Chambers estimated he procured documents from Hiss fifty-two times. But the same evidence that seemed to prove Hiss had been a spy now also exposed Chambers as a spy as well. If a statute of limitations of three years prevented his prosecution as a spy, Chambers was now indictable for having given false testimony to a grand jury, or to HUAC.

But Chambers had withheld yet more evidence: three metal cylinders of microfilm, and two developed strips of film wrapped in wax paper which, because he feared his farmhouse would be raided by Hiss's defense or by Communist agents, he had concealed in a hollowed out pumpkin from a vine overgrowing a strawberry patch on the farm. These were the famous "Pumpkin Papers," or, in actuality, the Pumpkin microfilms. As investigators developed the film, the words they saw on the first frame were "Strictly Confidential."

Pat and Dick Nixon were taking a long-delayed vacation cruise on the steamer *Panama*. Nixon had undertaken the cruise knowing in advance that more evidence was coming. With his canny sense of theater he anticipated that he would be summoned back. Just before he left for the cruise, he told the House doorkeeper, Fishbait Miller, "I'm going to get on a steamship and you will be reading about it. I'm going out to sea and they are going to send for me."

Sure enough, a Coast Guard seaplane was sent to the Bahamas to extract Congressman Nixon from his vacation to preside again over a big break in the Hiss case.

The Pumpkin Papers and the urgent recall from the Bahamas—Nixon in a suit coat, hunched in a dinghy, whisked off in a seaplane on the Republic's business, *nothing so frivolous as a vacation for the indispensable young man*—made wonderful theater. But the script went terribly wrong for a moment when, on December 6, Nixon and his investigators were studying the Pumpkin evidence (an investigator holding up a strip of microfilm while Nixon posed like Sherlock Holmes with a pocket-size magnifying glass, pretending for photographers that he was reading purloined top-secret text). A photographer asked casually, "What's the emulsion figure on those films?" Meaning, what was the date of the film's manufacture.

In a phone call, Eastman Kodak's Rochester headquarters said that the film had been manufactured in 1945. It could not be genuine.

Richard Nixon exploded: "Oh my God, this is the end of my political career." He placed an enraged phone call to Chambers, who sputtered, "It cannot be true . . . God must be against me."

Nixon and Stripling were about to go back to the reporters and "face the music and . . . tell them that we were sold a bill of goods," when Eastman Kodak called back and said they had made a mistake. The microfilm dated from 1937. Chambers was telling the truth.

In the space of something less than five months in 1948, Richard Nixon had grasped the political opportunity that Whittaker Chambers had brought to him and had (with a fine sense of timing and theater, considerable confusion, some false leads, and extraordinary luck) turned himself from a promising, earnest freshman into a national figure. He did not save the Republic from Communist espionage (Hiss was hardly a threat in the late forties), except to the extent that the Hiss case aroused Americans to greater vigilance and anxiety about the Communist threat, and, in a darker way, prepared the way for Joseph McCarthy.

LYNDON VS. COKE

THE FIASCO OF THE KIDNEY STONE had cost Johnson two precious weeks of campaign time; at all costs, Johnson had wanted to avoid surgery, which would have cost him a period of recuperation that he could not afford before the July 24 primary. Among other things, Johnson tried to knock the stone loose by having himself driven, bouncing and jostling, over rough rural roads. The problem was resolved only when Johnson was flown up to the Mayo Clinic in Minnesota and doctors there used a technique called cystoscopic manipulation to dislodge the stone from its location high in the ureter.

Back on the campaign trail in early June, Johnson confronted a desperate political problem. He was far behind Coke Stevenson. Recovering at the Mayo he even lashed out irrationally at Woody Woodward for not sending the statement of withdrawal as he had been ordered to do back in Dallas. "I know you didn't send that," Johnson snarled at the long-suffering Woodward, who had, in fact, saved Johnson's career that night. "And I won't forget."

His entire future depended on his beating Coke Stevenson. The deadline for filing to run again for his congressional seat had passed. He had to win the Senate or else get out of politics. He said later, "I just could not bear the thought of losing everything."

But how to win?

No one had ever campaigned by helicopter before. Either John Connally or Woody Woodward came up with the idea. Woodward was familiar with helicopters from his service in the air force. Someone may have remembered Frank Capra's 1936 movie *It Happened One Night,* in which the heiress' bridegroom-to-be, the aviator King Wesley, arrived at the fancy wedding, to great excitement, by descending upon the bride's lawn in an "Auto-Gyro."

Over half the population of Texas still lived in small towns. The state's roads system was in many places rough and inadequate. The helicopter would be a novelty that would allow Lyndon Johnson, still relatively unknown outside his own congressional district, to move rapidly across the expanses of Texas (a state eight hundred miles long and almost as wide), making as many as thirty stops a day at widely spaced towns, whipping up a crowd every time with the spectacle of his descent from the big blue Texas sky in a machine that almost none of them had ever seen before.

Pappy O'Daniel's famous hillbilly band had worked to attract crowds, but this was even more effective. A powerful loudspeaker was attached to the undercarriage and, as the chopper circled overhead, Johnson would shout greetings. Sometimes he had the pilot hover over a farmer in a field just to introduce himself and ask for the farmer's vote. If the farmer had written a letter to his campaign, Johnson would address the man by name. He would say, "I'm up here thinking of you and your kind letter and comments. I just wanted you to be sure and tell your friends to vote for me at election time."

The helicopter was an expensive logistical nightmare for Johnson's campaign staff. Helicopters of that early generation had a range of only about 150 miles. They used only ninety octane gas; some airports stocked it, some did not. Few Texas towns had airports anyway. The chopper would therefore have to be refueled by trucks carrying gas in fifty-gallon drums and leap-frogging across the state from stop to stop, racing to keep up with the candidate.

The chopper would need a mechanic because the machine would require servicing every night. And who would hold the crowds back on the ground to prevent a kid from wandering too close to the rotor blades and getting killed?

But Johnson thought the risk and difficulty of the helicopter would be worth it. He was in a desperate frame of mind. The last poll taken, in mid-May, showed that Coke Stevenson was the choice of 64 percent of the voters, and Johnson of 28 percent.

What were the possible issues? Communism? Stevenson was deeply conservative. The character of Stevenson himself? Coke seemed to most Texans to be an admirable figure of probity, a self-made success as rancher, lawyer, and politician: capable, honest, and even shading over a little into folklore as an icon of the old virtues, implicitly fearless, his leathery face weathered, his back ramrod straight when he rode a horse.

On June 1, when Johnson was still at the Mayo Clinic, he listened to Stevenson's first campaign speech on the radio, a moderate and sensible discussion of the subject of the Communist threat. Without mentioning Johnson, Stevenson talked about the congressman's references to "the barbaric hordes of godless men in Eurasia."

Stevenson said: "There are men in this nation today who go about over the country as apostles of fear. They tell us another war is just around the corner. They are prophets of doom, howlers of calamity." People like that—like Johnson!—were hysterical about the Red menace. "We can be vigilant without being frightened . . . I don't believe you are afraid. We are descendants of men and women who have fought and won both the battles of war and the battle of peace."

Lyndon Johnson was made daring by his own desperation, by his sense of having nothing to lose. He decided on the helicopter. And he decided on an approach to Stevenson that was just as daring. Audaciously, he would attack Stevenson at precisely the point where he was strongest—would attack his character, his reputation, his honesty, even his conservatism and his anti-Communist credentials.

It was an astonishing strategy. It appalled Johnson's own handlers, who thought it was suicidal.

Embarking on his first speech after leaving the Mayo Clinic, a radio address from Houston, Johnson began with a minor note of the self-pity that was always unattractive in him, especially when he fused the self-pity with viciousness: "While I was sick at Mayo's, a calculating, do-nothing, fence-straddling opponent of mine . . . got off the fence for the first time to oppose the teacher salary increase. I challenge my opponent to tell Texans tomorrow if he favors withdrawing federal aid from five hundred thousand world-war veterans, men who did not sit at home when Old Glory had to be carried to every corner of the globe."

This was the sort of smear-by-non-sequitur that Richard Nixon was also good at, although Nixon worked it a little more smoothly; Johnson as a Texan tended to throw a somewhat extravagant rhetorical punch ("Old Glory," for example).

The speech amounted to a perfect little model of the perverse device that Johnson would employ all through the summer to defeat Stevenson. The nuclear core of Johnson's device was the Big Lie.

It was totally false for Johnson to suggest that Stevenson opposed federal aid to veterans; in fact, he had already proposed that it be increased. Incredibly, Johnson was able in the course of the campaign to make it seem that "Calculatin' Coke" was soft on labor unions and implicitly on communism, that he lacked courage and honesty, and that at an extremely vigorous 60 he was a tired old man.

Robert Caro has analyzed the subtlety with which Johnson judged his opponent and turned his opponent's own virtues against him. Johnson—one of the shrewdest judges of character who ever entered politics—understood that Coke Stevenson was simply too proud to respond to his scurrilous charges. He knew that he could use Stevenson's integrity of character and self-esteem as weapons against him—could make his silence appear to voters to be, not a reflex of dignity in the face of vicious charges, but rather a sign of guilt and shame and weakness.

When Johnson spread rumors against Stevenson that involved alleged corruption in leases that Magnolia and other oil companies had purchased to test for oil on land Stevenson owned, Stevenson told reporters that he would not attempt to defend his honesty: "My private life is an open book and my record of public service is too well known to the people of Texas to require repetition. . . . If my record does not warrant my election to the Senate, then I ought to stay at home. The people know enough to make their own choice."

There was a touchingly dignified innocence in Stevenson's certainty—in his inability to see (who could have foreseen it?) that Lyndon Johnson was about to explore a new dimension in the amoral possibilities of Texas politics, and that Stevenson's sterling and stolid probity would lose in the end to LBJ's ruthless and unorthodox desire.

The helicopter, for one thing, seemed to announce a new metaphysics in fundamentalist regions where people were hospitable to wonders. A woman in Blanco, Texas, told Caro: "After it [the helicopter] left, a Bible student said that the Bible says that people will float through the air. He said, 'This is the beginning. This is the beginning of a new era. We will see all sorts of changes from now on.'"

As part of his rightward maneuver after the war, Johnson had voted in favor of the union-curbing Taft-Hartley Act. Now the Texas chapter of the American Federation of Labor, bitter about the apostate New Dealer, endorsed Coke Stevenson for senator— not out of great enthusiasm for the conservative Stevenson but merely on the principle that the enemy of our enemy is our friend-of-convenience. Johnson immediately charged that Stevenson and the AFL had made a secret deal—the AFL would endorse Stevenson and Stevenson would vote to repeal Taft-Hartley.

In actuality, Stevenson favored Taft-Hartley, and was if anything more anti-labor than Johnson, but he was reluctant to antagonize labor. Besides, as Johnson had foreseen, the more outrageous the charge LBJ leveled against him, the more Stevenson would disdain to answer it.

There was no "secret deal." Johnson knew the charge was false. But he hammered away. As the campaign went on, he managed to create, to spin, great dust-devils of plausibility that jittered and whirled around Stevenson's good name. Johnson demanded, in speech after speech, that Stevenson "tell the truth" about this "secret deal" he had made with "labor dictators." He said that Stevenson had sold his soul for the labor vote: "He's a yearling with the labor boss brand on his hip."

Not the least irony of this was that Johnson himself was receiving substantial amounts of labor union cash from outside the state, from John L. Lewis's United Mine Workers, for example; this was money sent to support the old New Dealer friend of labor, Lyndon Johnson, against the man, Stevenson, who, as Johnson's liberal friends in Washington had convinced everyone, was a "Neanderthal" and must be defeated.

Johnson embroidered his war record, making himself sound like a hero. He mocked Stevenson and mimicked him in front of campaign crowds—Johnson was very funny and talented at impersonation.

Stevenson was outraged but not inert. He compared Johnson to the left-wing congressman from Brooklyn, Vito Marcantonio, who was proving to be a convenient Red standard in postwar political campaigns; Nixon had cited Marcantonio in the 1946 Voorhis campaign, and would do it again in attacking Helen Gahagan Douglas in 1950.

On Primary Day, July 24, Stevenson won 40 percent of the vote; Johnson won 34 percent, and a third candidate took 20 percent. There would have to be a runoff between Stevenson and Johnson.

It came on August 28. Johnson and Stevenson ran neck and neck, one pulling ahead, then the other. The count took days, in part because, by old Texas political tradition, extra votes can always be found to tip a close race one way or the other, and a drawn-out process of see-you-and-raise-you may ensue.

At last, George Parr, the political boss of the south Texas counties of Jim Wells, Zapata, and Duval, weighed in with returns that corrected a "mistake" from a ballot box in Alice, in Duval County, Precinct 13—a correction that shifted two hundred votes from Stevenson to Johnson and thus seemed to put Johnson over the top. The Texas State Democratic Convention, in melodramatic session, gave the victory to Johnson.

Both sides were undoubtedly stealing votes. The Johnson biographers Irwin and Debi Unger wrote: "The number of votes stolen by the Stevenson forces has been glossed over in most biographies of Johnson. But they were substantial."

Stevenson challenged the results. But finally, U.S. Supreme Court Justice Hugo Black—influenced, it may be, by friends from the Roosevelt and Truman administrations—decided in Johnson's favor. Black ruled: "It would be a drastic break with the past, which I can't believe Congress ever intended to permit, for a federal judge to go into the business of conducting what is to every intent and purpose a contest of an election in the state." In those days, winning the Democratic primary was tantamount to winning the November election itself.

Lyndon Johnson, just turned forty, had brought himself back from the political dead. It was not a pretty performance, but, in January, he would be going back to Washington as a United States senator.

EPILOGUE

WALT WHITMAN WROTE that it does not matter what disease you have, for when you die, the disease is gone, and the body, the life, is purified. If you visit Richard Nixon's modest grave in Yorba Linda, in a peaceful corner of the Richard M. Nixon Library courtyard, an almost unexpected *nil nisi bonum* arises in the mind. Nixon is buried beside his wife, Pat, each grave marked only by the simplest of polished black headstones that lie almost flush to the grass. Nixon's stone is engraved with a Quaker thought: "The greatest honor history can bestow is the title of Peacemaker." A hundred yards away stands the little craftsman kit house—neat and trim, unexpectedly tiny and feminine, like a doll's house—that Frank Nixon had constructed. Nixon began his memoirs: "I was born in a house my father built." Nixon wrote that in that house, "sometimes at night I was awakened by the whistle of a train, and then I dreamed of the far-off places I wanted to visit someday."

When Nixon died, Bob Dole broke down and wept at his funeral—saturnine Republican Bob Dole of Kansas, who, on one ceremonial occasion, beholding ex-Presidents Carter, Ford, and Nixon standing solemnly in a row, remarked: "There they stand: Hear No Evil, See No Evil, and Evil." Dark Dole humor—an astringent prairie wind cutting through it.

But at the gravesite in Whittier at the funeral in 1994, Dole wept. The only epitaph said "peacemaker." The better side of Nixon began to emerge in memory. The poison of the anger (his own, and that of those who hated him) began, as Walt Whitman foresaw, to drain away from the subject of Richard Nixon. It may be that history was able to forget, or to put into perspective, the uglier or stranger sides of his character and political behavior—paranoia, dirty tricks, the mess and disgrace of Watergate.

Which of the three was the best man?

Eventually, ideology fades—Was Alger Hiss guilty? Was Vietnam the wrong war?—and what remain are characters and stories, deeply absorbed; they may eventually turn into gods and myths that, as the Greeks thought, were cast into heaven as constellations. The American way is to cast these gods and myths about the landscape as presidential libraries, airports, high schools, highways.

THE SEVEN DEADLY SINS are lust, gluttony, avarice, anger, pride, envy, sloth. In the fifth century, the Christian allegorist Prudentius proposed the Seven Contrary Virtues—chastity as protection against lust, abstinence against gluttony, generosity against greed, humility against pride, patience against anger, diligence against sloth. Kindness against envy.

Richard Nixon's defining deadly sin was surely anger—or envy.

Kennedy's deadly sin was lust.

Johnson's deadly sin was greed—for power, for money.

Nixon's virtue was diligence—an asset that did not, however, check his anger and envy. His anger and envy sank him in Watergate. But his diligence in the years thereafter enabled him to restore his reputation and achieve what might be called a limited, modified apotheosis as elder statesman.

Kennedy's virtue was courage: he called the book *Profiles in Courage.* It was the quality he most admired. Courage did nothing, of course, to check his lust. If anything, a form of fatalistic or devil-may-care courage accounted for his need to take risks in his sex life.

But Johnson was a case of deadly sin deadlocked with contrary virtue. His great virtue of generosity was at lifelong war with his deadly sin, which was greed. That may have been the secret key to Johnson's mysterious character: that he indulged his sin, greed for power, so that it might implement his virtue, which was generosity. At his best, he sought power in order to do good things—even grandiose things, "the Great Society." At his worst, the stalemate of his impulses mired a nation in a war he could neither win nor quit.

Nixon's were the Orthogonian values—square, straight, middle class, orthodox: but with a defensive/aggressive combative edge. Nixon was a Quaker boy who put rocks in his snowballs. There was something, some obscure affront that he never forgave.

Johnson's values amounted to a complex modification of the Texas self-image (which is itself a lot more complicated than people think.) His swaggering, exhibitionist manliness had a tendency to turn rancid, and to undo (in vicious politics, in Vietnam) the side of him that was the Great Mother and wished to nurture and love all the children of the Earth.

The life of Kennedy—Anglophile, Irish pol, secret invalid, sexual Mucker slipping through the service tunnels of New York's Carlyle Hotel for a rendezvous upstairs with a blonde—was an unfinished work. Would the substance of it, had he lived, eventually have managed to match the shining rhetoric and façade and public relations? Or would history have torn the façade aside and exposed him? If he had lived, John Kennedy's second term would have run to the end of 1968—and there have been few years in American experience that were as messy and destructive as 1968. Of course, Kennedy might have avoided the mistakes that Johnson made. On the other hand, his incredible sex life might have been revealed, and his James Bond/John Buchan love of counterinsurgency might have conspired with his anti-Communist orthodoxy to bring the United States just as deeply into Vietnam.

Was it possible to foresee, in 1948, what the three would become—their interbraided ascents to power (a sort of triple helix of ambition), and the ruin of them?

Some, in 1948 and before, had predicted great success. Joe Kennedy saw a president in his second son, after the first one died. People who knew young Nixon in Whittier and Washington talked about coming to see him, one of these days, in the White House. Lyndon Johnson all along had cherished what might be called a firm yearning, a desire amounting to a conviction that he would be president.

None of them was a great man. Each was incomplete and defective. Sometimes, great occasions and crises raise up great leaders: Abraham Lincoln and Franklin Roosevelt come to mind. Sometimes great crises miserably fail to raise up adequate leaders—as in, say, the American drift toward civil war in the 1850s, when all the nation could manage was Franklin Pierce and James Buchanan. America produced Martin Luther King Jr. in the sixties, but otherwise the story of the decade was precisely the toppling of authority, everywhere (in the presidency, in government, in the military, in the universities, in the family) by the immense new commercial and moral and cultural authority of the generation born just after World War II.

Nineteen forty-eight was the seedbed, both of the three men's political futures and more broadly of the immense decade of change that would at last, in different ways, overwhelm all three.

Nineteen forty-eight was when we started to become . . . what we became.

NOTE ON SOURCES

This book is not a work of original scholarship but rather an extended essay on the meaning of the year 1948 and on the characters of three men who would go on to become president of the United States. All three have been the subject of hundreds of books—thousands—so that their stories have become classics, like those of, say, Agamemnon, Menelaus, and Odysseus: told and retold by many authors in many forms, the same anecdotes worked and reworked, held to the light at different angles.

In preparing the narrative portions dealing with Lyndon Johnson, I have drawn extensively upon Robert Caro's distinguished, exhaustively researched biography, *The Years of Lyndon Johnson,* which now runs to three volumes, the second of which, *Means of Ascent,* describes 1948 and the Coke Stevenson race in detail.

I have also relied upon Robert Dallek's excellent *Lone Star Rising, Lyndon Johnson and His Time;* upon *LBJ: A Life,* by Irwin Unger and Debi Unger, as well as upon a number of other Johnson biographies. I learned much about the character and personality of LBJ from Doris Kearns Goodwin's portrait *Lyndon Johnson and the American Dream.*

In the narrative portions on John Kennedy, I have relied, like many Kennedy biographers, upon the thorough legwork done by Joan and Clay Blair Jr. for *The Search for J.F.K.* Doris Kearns Goodwin's fine and sweeping history, *The Fitzgeralds and the Kennedys,* has been the source of much detail. Robert Dallek's *The Unfinished Life of John F. Kennedy* has been invaluable—as, in various ways, have other studies listed in the selected bibliography.

For my narrative sections on Richard Nixon, I am indebted especially to Roger Morris' magisterial and densely detailed biography, *Richard Milhous Nixon: The Rise of an American Politician,* as well as to Stephen Ambrose's biography of Nixon and to Tom Wicker's acute reading of the man in *One of Us*. Earl Mazo's early biography, published when Nixon was still vice president, supplied much interesting detail, especially about Nixon's South American trip and the events in Caracas, which Mazo witnessed.

In writing about the Hiss case, I have relied upon Sam Tanenhaus' splendid biography, *Whittaker Chambers*; on Chambers own book, *Witness,* and other sources. Material for the narrative section on Brumidi was drawn from *Constantino Brumidi, Artist of the Capitol*, by Barbara Wolanin. In writing about Homer Capehart, I have drawn much information from *Homer E. Capehart: A Senator's Life*, by William B. Pickett.

I have also drawn, inevitably, upon my personal impressions of Kennedy, Johnson, and Nixon, formed over many years. Both of my parents were journalists in Washington in the forties and fifties, and knew all three men. During summers in the early fifties, when I was 13 and 14, I worked as a Senate page boy. Johnson was the Senate Democratic leader and Nixon, as vice president, was the presiding officer; Kennedy was the junior senator from Massachusetts. I sat literally at their feet, on the steps of the Senate rostrum, where pages wait to be summoned by the snap of a senator's fingers. Sometimes on Saturday mornings I played touch football with the Kennedys and their gang (the star was Byron "Whizzer" White, former All-America and future Supreme Court justice) at a playground at 34th and Q Streets in Georgetown—Bobby playing quarterback but John Kennedy mostly watching from the sidelines because of his bad back. Later, as a journalist myself, I wrote extensively about the three for *Time* magazine, and spent a certain amount of time—especially in the sixties, before he became president—talking to Richard Nixon, or, more often, simply watching him and listening as he held forth at meetings with a few *Time* editors and writers in a private dining room at the top of the Time-Life Building in New York. Nixon sometimes talked about himself in the third person: "Now, if Nixon wins in those three states, then. . . ." A friend of mine, Chuck Houghton, whose father was one of Kennedy's roommates at Harvard, tells me that Kennedy sometimes did the same thing, talking about himself in that coldly appraising, disembodied way.

What follows is a partial list of books I have used in the preparation of this study:

On Kennedy

Joan and Clay Blair, Jr., *The Search for J.F.K.* (New York: Berkley, 1976)

Benjamin C. Bradlee, *Conversations with Kennedy* (New York: Norton, 1975)

Peter Collier and David Horowitz, *The Kennedys, An American Drama* (San Francisco: Encounter Books, 1984)

Robert Dallek, *An Unfinished Life, John F. Kennedy, 1917–1963* (Boston, Little Brown, 2003)

Paul B. Fay, Jr., *The Pleasure of His Company* (New York: Harper & Row, 1966)

Nigel Hamilton, *JFK, Reckless Youth* (New York: Random House, 1992)

Doris Kearns Goodwin, *The Fitzgeralds and the Kennedys, An American Saga* (New York: Simon & Schuster, 1987)

John F. Kennedy, *Profiles in Courage* (New York: Harper, 1956)

Thomas Maier, *The Kennedys, America's Emerald Kings* (New York: Basic Books, 2003)

Christopher Matthews, *Kennedy & Nixon, The Rivalry that Shaped America* (New York: Touchstone, 1996)

Ralph G. Martin, *A Hero for Our Time: An Intimate Story of the Kennedy Years* (New York: Macmillan, 1983)

Thomas C. Reeves, *A Question of Character, A Life of John F. Kennedy*, (New York: Free Press, 1991)

Garry Wills, *The Kennedy Imprisonment* (Boston-New York: Houghton Mifflin, 1981)

On Johnson

Robert A. Caro, *The Years of Lyndon Johnson: The Path to Power* (New York: Knopf, 1982)

Robert A. Caro, *The Years of Lyndon Johnson: Means of Ascent* (New York: Alfred A. Knopf, 1990)

Robert Dallek, *Lone Star Rising, Lyndon Johnson and His Times 1908–1960* (New York: Oxford University Press, 1991)

Doris Kearns Goodwin, *Lyndon Johnson and the American Dream* (New York: St. Martin's Press, 1976)

Irwin Unger, Debi Unger, *LBJ, A Life* (New York: John Wiley & Sons, 1999)

On Nixon

Stephen E. Ambrose, *Nixon, Volume I — The Education of a Politician 1913–1962* (New York: Touchstone, 1988)

John Erhlichman, *Witness to Power, The Nixon Years* (New York: Simon and Schuster, 1982)

David Greenberg, *Nixon's Shadow, The History of an Image* (New York: W. W. Norton, 2003)

Earl Mazo, *Richard Nixon, A Political and Personal Portrait* (New York: Harper and Brothers, 1959)

Roger Morris, *Richard Milhous Nixon, The Rise of an American Politician* (New York: Henry Holt, 1990)

Richard Nixon, *RN, The Memoirs of Richard Nixon* (New York: Grosset and Dunlap, 1978)

Tom Wicker, *One of Us: Richard Nixon and the American Dream* (New York: Random House, 1991)

Garry Wills, *Nixon Agonistes, The Crisis of the Self-Made Man* (New York: Houghton Mifflin, 1969)

On Chambers and Hiss

Whittaker Chambers, *Witness* (Washington, D.C., Regnery, 1952)

John Chabot Smith, *Alger Hiss: The True Story* (New York: Holt, Rinehart, Winston, 1976)

Alonzo L. Hamby, *Man of the People: A Life of Harry S. Truman* (New York: Oxford University Press, 1995)

C. David Heymann, *The Georgetown Ladies' Social Club* (New York: Atria Books, 2003)

Andrew Lownie, *John Buchan, The Presbyterian Cavalier* (Jaffrey, N.H.: David R. Godine, 2003)

William Manchester, *The Glory and the Dream, A Narrative History of America — 1932–1972* (Boston, Little Brown, 1973)

David McCullough, *Truman* (New York: Simon and Schuster, 1992)

William B. Pickett, *Homer E. Capehart: A Senator's Life* (Indiana Historical Society, 1990)

Forrest C. Pogue, *George C. Marshall* (New York: Viking, 1973)

Thomas C. Reeves, *The Life and Times of Joe McCarthy* (Lanham, Md.: Madison Books, 1997)

Lana Turner, *Lana: The Lady, the Legend, the Truth* (New York: E. P. Dutton, 1982)

Richard J. Whalen, *The Founding Father, The Story of Joseph P. Kennedy* (New York: New American Library, 1964)

Barbara Wolanin, *Constantino Brumidi, Artist of the Capitol* (Washington, D.C.: U.S. Government Printing Office, 1998)

The WPA Guide to Washington, D.C. (New York: Pantheon, 1983)

Howard Zinn, *Postwar America: 1945–1971* (Bobbs-Merrill, 1973)

I am especially indebted to my son James Morrow for his invaluable help in preparing this study.

Sam Tanenhaus, *Whittaker Chambers* (New York: Random House, 1997)

Allen Weinstein, *Perjury, The Hiss-Chambers Case* (New York: Random House, 1978)

On Henry Luce

Robert E. Herzstein, *Henry R. Luce* (New York: Charles Scribner's Sons, 1994)

W. A. Swanberg, *Luce and His Empire* (New York: Charles Scribner's Sons, 1972)

Others

Bill Adler, *Washington, A Reader* (New York: Meredith Press, 1967)

Carl Bernstein, *Loyalties, A Son's Memoir* (New York: Simon and Schuster, 1989)

Raymond Borde and Etienne Chaumeton, *A Panorama of American Film Noir, 1941–1953* (San Francisco, City Lights Books, 2002)

Paul Boyer, *By the Bomb's Early Light: American Thought and Culture at the Dawn of the Atomic Age* (Univerity of North Carolina Press, 1994)

David Brinkley, *Washington Goes to War* (New York: Knopf, 1988)

John Buchan, *The Four Adventures of Richard Hannay* (Godine, 2002)

Frank Capra, *The Name Above the Title* (New York: Macmillan, 1971)

Lord David Cecil, *Melbourne* (Indianapolis/New York: Bobbs Merrill, 1939)

Thurston Clarke, *Ask Not* (New York: Henry Holt, 2004)

Edward Cray, *General of the Army* (New York: Simon and Schuster, 1990)

Robert H. Ferrell (ed.), *Off the Record: The Private Papers of Harry S. Truman* (New York: Harper & Row, 1980)

Katharine Graham, *Katharine Graham's Washington* (New York: Knopf, 2002)

INDEX